To Jim —

on your 75th Birthday

Love,

Mary

September 15, 2012

Resurrection, Apocalypse, and the Kingdom of Christ

Princeton Theological Monograph Series

K. C. Hanson, Charles M. Collier, D. Christopher Spinks,
and Robin Parry, Series Editors

Recent volumes in the series:

Paul G. Doerksen
The Church Made Strange for the Nations:
Essays in Ecclesiology and Political Theology

Lisa M. Hess
Learning in a Musical Key: Insight for Theology in Performative Mode

Jack Barentsen
Emerging Leadership in the Pauline Mission: A Social Identity Perspective
on Local Leadership Development in Corinth and Ephesus

Matthew D. Kirkpatrick
Attacks on Christendom in a World Come of Age: Kierkegaard,
Bonhoeffer, and the Question of "Religionless Christianity"

Michael A. Salmeier
Restoring the Kingdom: The Role of God as the "Ordainer of Times
and Seasons" in the Acts of the Apostles

Gerald W. King
Disfellowshiped: Pentecostal Responses to Fundamentalism
in the United States, 1906–1943

Timothy Hessel-Robinson
Spirit and Nature: The Study of Christian Spirituality
in a Time of Ecological Urgency

Paul W. Chilcote
Making Disciples in a World Parish:
Global Perspectives on Mission & Evangelism

Resurrection, Apocalypse, and the Kingdom of Christ

The Eschatology of Thomas F. Torrance

STANLEY STEPHEN MACLEAN

PICKWICK *Publications* · Eugene, Oregon

RESURRECTION, APOCALYPSE, AND THE KINGDOM OF CHRIST
The Eschatology of Thomas F. Torrance

Princeton Theological Monograph Series 181

Pickwick Publications
An Imprint of Wipf and Stock Publishers
199 W. 8th Ave., Suite 3
Eugene, OR 97401

www.wipfandstock.com

ISBN 13: 978-1-61097-394-6

Cataloguing-in-Publication data:

MacLean, Stanley Stephen.

    Resurrection, Apocalypse, and the Kingdom of Christ : The Eschatology of Thomas F. Torrance / Stanley Stephen MacLean.

    xviii + 216 pp. ; 23 cm. Includes bibliographical references.

    Princeton Theological Monograph Series 181

    ISBN 13: 978-1-61097-394-6

    1. Torrance, Thomas F. (Thomas Forsyth), 1913–2007. 2. Eschatology. 3. Church. I. Series. II. Title.

BT220 M165 2012

Manufactured in the U.S.A.

To my parents

Angus James MacLean (d.1995)

&

Flora Ann (nee MacDonald) MacLean

Contents

Acknowledgments

I WOULD LIKE TO EXPRESS MY GRATITUDE TO THOSE WHO HELPED ME to complete this dissertation. In particular, I want to thank a number of people at Princeton Theological Seminary, where I spent six weeks doing research on the topic. Special thanks go out to Dr. Iain Torrance for his guidance, encouragement, and for kindly granting me permission to use his father's unpublished writings. Thanks also to the staff in the archival section of the Princeton Seminary Library, especially to Dr. Clifford Anderson and Kenneth Henke for all their assistance. All the staff there helped to make my visits to Princeton both productive and pleasant.

I also profited from the assistance of two archivists overseas. Thanks to Sarah Duffield at the Church of England Record Centre and to Hans-Anton Drewes at the Karl Barth *Archiv* for kindly responding to my requests.

There are a number of people in Canada I must mention. I am especially grateful to my former pastor, Dr. Richard Topping, for taking the time out of his summer vacation to proofread carefully the entire manuscript. His support and friendship over the years have also meant a lot to me. A word of appreciation also goes out to Dr. Joseph McLelland for sharing his first hand knowledge of Torrance's lectures on eschatology in 1952. Finally, I would like to thank Dr. Douglas Farrow, my supervisor at McGill University, for introducing me to Torrance's eschatology many years ago and for helping me to complete a dissertation on this topic.

Introduction

THOMAS TORRANCE (1913–2007) HAD A LONG AND ILLUSTRIOUS career, spanning six decades. He penned over 600 works and covered a wide range of subjects in Christian theology, often making original contributions to them. Eschatology was one of these subjects, although it is not one we associate with Torrance. He is famous for his contributions to trinitarian thought and theological method, and especially for his penetrating investigation of the relationship between science and theology.

To date, there are around fifty studies on Torrance. So far, none has focussed on his eschatology. Many, understandably, deal with his theological method or his scientific theology. A number of these have been published: Wolfang Achtner, *Physik, Mystik and Christentum: Eine Darstellung und Diskussion der naturlichen Theologie bei T. F. Torrance* (Frankfurt, 1991); John Douglas Morrison, *Knowledge of the Self-Revealing God in the Thought of Thomas Forsyth Torrance* (New York, 1997); Colin Weightman, *Theology in a Polanyian Universe: The Theology of T.F. Torrance*; Elmer Colyer, *The Nature of Doctrine in T. F. Torrance's Theology* (Eugene, OR, 2001); and Tapio Luomo's *Incarnation and Physics: Natural Science in the Theology of Thomas F. Torrance* (Oxford, 2002).[1]

A number of studies focus on theological loci. The earliest of this type is Johannes Guthridge's *The Christology of T. F. Torrance: Revelation and Reconciliation in Christ* (Melbourne, 1967). Perhaps the most comprehensive is Won Kye Lee's *Living in Union with Christ: The Practical Theology of Thomas F. Torrance* (New York, 2003). Lee's study

---

1. To this class we can add the unpublished dissertations of Bryan Gray, "Theology as Science: An Examination of the Theological Methodology of Thomas F. Torrance"; Dennis Sansom, "Scientific Theology: An Examination of the Methodology of Thomas Forsyth Torrance"; Douglas Trook, "The Unified Christocentric Field: Toward a Time-Eternity Relativity Model for Theological Hermeneutics in the Onto-Relational Theology of Thomas F. Torrance"; F. Leron Shults, "An Open Systems Model for Adult Learning in Theological Inquiry"; Jason Hing-Kau Yeung, "Being and Knowing: An Examination of T. F. Torrance's Christological Science"; Kurt Richardson, "Trinitarian Reality: The Interrelation of Uncreated and Created Being in the Thought of Thomas F. Torrance."

builds upon a slightly earlier study with a similar title: William Rankin's "Carnal Union with Christ in the Theology of T. F. Torrance" (University of Edinburgh, 1997). One of the most specialized is Robert Stamps' "'The Sacrament of the Word Made Flesh': The Eucharistic Theology of Thomas F. Torrance" (University of Nottingham, 1986). There has been a good deal of scholarly interest as well in Torrance's theological anthropology. This has been epitomized in Phee Seng Kang's "The Concept of the Vicarious Humanity of Christ in the Theology of Thomas Forsyth Torrance" (University of Aberdeen, 1983) and in the recent publication of Myk Habets, *Theosis in the Theology of Thomas Torrance* (Farmhan, UK, 2009).

Won Kye Lee's study is one that at least underlines the significance of Torrance's eschatology. Eschatology, we learn, has an important role in our union with Christ. This union, he concludes, "is quasi-hypostatic and eschatological."[2] Yet even in Lee's broad systematic study, eschatology occupies only a few pages.

This book deals with a neglected subject in Torrance's theology. I have chosen eschatology, though, not just because it has been neglected but because it is a prominent subject both in Torrance's theology and in modern theology in general. In 1901 James Orr rightly predicted that the twentieth century would be the age of eschatology.[3] Unlike preceding centuries, this century is one where eschatology is a central theme for theologians. Near the end of it, the Lutheran theologian Carl Braaten spoke about the "eschatological renaissance in Christian theology."[4] Jürgen Moltmann (1926–) surely represents the high point of this renaissance. He has insisted that eschatology is not "one element of Christianity" but "the medium of Christian faith."[5] It is, he adds, "characteristic of all Christian proclamation, of every Christian existence and of the whole church."

It is recognized that the renaissance began with Karl Barth, Moltmann's teacher at one time. In his *Epistle to the Romans* (1922) Barth asserted that "Christianity that is not entirely and altogether eschatology has entirely nothing to do with Christ." Torrance was not only a student

---

2. Lee, *Living in Union with Christ*, 308.

3. Orr, *The Progress of Doctrine*, 345.

4. Hodgson and King, *Christian Theology*, 275.

5. Moltmann, *The Theology Hope*, 16.

of Karl Barth but a close disciple. Eschatology, then, should have been important to him as well.

Why did eschatology suddenly come to the forefront of theology in the twentieth century? There are theological and historical reasons, which we can only sketch out here.[6] Theologically, the change begins with the German scholars Johannes Weiss and Albert Schweitzer. Their biblical research showed that an apocalyptic eschatology was at the core of Jesus' preaching.[7] Jesus expected God's kingdom to break dramatically into history in his lifetime.

The conclusions of Weiss and Schweitzer turned on its head the liberal theological establishment, which had dismissed biblical eschatology as part of an outmoded Hebraic world-view. Albert Ritschl was one of the first to identify the kingdom of God as the central idea in Jesus' teaching, but he construed this as "moral society of nations" that can be realized on the basis of the Christian motive of love.[8] For Troeltsch, in the same vein, the kingdom of God is an "ethical ideal" within us; and while this ideal can never be realized absolutely in this world, it "drives man onward" and has a transforming effect on society at large.[9] In general, Christian eschatology in nineteenth-century Western Europe had become confused with the idea of worldly "evolutionary progress" that was characteristic of that time period.[10] It had nothing to do with God's intervention in history or the return of Christ.

While it became clear, after Schweitzer and Weiss, that Jesus could no longer be understood apart from his apocalyptic eschatology, the modern view of the world made this eschatology look untenable.

6. For a broad survey of Christian eschatology, see Hebblethwaite's *The Christian Hope*. A helpful guide to modern eschatology, including Roman Catholic forms, is La Due's *The Trinity Guide to Eschatology*. Moltmann's *The Coming of God* contains a trenchant, though tendentious, survey of German eschatology in the first half of the twentieth century, 3–22. For the latter half of the century, and for a sample of Dutch eschatology, see Runia, "Eschatology in the Second Half of the Twentieth Century," 105–35. The only author from this group, however, that even mentions Torrance is Brian Hebblethwaite.

7. Johannes Weiss, *Jesus' Proclamation of the Kingdom of God*; Albert Schweitzer, *The Quest of the Historical Jesus*.

8. Ritschl, *The Christian Doctrine*, 10, 290.

9. See Troeltsch, *The Social Teaching*, 1013.

10. See John Baillie, *The Idea of Progress*; also H. E. Fosdick, *Christianity and Progress* (1922). Fosdick reports that in his day the Church is viewed as "primarily an instrument in God's hands to bring personal and social righteousness on earth," 114.

Schweitzer himself became a mystic, for Jesus was deluded: the kingdom did not break in as he had expected; nor could it. Jesus was just another tragic hero, crushed by the "wheel of the world" which continued to run its course as it always has.

World War I brought an end (in Europe at least) to the "age of optimism." Not only was the "consistent eschatology" of Jesus untenable now, so was faith in the natural upward ascent of humankind. Under the leadership of Karl Barth, the "theology of crisis" promised a solution to the crisis in eschatology. Eschatology is central here. However, it is an eschatology shorn of temporality. It does not have much to do with apocalyptic, with history or the future. It is about "Eternity," as the judgment of God, breaking into time. Contrary to Schweitzer, there is no problem of the delay of the *parousia*. That is because the kingdom of God presses down from above onto every moment of our existence. After all, Eternity surrounds time.

Rudolph Bultmann had his own ingenious solution to the eschatological problem. One could partake of the eschatology of the New Testament without partaking of its primitive cosmology. The key was to "demythologize" the message of the gospel (the *kerygma*).[11] What is really important in eschatology, the reasoning goes, is the "existential moment," an encounter with God through faith alone. Yet Bultmann drives a wedge between eschatology and history.[12] Eschatology has to do with Christ coming to us through faith, not with the coming of Christ on the clouds of heaven. Therefore, "every instant has the possibility of being an eschatological instant."[13]

From Torrance's own soil came an alternative to Schweitzer's "consistent" or "futurist" eschatology. This was C. H. Dodd's "realized eschatology," which, like Bultmann's eschatology, seeks to emancipate eschatology from future historical events. In *The Parables of the Kingdom* (1936) Dodd contends that the kingdom of God, the Day of the Lord, arrived fully in the person and ministry of Jesus. Jesus' miracle-working power, his judgment and overthrow of evil forces, and finally his resurrection all attest to the presence of this kingdom. There is no need to look for a second coming of Christ on horizontal plane of history. This

---

11. Bultmann, "New Testament and Mythology," 1–44.

12. See Bultmann, *History and Eschatology*.

13. Ibid., 154.

is not to say there is no eschatological reserve, but what remains will be realized in the "world beyond" this one.

Oscar Cullmann tries to do justice to both the realized and futurist elements that clearly seem to constitute New Testament eschatology.[14] For him the solution is in the recovery of the biblical concept of time. This is a linear conception (*chronos*). The Christ-event is the mid-point in salvation history (*Heilsgeschichte*). This point is in the past. The kingdom of God, then, has "already" come with the advent of Jesus Christ. He is Lord. But this kingdom has "not yet" fully arrived. We must look forward to the "last things," which include the second advent of Christ and the general resurrection of the dead. The church, therefore, has real grounds for hope.

The course of history in the twentieth century kept eschatology at the forefront. The spread of Communism in mid-century represented a complete secularization of Christ's notion of the coming of the kingdom of God. Communism, World War II, and the general crisis of civilization forced churches in the 1940s and 50s to ponder together the meaning of hope for both the church and the world. If the *bureau of eschatology* was closed in the nineteenth century, then by the middle of the twentieth century it was, in von Balthasar's words, "working overtime."[15]

This is, in a nutshell, the historical and eschatological background of Torrance's early career. This book uncovers Torrance's eschatology and examines its origin and development against this background. It begins (chapter 1) with Torrance's lectures at Auburn Seminary in 1938/39, for this is where his eschatology begins to take shape. Owing to the strong influence of Barth's *Church Dogmatics*, these lectures leave us with a strong sense that the kingdom has come in the "Person" and "Work" of Christ. Eschatology is determined by the incarnation, the cross, and resurrection. Yet on the basis of Christ's ascension and second advent we are given an equally strong sense that the kingdom is still to be consummated and that Christ is still carrying on his redeeming work.

We then (chapters 2 and 3) trace the development of his eschatology through his sermons at Alyth and Beechgrove. Grounded on the resurrection and ascension of Christ, this eschatology is practical and apocalyptic as well as personal and historical. Yet we find that same

14. See Cullmann, *Christ and Time.*

15. Sauter, *What Dare We Hope?* 27. The original source is von Balthasar, "Eschatologie," 403.

tension between the present realization of the kingdom and its future consummation, between the revelation of the new creation and the hiddeness of it. This tension is established by the actualization of the kingdom through the cross of Christ, which, in Torrance's words, is "still in the field."

Next, we examine Torrance's eschatology in the context of the ecumenical movement (chapters 4 and 5), as it takes shape through his work (1948–63) for the Commission of Faith and Order of the World Council of Churches. Here eschatology is vital to the nature of the church as the Body of Christ in time and space. Once again, we find a tension between the present, hidden realization of the kingdom and its future, full manifestation. The church is caught in the middle of this tension, for it represents the new creation and the new humanity. Its true nature (holiness and unity), however, is hidden in Christ, waiting to be revealed with his final *parousia*. There is an eschatological fulfillment of the Body through the resurrection of Christ and, correlative to the ascension, a teleological growth of the Body towards fullness (*pleroma*) in Christ. The church's eschatological reality is manifested in her sacraments, her ministry, and mission.

The book concludes with an overview of the results of this study, a look at the lasting significance of Torrance's eschatology, as well as some critical observations of it.

This book will show that Torrance's early theology is an imaginative attempt at recapturing the eschatological orientation of the early church. This means eschatology is not viewed as an appendix to the Christian faith. Instead every element of this faith is given an eschatological cast. The key is Torrance's Christology. Eschatology is a component of this Christology. Eschatology, he can say, is about the *parousia* (coming-presence) of Jesus Christ. For Torrance, there is no "delay of the *parousia*," since the *parousia* includes Christ's life, death, resurrection, ascension, and second advent as "one extended event." Eschatology is central to the church because, as the Body of Christ, it participates in Christ's death, resurrection, and movement toward fulfillment. The church is really the new humanity in concentrated form.

At the same time, one should not expect to find a comprehensive, systematic treatment of Torrance's eschatology in the following pages. We must bear in mind that Torrance did not leave us with a full-fledged eschatology. Much of his thinking on the subject was occasional; much of it was inchoate.

This study is more historical-descriptive than analytical-descriptive. Its primary aim is to demonstrate that Torrance was a first-rate eschatologist, a point that has scarcely been recognized.[16] A secondary aim is to show that Torrance's eschatology has been shaped—though not determined—by Torrance's historical context.

It is time to say a word about my method. I heeded Bruce McCormack's advice at the end of his intellectual biography on Barth. There he states that, "the most pressing need in contemporary theology is a historical one."[17] This is certainly true in regard to Torrance's eschatology, since it is occasioned by some of the greatest events of the century.

Rankin's study, "Carnal Union in Christ," is the first attempt to understand Torrance's theology in terms of its historical background. The great benefit of this work is that it helps us to see the role that Barth, Calvin, and Athanasius played in the genetic development of Torrance's concept of "carnal union." However, Rankin's thesis falls short in giving us a clear picture of the historical context of Torrance's theology. It gives too much attention to the theologian's unpublished papers (many of which have been published), while giving too little to his historical context. Lastly—and sadly—"Carnal Union in Christ" completely ignores Torrance's eschatology.

Alister McGrath's book *T. F. Torrance: An Intellectual Biography* (Edinburgh, 1999) represents the second attempt to understand Torrance's theology in its historical context. McGrath's book shed much needed light on Torrance's early career. However, his research in this area is far more biographical than theological, and far from complete. He fails even to mention Torrance's wartime sermons, which constitute *The Apocalypse Today* (1960). His treatment of Torrance's ecumenical work in the 1950s is spotty; though to his credit he does explain that a major part of this work involved the recovery of the eschatological element in the church.

---

16. Yet, just recently, in his lengthy synopsis of Torrance's doctrine of atonement, Robert T. Walker wisely identifies "the eschatological perspective" as one of the four leading themes in Torrance doctrine: Thomas F. Torrance, *Atonement: The Person and Work of Christ*, edited by Robert T. Walker. To support his claim, Walker includes a nearly fifty-page addendum on the subject.

17. McCormack, *Karl Barth's Critically Realistic*, 466.

Historical research on Torrance involves a broad range of sources, including unpublished articles, lectures, sermons, correspondence, and memoirs. The complete works of T. F. Torrance, along with his personal library, are now part of Special Collections (archives) at Princeton Theological Seminary. This collection includes all of Torrance's sermons from his years as a Church of Scotland minister at the Barony Parish Church in Alyth and at the Beechgrove Parish Church, Aberdeen. These sermons are the bases for chapter 2 and parts of chapter 3.

Prologue: From Edinburgh to Auburn, 1934–1939

A. Edinburgh and Basil, 1934–1938

WHAT WERE THE FORMATIVE INFLUENCES ON TORRANCE'S ESCHATOL-
ogy? One immediately thinks of Karl Barth's theology, but one cannot
underestimate the influence of Torrance's teachers at the University of
Edinburgh, where his theological education began (1934–37). The great
figure there at this time, and the one who had the greatest impact on
Torrance, was Hugh Ross Mackintosh (1870–1936), who held the Chair
in Systematic Theology.[1] He published a number of books, most notably
The Doctrine of the Person of Christ (1912), which became a standard text
for a generation of divinity students. Mackintosh's christocentric view of
grace and his evangelicalism seemed to have made a lasting impact on his
student. According to Torrance, it was Mackintosh's doctrine of atonement that explained the nature of his teacher's theology. The "nerve" of
all his teaching, he writes, was "the forgiveness of sins provided directly
by God in Jesus Christ at infinite cost to himself."[2] Torrance's tribute to
his teacher is appropriately titled "Hugh Ross Mackintosh: Theologian
of the Cross."

We should not gloss over Mackintosh's influence on the development of Torrance's eschatology. The cross is central to Torrance's apocalyptic eschatology, as we will discover. Years later, Torrance will cite
Mackintosh (along with another Scot, P. T. Forsyth) as one of those few
modern theologians who were able to follow the Reformers in preserv-
ing the "eschatological tension of faith."[3]

---

1. "Professor Mackintosh made a profound and lasting impact on my spiritual and
theological development . . . [He] had a vast and commanding sense of the grace of the
Eternal" (Torrance, "Student Years," 4).

2. Torrance, "Hugh Ross Mackintosh," 162.

3. Torrance, "The Modern Eschatological Debate," 45, 50.

However, Torrance's eschatology would develop into something very different in terms of form and content from what one finds in either Mackintosh or Forsyth. Whereas he would define eschatology as an objective application of Christology to history and the church, Mackintosh and Forsyth focussed on individual eschatology, which they interpreted in moral, psychological terms. And neither man showed much interest in the Apocalypse. From Forsyth's pen came *This Life and the Next* (London, 1918), which examines "the effect on this life of faith in another."[4] Mackintosh's weightiest contribution is *Immortality and the Future* (London, 1915). For him the criterion of truth in eschatology is "what is certified to the soul by faith in Jesus."[5] The way these men approached eschatology reveals the dead hand of German liberal theology. Forsyth had studied at Göttingen under Albrecht Ritschl; Mackintosh at Marburg under Wilhelm Herrmann.

By the 1930s, however, Mackintosh had developed a deep appreciation for Karl Barth's theology, which represented a repudiation of German liberalism.[6] Indeed Mackintosh would play a part in Torrance's decision to do post-graduate study at Basel (1937–38) under Barth.[7] There Torrance heard his series of lectures on the doctrine of God. These would become volume II.1 of the *Church Dogmatics*.[8] It was probably Barth's theological method that impressed Torrance more than anything. Barth treated the Word of God as the real and objective revelation of God himself, and understood dogmatics as a critical science. As a research project, Torrance chose the scientific structure of Christian dogmatics.[9]

4. In the same vein is John Baillie's *And the Life Everlasting* (1934), which is about "an inquiry into the nature of and grounds of Christian hope of eternal life" (ibid., 5).

5. Mackintosh, *Immortality*, 128.

6. See Mackintosh's *Types of Modern Theology*, where he devotes the final chapter to the theology of Karl Barth. Unlike some in his day, Mackintosh clearly expected Barth's influence on the Church to increase. For him the great benefit of Barth's theology is that it "forced men to take Revelation seriously, with a revival of faith as a consequence" (ibid., 253). It has been argued that Mackintosh's theology, with its strong emphasis on the free grace of Christ, anticipated Karl Barth's theology. This is the thesis of J. W. Leitch. See *A Theology of Transition: H. R. Mackintosh as an approach to Karl Barth*.

7. Torrance, *Karl Barth*, 121.

8. It seems that these lectures left a lasting impression on Torrance. Near the end of his career he revealed that CD II/1 was his favourite section of the *Dogmatics*. This is after he told Michael Bauman in an interview that Barth's "doctrine of God is simply the best thing of its kind." Michael Bauman, *Roundtable*, 112.

9. McGrath, *T. F. Torrance*, 45.

However, Barth dissuaded him and advised him instead, on the basis of his pupil's interest in the Greek Fathers, to write on the doctrine of grace among the second-century fathers of the church.[10] Torrance agreed. That was in 1938. The fruit of his labour is *The Doctrine of Grace in the Apostolic Fathers* (Edinburgh, 1946). Eschatology has an important place here. Torrance concludes that the apostolic Fathers misunderstood the "radical nature" of New Testament grace and its distinct "eschatological character," which sets believers free and translates them into a "completely new world."[11] But we are getting ahead of ourselves. These words were published in the mid-forties.

B. The Auburn Lectures on Christology, 1938–1939

The war interrupted Torrance's doctoral research, but it was not the first thing to interrupt it. This was his stint lecturing at Auburn Theological Seminary in upstate New York. He had planned on returning to Basel after a summer break in Scotland, but his plans changed when John Baillie, a professor of divinity at New College, persuaded him to fill temporarily a faculty vacancy at Auburn.[12] The seminary was long-regarded as a liberal institution. By 1938 it was at the vanguard of the so-called "New School" Presbyterianism, which positioned itself against the fundamentalism of the "Old School" Presbyterianism. Torrance arrived in the fall of 1938 and taught a full year of courses. Although he devoted most of his time to Christian dogmatics, he had to teach a whole range of subjects, including systematic theology, biblical theology and philosophy of religion.

1. Theological Method

So far, only his lectures on Christology and soteriology have been published.[13] It is not Torrance's finest work, as he admits. "They had been put together in a hurry when I was twenty-five years of age and were

---

10. Ibid., 46.

11. Torrance, *The Doctrine of Grace*, 139.

12. The seminary nailed its colours to the mast when it came out with the "Auburn Affirmation" in 1927. Baillie had also done a stint of teaching at Auburn. The campus closed in 1939, and the seminary moved to the campus of Union Theological Seminary in New York City.

13. Torrance, *The Doctrine of Jesus Christ*.

rather rough-hewn and jejune."[14] Nonetheless, they give us a precious insight into the genesis of his theology. Besides, these are the only lectures where you find "last things" discussed, albeit briefly. It is treated in the last lecture, titled "The Ascension of Christ and the Second Advent," but it occupies just three pages in a 200-page book. But it is not just these three pages that interest us. It is Torrance's whole Christology. For he would eventually define eschatology as a component of Christology: as the "application of Christology to the Kingdom of Christ and to the work of Christ in history."[15]

McGrath correctly observes that Torrance's lectures follow "broadly" the "structural framework and theological perspective" of Mackintosh's *The Doctrine of the Person of Christ* (1913) and Forsyth's *The Person and Place of Jesus Christ* (1909).[16] Not only does he cite these men frequently, he uses their motifs as his starting point. "In any discussion of Christian Doctrines I believe that central place must be given to the doctrine of the Person and Work of Jesus Christ."[17] It is the unity of the two that he is after. Why? Because, in his view, there has been a tendency to examine the person of Christ (Christology) apart from the work of Christ (soteriology). Again, he has in mind Forsyth and Mackintosh.[18] Forsyth treats the "person" of Christ under one title and his "work" separately under another: *The Work of Christ* (1910). As the title of his *magnum opus* indicates, Mackintosh had a great deal to say about the person of Christ; however, he did not have much to say about Christ's work. Torrance would find a better model in Brunner's *The Mediator*. Brunner underlines the need to see the person and the work of the Mediator as a unity.[19] Still, Torrance believes his former teacher laid the proper foun-

14. Torrance, *Royal Priesthood*, 43.

15. Torrance, *The Doctrine of Jesus Christ*, ii.

16. McGrath, *T. F. Torrance*, 51.

17. Torrance, *The Doctrine of Jesus Christ*, 1

18. It is quite probable that he also had in mind John Baillie's *The Place of Jesus Christ in Modern Christianity*. Baillie opens his study by stating that "there is no part of traditional religious belief which gives rise to so much complexity in the minds of the men of our time as does the part bearing on what is traditionally been called the 'Person and Work of Christ'" (ibid., 1). He explains that people in his day still revere the person of Jesus but have great difficulty accepting the doctrine of the "Trinity and the Incarnation and the Atonement" (ibid., 1). For Baillie, the answer lies in making these doctrines more acceptable to the sceptics instead of expounding them as the miraculous works of God, which is what Torrance does.

19. Emil Brunner insists that neither the Christmas message nor the Easter message

dation for Christology. In the preface to his first lecture, he writes: "Cf. H. R Mackintosh: 'In point of fact it is at the Cross that the full meaning of *God in Christ* has broken on the human mind.'"[20]

That being said, Torrance's Christology is patently different from Mackintosh's and Forsyth's. In their theological treatises the dead hand of German liberalism is again evident. The person and work of Christ tends to be conceived anthropocentrically, i.e. in moral and psychological terms.[21] Naturally, both men ignore the ascension and second advent of Christ. Torrance's approach, by contrast, reflects Barth's influence.[22] It is much more theo-centric. One gets a clear sense of the objective otherness of God. The real starting point is not our faith in God, though this is essential, but the Word of God—the concrete, historical actions of God in Christ as witnessed to in Scripture. Torrance underscores the notion that Christ is even the subject of faith. "Thus the central thing in faith, in acknowledgement of the Person of Christ is *Christ's own action*, his encounter with us, he who has come to save us."[23]

2. Christology and History

Torrance's method of reckoning with Christ and his action is laid out in his introduction. Jesus Christ is the "immediate Object of believing knowledge and worship."[24] This includes knowledge of God the Father and the Holy Spirit. But Christ is not simply a mediator of knowledge

---

can be 'separated from the other, for both mean this, that God comes" (Brunner, *The Mediator,* 409). However, Brunner responds to the other problem in Christology, the tendency to subordinate the person of Christ to his work (ibid., 407–9).

20. Torrance, *The Doctrine of Jesus Christ,* 1.

21. John McConnachie (1875–1948), who is recognised as the earliest exponent of Barth in Scotland, describes Mackintosh's Christology as following in the tradition of the great German liberal theologians Herrmann and Ritschl. McConnachie was in a position to judge. He had also studied under Herrmann. For his views on Barth and Mackintosh, see his book *The Significance of Karl Barth,* 120–21. Torrance adopted from Mackintosh the idea that Christ's "work is but his Person in action," but for Mackintosh this idea is discernible chiefly in Christ's "ethical supremacy", not in his historical actions. What this means is that Christ "inspires a new ideal of character and conduct," which we cannot possibly acquire apart from his help (Mackintosh, *The Doctrine of the Person,* 326).

22. On his voyage to America, Torrance brought with him *Die Kirchliche Dogmatik* I/1 & I/2.

23. Torrance, *The Doctrine of Jesus Christ,* 18.

24. Ibid., 1.

of God, "he is *himself very* God of very God."[25] As much as Christology deals with a person who is ontologically and objectively real to faith, it deals with a person who is historically real. "The central object of the Christian Faith is to be found in a *Person* who was without doubt historical; and it was his life and work carried out under Pontius Pilate that has been the pivot of the world ever since."[26] Christology by definition has a close connection with time and history. The work of the person of Christ is redemption wrought out in history.

But Torrance is aware that modernity militates against such an idea. It has made the historical nature of Christ's redemption into a "stumbling block" to faith in Christ. This is ironic, for modernity gave birth to a renewed interest in history. This led to the quest of the historical Jesus, a critical investigation into real life of the man who the church proclaims as Lord. This quest was predicated, though, on the idea, which stems from Lessing's "ugly ditch," that there is an unbridgeable gap between the Christ of faith and the Jesus of history. However, this search for the authentic Jesus of history has only meant a reduction of the Jesus of history. The modern historian presents us with a great religious teacher but not one defined by his great acts in history: the incarnation, the atonement, the resurrection, and ascension. We hear about a great moral leader, yet one who in the end was swallowed up by history. But we do not encounter the Son of God in the flesh; the God-in-time who triumphs over history in the end.

Against this view, Torrance calls for a Christian protest "in the strongest terms." Christianity declares that God has entered history, entered time, in Jesus Christ. And this means that "Redemption . . . has to be actualized in history and . . . mediated through history."[27] It even involves, as he will say later, the "reversal of history." Theologians, therefore, must pay greater attention to the role of history. It must be seen as the "sphere of God's operation and the medium of divine Redemption," where the *supreme fact* is not a symbol of a transcendent world but the "Person of God in Christ."[28] However, Torrance does not call for a new philosophical study of history. That may only serve to undermine the Christian faith again. The new emphasis on history must begin with

25. Ibid.

26. Ibid., 2.

27. Ibid., 4.

28. Ibid.

a greater appreciation of Jesus' relation to ancient Israel. He does not think Christ can be known apart from the Old Testament; because in the Old Testament history is "not merely contingent."[29] History is the sphere in which God acts, acts for the purpose of redemption. It is here where history points toward Jesus Christ, the historical fulfilment of Old Testament hopes. That explains why Old Testament eschatology stresses the future, and why it is essentially messianic.

But God's work in history did not end abruptly with the coming of Jesus the Messiah. Jesus Christ is also the Mediator between God and the whole world. "God was in Christ reconciling the world to Himself" (2 Cor 5:19). The world is reconciled to God through the cross, the supreme work of Christ, but the world still needs to be fully redeemed through Christ. Hence the ascension is a vital part of the work of Christ. It is from his heavenly throne that Christ actualizes his redemption in history. This is the meaning of the last book of the Bible, the Apocalypse. Moreover, the ascension gives the church the assurance that God is still "actually among us." After all, it is a "fundamental dictum" of Christianity that "in Christ we have God in history."[30]

When Torrance underlines the historical nature of Christ, one might assume he is on the side of American fundamentalists in their battle against the modernists. Not quite. He is on the side of certain European theologians. His understanding of Christ's relation to history owes much to Barth and Brunner. This means that history alone does not bear witness to the divinity of Christ. Jesus Christ was and is *in* history, but he is not *of* history. History is a predicate of revelation, but revelation is not a predicate of history. The divinity and lordship of Christ are not subject to historical verification. The results of the "quest of the historical Jesus" have proven that much. The historian can at most see only "Christ in the flesh." But, as Brunner put it, the "believer sees more than the 'Christ after the flesh' in the 'Christ in the flesh.'"[31] That is because the revelation of Jesus as the God-Man happens through faith alone.

3. Teleology

There is something else that gives Torrance's Christology a strong eschatological cast. This is teleology. Christology is about God-in-time,

---

29. Ibid.
30. Ibid.
31. Brunner, *The Mediator*, 156.

God-in-Action. But this action is for a purpose, a *telos* (an end). That *telos* is the redemption of the world. Christ in history is Christ in saving action. We can only know Christ's person from his work; his being from his action; his nature from his benefits. Torrance gets this epistemology from Barth, but also from Forsyth and Mackintosh. Citing the former, he writes: 'Theologically, faith in Christ means that the person of Christ must be interpreted by what that saving action of God in him requires, that Christ's work is the master key to His Person, that His benefits interpret his nature. It means, when theologically put, that Christology is the corollary of Soteriology."[32] Mackintosh saw it this way: "It is a feature of the best modern Christology that the person of our Lord has come to be exhibited as interpretable only through the medium of His redeeming work. There is a universal feeling that to know what He has done and does will reveal to us what He is."[33] In Torrance's words, "He is the *Redeemer*—God; and apart from his Redemption we know really nothing of him."[34] Torrance also gives a nod to Cullmann's christological principle.[35] He claims that Christ "is to be understood functionally and not metaphysically, dynamically rather ontologically."[36]

Redemption is the *telos* of God's action in Christ. But redemption involves more than the release from guilt, much more than what the individual can experience here and now. Teleology must not be anthropocentric, for it does not terminate in the soul of the individual. It also involves the reversal of history, a new time, a new heaven and earth. In fact redemption terminates in the glory of God. Torrance writes that "the primary object of God . . . is not salvation but the Glory of God, for God does not seek an end less than his own Being, else he would not be God. But the Glory of God includes our salvation, and we must learn always to think of God as at the Centre."[37] Since the glory of God is the real end or *telos*, then Christology must strive to give an account of those last things—resurrection, ascension, parousia, judgment—which extend beyond the scope of humanity's present concerns and beyond the world's

32. Torrance, *The Doctrine of Jesus Christ*, 13.

33. Mackintosh, *The Doctrine of the Person*, 321.

34. Torrance, *The Doctrine of Jesus Christ*, 184.

35. "When it is asked in the New Testament 'Who is Christ?,' the question never means exclusively, or even primarily, 'What is his nature?,' but first of all, 'What is his function?'" Cf. Cullmann, *The Christology of the New Testament*, 4.

36. Torrance, *The Doctrine of Jesus Christ*, 165.

37. Ibid., 18.

myopic conception of what is possible. For these things centre on the Last One (*Eschatos*) who brings glory to God.

4. Eschatology as the Presence of the Kingdom of God

For Torrance, though, eschatology is not only about things in the future and about movement towards an end. It concerns things that are present, that have been realized. In a sense the end has already come with the incarnation of the Son of God. In him the glory of God has been revealed. Following Barth, Torrance insists that the incarnation is essentially a "movement of Eternity into time."[38] It means "God is present, actually present in Christ."[39] Christ is Immanuel, "God with us." The incarnation makes Christianity "pre-eminently the religion of the Parousia of God, of an actual coming of God and of a real presence of God held together in the same thought: in Jesus Christ the Son of God."[40] But if Jesus Christ is not of God, then there is no presence of the kingdom of God in the world. The kingdom is only a hope, something wholly in the future. If that be the case, then Christianity is no advance upon Judaism, which still longs for the Messiah. Torrance laments the loss of faith in the presence of God in his own day, and he attributes this loss to a denial of the deity of Christ.

This presence of God in Christ, this coming of the kingdom, has negative and positive consequences. Negatively, it means the judgment of humankind. The coming of God in Christ presupposes a separation between humankind and God, one caused by humankind's rebellion against God. This is the meaning of original sin. In short, the incarnation presupposes a *fallen* human nature. The incarnation tells us that God came to judge sin and put it away, to overcome that chasm between humankind and God. But the judgment that comes from the revelation of God in Christ is redemptive. It is not only a judgment of individual sins but a judgment of all collective attempts to build a kingdom of God apart from God. "It means ultimately the disqualification of civilisation and the great and magnificent tower of Babel."[41] All cultures of progress are doomed to fail in the end. This is why in his sermons on the Apocalypse

38. Ibid., 74.
39. Ibid., 142.
40. Ibid.
41. Ibid., 77.

Torrance shows a suspicion towards the "new world order" that emerges after the war and why, unlike many of his contemporaries, he will not be deeply disturbed by the crisis of civilization that will grip Europe in the middle of the century.

On the other hand, the incarnation means God takes time seriously and has a "gracious attitude" towards it. We are redeemed in time and with time, not from it or outside it. Time in fact, like human nature, is restored in the incarnation. It is even given "a place in Eternity."[42] Indeed Christ's kingdom is really about a new time. "While Jesus came to over-throw the old order, he came to set up a new one, a new Kingdom, a new time."[43]

As for the benefits of the presence of God, Torrance, relying on John's Gospel, summarizes them as "Love," "Life," and "Light." The incarnation is more than a sign of the fact that God loves us. It is *the fact that* God loves us, that he gives himself fully, that he holds nothing back from us. "In Him dwells all the fullness of the Godhead bodily" (Col 2:9). The love behind the incarnation is a totally free act of God. However, God cannot be reduced to love (a tendency in modern theol-ogy). Love can be called the "bestowal of self" of God, but God's self is the "prius" or "ultimate fountain" of this bestowal.[44] The incarnation is the "real coming of God to man, in which God gives himself *for* and *to* man."[45] We think instantly that this means God loves us. He does; but that "for" must first be understood as something *for our redemption.* The love shown in the incarnation is a pure gift love; it is neither caused nor merited by its object. In sum, we can find no reason for this love because there is no adequate human analogy for it, as the New Testament writers discovered. The best word for it was "agape." The incarnation forces us to acknowledge this love as arising from the "self-grounded will of God," as an "ultimate fact" that "knows no 'why?'"[46] "If we do not see God's incar-nate love this way we risk betraying the central message of Christianity: Grace—the utter God-centeredness of revelation and redemption, the unconditioned coming of God to man in Christ."[47]

42. Ibid., 78.

43. Ibid.

44. Ibid., 86.

45. Ibid., 83.

46. Ibid., 87.

47. Ibid.

If the incarnation is about love, it is about life too. For Torrance, the essence of human life is communion with God. Sin disrupted this communion, but the incarnation restores it. This, of course, does not happen immediately. The incarnation is the first stage in our redemption. This is followed by the remission of sins, the Spirit of adoption, the transformation into the image of Christ and the resurrection of the body. From this perspective, the resurrection is in a "real sense" the "completion of the Incarnation."[48] The incarnation also brings God to light. "I am the Light of the World" (John 8:12). Knowledge of God follows from the incarnation. It means God has accommodated himself to our senses by assuming a human form. Real theological knowledge is now possible, not through any human form but only through the specific form of Jesus Christ. The coming of God in the flesh compels us to think of God "exclusively" in terms of Christ.

But knowledge of God through Christ becomes actual only after we have heard and accepted the Word of God in faith and through the Holy Spirit. The Spirit of God is the light that discloses God to us in the human form of Christ. More precisely, the Holy Spirit turns the "objective revelation of God in Christ . . . into a subjectively real revelation."[49]

The incarnation, as the *parousia* of God, therefore has a "two-fold" meaning: as a witness both to God's holiness and love. Christ is the incarnation of Holy Love. It is the incarnation of the God who in his goodness creates life but who in his righteousness can take life away. His holiness leads to the crucifixion of our sinful nature in the incarnate One; his love leads to the resurrection of our flesh through this same One. For Torrance, the "two-fold" meaning of the incarnation instructs us that we cannot understand the incarnation without the atonement; nor can we understand the atonement without the incarnation. This is why he believes a proper doctrine of atonement has to consist not only of Christ's substitutionary work but of Christ's "vicarious life of obedience to the Father."[50]

The organic connection between incarnation and atonement explains the unity of the "Person and Work of Christ." This relationship is also the linchpin of Torrance's Christology and soteriology.

48. Ibid., 78.

49. Ibid., 100.

50. Ibid., 151. In the Scottish Reformed tradition he sees these two aspects of atonement represented by R. W. Dale and John McLeod-Campbell respectively.

5. The Work of the Cross

Recall that Torrance began his lectures under the claim that it is at the cross that *the full meaning of God in Christ has broken on the human mind.* The cross is the principal work of Christ. This is good Reformed theology. But Torrance is not a typical Reformed theologian, since for him the cross stands for more than penal substitutionary atonement. More than any other work of Christ, it discloses the mystery of the person of Christ. "It is there [at the cross] in his sacrificial passion that the whole divine-human nature of Jesus' Person as the incarnate Son of God is revealed to the understanding of saving faith. It is there at the cross that the meaning and the purpose of his incarnation really become revealed to us."[51] The cross may be understood as a "cross-section" of the life and ministry of the incarnate Son.[52] It signifies Christ's vicarious death for our sins, but it stands equally for the Son's vicarious life of obedience to God the Father. On this score, Jesus' entire life is a vicarious offering for us. "The Cross is the outworking of a decision that constitutes the Person of the Mediator himself in the incarnation."[53]

For Torrance, the problem with the penal-substitutionary model of the atonement is that it gives the impression that God's redemption is merely a legal transaction, that God's redemption has no material basis in the person of Christ. In his view, the only way to correct this is by taking into consideration Christ's whole life, so that his atoning work begins at birth, increases in intensity in correlation with maturation as a real person, until it reaches a climax at Golgotha. To help us conceive the person and work of Christ together, the incarnation and the cross, Torrance—borrowing Mackintosh's words—would have us think of the work of Christ as his "Person-in-movement" or his "Person-in-saving action."[54] As well, Torrance draws attention to the unity of this action. Christ's saving actions should be understood, then, as "one supreme comprehensive act of God's Self-humiliation from the Cradle to the Cross."[55]

---

51. Torrance, *The Doctrine of Jesus Christ,* 165.

52. Ibid., 153.

53. Ibid., 151.

54. Ibid., 149.

55. Ibid., 85.

Yet Torrance does not stop at the cradle. How could he, if he insists that Christ is "very God of very God," the actual coming of God in flesh and time? Thus the cross discloses not only the "secret" of the person of Christ. It discloses the "secret" of God. The great news revealed is that the cross of Christ is "eternal in the heart of God."[56] As Torrance learned from Barth, our understanding of God can be neither greater nor less than what Christ is for us and does for us. This means the whole work and person of Christ is best understood as a manifestation of the act and being of God. "The Act of God in Christ on the Cross must be thought of in accordance with his Being which is itself God's reality in action, for it is in the Cross that there was manifested his supreme self-assertion as Holy God and God's supreme self-bestowal as Holy Love."[57]

Eschatology is ultimately about the glory of God. Even the cross of Christ, in Torrance's view, is a witness to this. The holiness and love of God that comes to us in Christ may be understood as "the Dominion and Communion of God," which is the essence of the kingdom of God.[58] Still, the news of the arrival kingdom of God, the gospel, is really the establishment of the kingdom of God through the act of God the Father in Christ. And nowhere is the holiness and love of God, his dominion and communion, greater that at the cross of Christ. "It is here in fact that God both gives himself in his Holiness *to* men and asserts himself in his Holy Love to be *for* mankind."[59]

The cross stands for God's judgment of sin. It is the sure evidence that God in his holiness will not tolerate forever the presence of sin in his creatures. The cross, then, is God's holiness in action, his self-assertion in the face of man's rebellion and private self-assertion. And God succeeds. He effectively asserts his holiness by putting to death Christ, man's representative and substitute before God. At the cross the holiness of God is revealed in all its truth and in all its glory. The judgment of the cross is also paradoxically a revelation of the love of God. For this judgment is the first act in God's atonement for sins. The cross not only reveals how far we have fallen away from God, but also how close God has come to us. It testifies that God is no longer against us, that he has not abandoned

56. Ibid., 153.
57. Ibid., 168.
58. Ibid.
59. Ibid., 169.

us. It shows that he has made the greatest stride towards the reestablishment of his "Dominion" over us and his "Communion" with us.

6. The Resurrection: fulfillment of the Person and Work

It is understandable that the lecture on the resurrection of Christ is near the end of the series. Its location, though, belies its importance. For Torrance, the resurrection is actually the starting point in Christology. With Barth he believes that it is in the light of the resurrection that the person of Christ is truly comprehended.[60] He is not concerned with the "how" of Christ's resurrection. Like Christ's virgin birth, he sees it as an absolute miracle. There is no natural cause behind it. Torrance pursues the significance of the resurrection for understanding Christ's person and work. The significance is that the resurrection illuminates and validates the person and work. In his view, it was the resurrection of the crucified Jesus that convinced the first disciples that this man was not just another prophet of Israel, but the Lord Jesus Christ and Son of God. "It is in the Resurrection that Christ comes out of his *Incognito*, as it were, and we behold his transcendent glory; it is at the Resurrection that we learn the real secret of Christ's Person to be not human but divine."[61] When the disciples recognized Jesus as divine, as Lord and Son of God, the events of his life took on a whole new meaning. They became revelatory and redemptive. "The significance of the resurrection . . . lies in the conjunction of Person and Work of Christ . . . Some have preferred to discuss his Person and teaching, some have laid emphasis on his work almost exclusively. The truth is that are rightly seen only together in their proper perspective and significance here: at the Resurrection."[62]

They are seen together because they are really brought back together in the resurrection. From an historical perspective, the cross marks the separation of the person and his work, a break in the unity of the incarnation and atonement. By becoming a sacrifice for sins the person is lost to death. The resurrection, however, reunites the person and work of Christ.

---

60. Barth had stated that "the whole life and death of Jesus are undoubtedly interpreted in the light of His resurrection" (Barth, *Credo*, 96).

61. Torrance, *The Doctrine of Jesus Christ*, 189.

62. Ibid., 187.

The resurrection represents eschatological fulfillment. For it shows Christ to be not only the source of our redemption but also the fulfillment of it. The resurrection means "power . . . triumph . . . victory."[63] Christ is the one who rose from his sacrifice on the cross "triumphant in the Kingdom of God."[64]

7. The Ascension: The Continuation of the Person and Work

It was Torrance's intention to describe the full import of the resurrection on the person and work of Christ. Unfortunately, most of the lecture material on the subject is lost. However, we do learn something about the significance of the resurrection, but this comes in the next—and last—lecture: "The Ascension of Christ and the Second Advent." In choosing to expound on the ascension, Torrance knows he is going against a tendency in modern theology to neglect the ascension. For example, Forsyth and Mackintosh ignore the subject altogether, while Emil Brunner downplays its significance. For Brunner, the ascension means that "He has His Face turned in the other direction, away from us. The story of Christ has now reached an end."[65]

For Torrance, by contrast, the story of Christ continues with the ascension. Indeed it must continue by this way if we really believe in the resurrection of Jesus from the dead. Faith in the resurrection entails that Jesus Christ continues to live as God and man. But on top of the biblical witness to this "Continuous Living Reality," Torrance finds ontological reasons. It is obvious, then, that Christology for him is not *only* functional. With the Nicene Fathers he argues that this hypostatic union of God and man is one that "was/is eternal and never-ending."[66] Theology as Christology therefore can continue. It means too that eschatology is not simply a matter of conjecturing about the future, but is about what Christ is doing and will do.

> Christian theology, centred in the Lord Jesus Christ, can have a proper place only where the reality of his human nature continues. Just as there only can be revelation to us where revelation takes human form, because humanity cannot think outside of

63. Ibid.

64. Ibid., 188.

65. Brunner, *The Mediator*, 156.

66. Torrance, *The Doctrine of Jesus Christ*, 190.

itself, so here where the form and reality of Christ as *God-Man* continues, . . . there theology as Christology must persist in its efforts to gain a clear understanding of the risen and ascended Lord Jesus and all that he means for us in the Church and the world.[67]

Since the ascension is about the life and ministry of Jesus after the resurrection, Torrance prefers to speak of the "risen and ascended Lord Jesus" (cf. Eph 1:20). Recall that the cross had to be seen in conjunction with the incarnation, in order to comprehend the person and work of Christ in his humiliation and in his past. Likewise, we must think the resurrection and ascension together in order to comprehend his person and work in his exaltation—in his present and his future.

This is not to deny any difference between the revelation that comes from the resurrection and the one that comes from the ascension. The object of faith, Christ Jesus, remains the same, and the ascension is within the "same realm of revelation as that enjoyed by the disciples of Jesus before and after his resurrection."[68] There is a difference, however, in the mode of apprehension of Christ, due to the descent of the Spirit at Pentecost. Excepting Paul's Damascus road experience, the ascension tells us that Christ is no longer visible to the naked eye, but only through the eye of faith, which is a work of the Holy Spirit—Christ's "other self."

For Torrance, the function of the risen and ascended Christ is no different substantially from the function of the incarnate Christ on earth. This is nothing less than the revelation of God to humankind and the redemption of humankind. The ascension reveals that Christ has returned bodily to the throne of God, confirming that Christ and his saving work on earth have their beginning and end in God. It can be understood as the "visible experience given to the disciples to assure them, as Jesus Christ on earth, he for ever is and will be in and with God in Glory."[69] It reveals that there is "a MAN in heaven today" and that all that constitutes our humanity in terms of mind, body, spirit, and relationships has been raised and carried up into heaven by Christ. Christ was, is, and always will be close to us; and thus he is truly qualified and ready to function as our compassionate High Priest before God the Father.[70]

67. Ibid.
68. Ibid., 191.
69. Ibid., 193.
70. Ibid.

The ascension gives us the knowledge also that time has a place in eternity. Christ's heavenly session means time is "real for eternity," not "illusory."[71] In asserting this Torrance is challenging Kant's philosophy of time. Kant probably did not regard time as an illusion, but he did insist that time is an "internal sense" that applies only to phenomenal reality. Therefore, whatever that does not affect our senses, such as eternity or God, cannot be in time. For Torrance, the ascension means not only that time is real for the eternal God; it also means time has been redeemed. We can now look forward to a redeemed time in the kingdom of God. Indeed the presence of the Holy Spirit in the church indicates that this new time has already "invaded" this present fallen, sinful time.

Above all, the ascension reveals that Christ is God's "Right Hand." The ascension should dispel any lingering doubts about the deity of Christ, and especially doubts that Christ is the "Act" and "Being" of God. Just as the incarnation confirms the humiliation of God in Christ, the ascension confirms the exaltation of God in Christ. God in being and act is none other than Christ in his person and his work. "What Christ IS, God IS, because Christ IS God's Right Hand."[72] The ascension guarantees that there is no other God hiding behind Christ, "no dark spots" remaining in the revelation of God, in the being and act of God. If the incarnation and cross show the humiliation and weakness of Christ, then the ascension shows us that the "act of Christ is actually the very omnipotent action of God-and that there is no other power or 'potence' in God which has not and is not revealed in Christ."[73]

In order to explain how the ascension is part of Christ's redemptive work, Torrance employs the three offices of Christ, the triplex *munus*, which have been important in Reformed dogmatics.[74] Taking Christ to

---

71. Ibid., 192.

72. Ibid., 193.

73. Ibid., 194.

74. The offices of Christ have their basis in the Old Testament, but Calvin was the first to distinguish the three offices and to give them a role in a systematic theology. See *Institutes*, II, 15. Ever since, Protestant theologians have in general recognized the validity of the offices, even though they have had great difficulty finding agreement on their function, interrelation, and even their number. Given the neglect of the ascension in modern Christologies, it is no surprise that the offices of Christ fell into desuetude with it. Torrance did, however, find inspiration for the recovery of the offices in Barth's *Credo*. For a good general survey of the offices of Christ, see Louis Berkhof, *Systematic Theology*, 356–66; 406–11; also Emil Brunner, *Dogmatics*, vol. 3, 271–307.

be Prophet, Priest, and King, permits one to think about his redemptive work as a unity with differences. In light of the resurrection, he defines the teachings of Christ as the work of his prophetic office, and his humiliation and cross as the work of his priestly office. Christ's kingly office is fulfilled through the ascension, but Torrance prefers to call this office his "Royal Priesthood," since he is a King still carrying out the work of redemption for the cosmos.

The central work of the priestly office is the cross. Therefore, even in his kingly office Christ bears the effects of the cross. "Jesus, yes, he Jesus, is now at the right hand of God holding the reins of the world in his hands, the hands that bore the imprint of the nails hammered in them on the cross."[75] This fact reveals the humanity of Christ the King, but it also determines the mode of his redemption in the world. Humankind will not be redeemed by means of the progress of civilization. It will be redeemed along the pattern of the cross. Redemption means ultimately redemption from suffering, but redemption takes place *through* suffering first.

It goes against the gospel to think that Christ's redemption of the world can take place without serious interruptions in the world's so-called development, without judgments upon the evils in the world. This *cross-view* of world redemption will come sharply into focus in Torrance's sermons on the Apocalypse in 1946, just after his experience as a war-time pastor and army chaplain. Yet the rumblings of war in Europe in 1939 forced him even then to ponder the relationship between the ascended Christ and the course of history. "We may not now understand all that happens and can happen in the world of today offers; it is black—and when has it been blacker than this moment? [i.e., 1939]—but of this we are assured by the Ascension that the Lord Jesus Christ is reigning over the kingdoms and nations of the world and working out his redeeming purpose for redemption."[76]

If God elects Christ Jesus to carry out the redemption of the world, then Christ elects a special people by which he fulfills this mission. This is the church on earth and in history. Here Torrance describes the church as the "visible incarnation of Christ on earth in lieu of his very Self"[77]—although later, during the 1950s, he will inveigh against the

75. Torrance, *The Doctrine of Jesus Christ*, 194.

76. Ibid.

77. Ibid.

"Catholic" idea that the church is a *Christus prolongatus*, or extension of the incarnation.

As the "visible incarnation of Christ," the church must conform to Christ and share in the sufferings of his cross; not as atonement, but as a judgment and chastisement in preparation for an existence lived in the power of the resurrection. Just as Christ identified with us as sinners, we are called to identify with him in his humiliation on the cross. Redemption for the church involves encountering the man on the cross. Knowledge of Christ also involves the cross, for Christ "still is the Crucified One though risen from the dead."[78]

Here we have a genuine *theology of the cross*. Christ has risen in triumph, power, and victory; he has ascended in glory to the throne of God, where he is now God's "Right Hand," Christ the King. However, the church and individual believers cannot yet know Christ as this glorious King. Until his coming again, they can only know him as the Crucified One, as their Lord and Savior through faith.

The church lives, in Barth's words, "*Zwischen die Zeiten*," between the time of the ascension and the second advent. It is a time of grace, a sign of God's patience, in order that the world will exercise repentance. Otherwise, divine judgment would be immediate: Christ's "Advent Presence would decide things finally there and then once and for all."[79] As in primitive Christianity, the central message of the church today should be "repent for the Kingdom of God is at hand."

Christ's visible absence from the world is not a sign he has abandoned the world, that he no longer loves it. On the contrary, he ascended for the sake of the church and the world, so that he could reach the whole world through the church with the message of the gospel.

8. The Second Advent

We have finally come to a traditional topic in eschatology. However, Torrance did not leave us with much to reflect on—just three pages. Still, we get to the heart of his eschatology, since eschatology (like theology in general) has to be centered on Christ and his actions. It is mainly about the *Eschatos* (Last One), not the *eschata* (last things).

78. Ibid.
79. Ibid., 196.

There are several ways to approach the second advent. In line with Torrance's earlier stress on the unity of the person and work of Christ, we may look at it as the final act of that "Person-in-saving-action." Or, in creedal terms, we may think of it as the coming of the Judge of the living and the dead. Here Torrance prefers the theocentric terms he used to describe the cross of Christ. The second advent is the "self-impartation of God" and the "self-assertion of God." Again, these movements imply the redemption of God through "the bestowal of himself in holy love" and of the judgment of God "through his holy self-assertion."[80] But these are not a set of isolated movements in God; they are connected with God's earlier movements in Christ. God's holy self-assertion at the second advent is the "final reaction" of God against sin.[81] It will be a reaction through Christ, on the ground of his cross, because he is the one who has ascended to the "very Throne of God," where God has entrusted all power and judgment to him.

Apart from the ascension of Christ, the church has no basis for its hope in Christ's return—nor either in the resurrection of the dead or the new heaven and earth. Although Christ delays his return, Torrance is confident that Christ "will come again in like manner" to his ascension before the disciples. The primary meaning of this "in like manner" is not cosmological but Christological and soteriological. It means Jesus will return as the crucified and risen Lord, as the man who was born of a virgin, who was crucified, left to die, and then buried, but who rose bodily from the grave. Soteriologically, Christ's return will mean the "fulfilment of all his saving and redeeming life and work."[82] Like his other redeeming acts, this act will also have a relation to time and history. In this case, however, the sudden return of Christ will bring an apocalyptic end to history. It will bring to pass its "final consummation in a great act of crisis in which all time will be gathered up and changed."[83] The crisis will be generated by the appearance of Christ, for this means that eternity will break into time. The whole effect will be a sudden "catastrophic" judgment and redemption of our corrupt time. "When Eternity enters time, Eternity with which there is no past, present, future, it must travel in and through time and gather it all up into a great catastrophic crisis in

80. Ibid., 197.
81. Ibid.
82. Ibid., 196.
83. Ibid., 197.

which time will pass away in its fallen condition, but judged, and slain, as it were, and a new time will be born in the Kingdom of God."[84]

One can find grounds in the bible (Mark 13 and par.; 2 Pet 3) for a catastrophic end to the world, but this notion that it will be the consequence of eternity entering time is Torrance's own extrapolation. His argument is based on his earlier assertion that the key fact about the incarnation is the movement of eternity into time. The ascension does not abrogate this new connection made between eternity and time; it only reaffirms that time is real for eternity, not an illusion.

In fact, the ascension of Christ refers to the movement of all human "conditions"—including time—into eternity, within the realm of "God's sovereign purpose."[85] But if this is really the nature of the case, then Torrance is stuck with an inconsistency. The effect of the second advent does not correspond to the effect that the incarnation and ascension had on time. How can one say that eternity "has no present, past or future" and thus must "gather" these all up at the end, if the God in Christ represents eternity, and the ascension of Christ is the sign that eternity is forever united to time? It seems that the significance of the ascension for the second advent is not commensurate with its christological and soteriological significance.

Like the first advent of Christ, the second will be a "self-bestowal and self-assertion of Christ." It will be the "final revelation of God's Love and Holiness in the Advent of Christ which completes the incarnate revelation . . . and the redemption accomplished in Christ Jesus."[86] This second self-assertion of Christ will be the final judgment of sin in the world. But those who are in Christ need not fear condemnation for their sins, since these have been atoned for by Christ's death. However, the self-assertion of Christ will effect in them both the immediate eradication of those sins the sanctifying Spirit has not destroyed and the cancellation of all "penalties incurred" from remitted sins.

The advent of Christ will also be the end of the time of grace, the time for repentance and of God's patience. There is no assurance of universal salvation.[87] Sinners who "resist" Christ and "persist in their

84. Ibid., 197.

85. Ibid., 192.

86. Torrance, *The Doctrine of Jesus Christ*, 198.

87. A number of years later, Torrance would write an article in refutation of J. A. T Robinson's case for universalism. See "Universalism or Election ?" 310–18.

resistance" to the end cannot expect one last offer of grace from God but only a final self-assertion or judgment from him. Indeed this will be the "Apocalypse of the Wrath" that leads to condemnation.[88]

The faithful in Christ, on the other hand, can look forward to God's final self-bestowal, the final revelation of his love. After God has asserted himself against all the remnants and effects of sin in his people, he will consummate the union he has with them in Spirit "with his very Presence."[89] They will be transformed "in the twinkling of an eye," and so the need for faith will cease.

Of course, any talk about the second advent naturally leads us into a consideration of things that have not happened, that are wholly in the future. But Torrance does not venture to speculate on details surrounding the second advent. This should not surprise us. As indicated above, his theology is governed by a scientific realism. This, though, does not rule out divine revelation. Calvin believed that God in his revelation must accommodate himself to our feeble human capacity. Torrance agrees. Revelation must take a "human form," since the human mind cannot "think outside of itself." The "consummation of faith," then, "does not lie completely within human knowledge and experience here and now. This is where we trespass on eschatology or the fulfilment of our hope in Christ which transcends earthly existence in the form we know it here and now."[90] To be sure, a Christian theologian also has the Spirit of God and faith to assist him; yet Jesus Christ is both the source of the Spirit and the object of faith. So any discussion about the Christ who will come again must, if it is to be real theological talk—and not speculation or mythology—be anchored to this man Christ Jesus who has risen and ascended.

This is why Torrance turns to the apocalyptic side of eschatology. For him the language of the Apocalypse is not the stuff of mythology. Rather, it points to the second advent of Christ, whose coming is revealed in his ongoing work of redemption. "The future reality of which they speak is continuous with the work of Christ on earth, with our knowledge and experience of him here and now today."[91]

---

88. Torrance, *The Doctrine of Jesus Christ*, 199.

89. Ibid., 198.

90. Ibid.

91. Ibid., 198.

Conclusion

This lecture by Torrance on the ascension and the second advent is one of the shortest in his Auburn series, yet it is the most original and visionary. He takes Christology beyond the boundaries set by contemporary theologians such as Forsyth, Mackintosh, and Brunner. Barth may have pushed the boundaries with his lectures on the Apostles' Creed in 1935 and his section on "The time of revelation" in *Die Kirchliche Dogmatik* II/1, but even he had not given much thought to the work of the risen and ascended Christ, or to the nature of the second advent itself.

Torrance left Auburn in the summer of 1939. He would not return to academia until he accepted the Chair in Church History at New College in 1950. In the meantime he was a parish minister for the Church of Scotland and a chaplain briefly in the British Army. Yet his theological activity did not cease. Indeed the horrors of war, the threat of communism, and the general crisis of civilization that marked this period became a crucible for Torrance's Auburn Christology, especially for that remarkable last part of it. In the pulpit at Alyth and on the battlefield of Italy, Torrance would have to cling tenaciously to the idea that "there is a MAN in heaven today," Christ the God-Man, who is truly "reigning over the kingdoms and nations of the world and working out his redeeming purpose for redemption." But he would do more that just cling to an idea; through deeper biblical and theological study he would explicate the meaning of it.

The lecture on the second advent is one of the few times Torrance discusses last things, as traditionally understood. There is an epistemological reason for this. As long as we live in the time of the church the "consummation of faith" is beyond our ken. Eschatology, then, if we define it strictly in terms of the last things, is bound to be an uncertain dogmatic science. But Torrance does not cease from thinking about eschatology. That is because he redefines it accordance with his Christology and soteriology. It becomes less about the "end time" and more about the "between the times," the time between the ascension and second advent, the time of the church, the time of grace.

The second advent remains important, but it is something that approaches us and something that we move towards. But this approach, this movement is not something that happens on the plane of history as we know it. The second advent is about Christ, the risen Lord and King who has ascended above the plane of history. His sudden advent would mean the reversal of history as we know it. Christ represents the new creation and the new age. The eschatological tension is therefore dual: it is "between the new and the old here and now," and "between the present and the future." That is why instead of the second advent Torrance will tend to speak of the one *parousia*—as a coming-and-presence of Christ—with two particular moments. Christ's kingdom, therefore, is not merely a future reality. It is equally a present, hidden reality, which unveils itself in the church—through the Spirit, the Word, and the Sacrament. Yet the full unveiling of Christ and his kingdom is reserved for the final *parousia*. But, as we will see, there are also practical and historical reasons why Torrance redefines eschatology.

2

Practical Eschatology

Alyth, Scotland 1940–1943

WE MUST LOOK TO TORRANCE'S SERMONS IF WE WISH TO LEARN ABOUT his eschatology in the 1940s. *The Apocalypse Today* (1960), one of his most eschatological works, is actually a collection of sermons from this period. Torrance published a number of papers in this decade, but they contain relatively little in the way of eschatology. He probably did not intend on expatiating on the subject, but historical and pastoral circumstances dictated otherwise. The principles of it—Christ's resurrection and ascension—were certainly in place at Auburn. Yet his eschatology flowers as he engages with the events of his time and the spiritual needs of his parish members. His sermons, he recalls, "seemed to reflect themselves in answer to concerns in the congregation."[1] This eschatology is not only deeply theological; it is also practical and pastoral. McGrath wisely observes that Alyth and Beechgrove were to Torrance what Safenwil was to Karl Barth.[2]

Although this eschatology comes from Torrance's sermons, that does not mean we can discount it. If anything, reading his sermons brings us to the heart of his eschatology. For Torrance, the sermon was the supreme test for theology. He learned this point from his great teachers. Mackintosh had insisted that true theology is theology that can be preached. Barth had stated that "in conformity with its object, the fundamental form of theology is the prayer and the sermon."[3] It seems that

1. Torrance, "My Parish Ministry," 11. He also relates that he could not separate preaching from his house visits any more than he could separate his lectures on Christian doctrines from the "pastoral and personal power" of the gospel (Torrance, "My Parish Ministry," 9).

2. McGrath, *T. F. Torrance*, 60.

3. Barth, *The Humanity of God*, 57.

years in the pulpit drove home these truths to Torrance. While lecturing on Reformation eschatology in 1952, he insists that "Grace today is the mighty Word of God, not a *verbum* (statio) but the *sermo* (active)."[4]

A. Resurrection

1. "The Personal Touch of the Risen Lord"

On March 20, 1940, Thomas Torrance realized his goal of becoming a minister for the Church of Scotland. He was ordained and inducted into the vacant charge at Alyth Barony Parish Church.[5] Alyth is located about forty miles from Edinburgh on the north side of the Forth estuary, between Perth and Angus. Torrance remembers it as "a lovely old town," with about 3,000 souls and a "distinguished church history."[6]

He began his ministry of the Word at about the point he left off in his Auburn lectures, on the resurrection of Jesus Christ. His very first sermon was on Easter evening, and contains words taken straight from those lectures: "The Resurrection of Jesus of Nazareth from the dead dynamited the whole world."[7] Torrance could not have begun his ministry on a more fitting day on the church calendar. His preaching was essentially *kerygmatic*, and Christ's resurrection is the ground of the *kerygma*. Luke 24, the basis for his first sermon, was one of his favorite chapters in the Bible. He would preach from it seven times.[8] The essence

4. T. F. Torrance, New College lectures on eschatology. See also Torrance's review of *The Oracles of God*, 212–14. He applauds the author for exposing the link between Calvin's sermons and his theology. "Another fact expounded in these pages is that the formulation of theology is the task of the pastor—hence Mr. Parker gives over a whole chapter to delineating the theology of Calvin as it arises out of his preaching." "For him [Calvin] the relevance of theology lay in the fact that it is the servant of the preacher."

5. For these biographical details, and others surrounding his ministry at Alyth, see McGrath, *T. F. Torrance*, 60–69.

6. Torrance, "My Parish Ministry," 3, 5. This autobiographical essay is now a chapter in a book that is an assortment of Torrance's papers on ministry and the church. Torrance, *Gospel, Church, and Ministry*.

7. Torrance, Sermon on Luke 24.30ff.

8. The Gospel of Luke as whole was a favourite source for sermons. Torrance preached forty sermons from it between 1940 and 1949, though a good portion of these were recycled ones. This attention he gave to Luke 24 is a good barometer of his theological priorities, when one compares it with the attention (or lack thereof) he gave to other parts of the New Testament. From the whole of Philippians, he gave eight sermons; from Rom 8–16, nine sermons. Yet in Torrance's eight years in the pulpit he avoided the Sermon on the Mount.

of the *kerygma* should always remain the same, yet—as every minister knows—it has to be adapted to constantly changing socio-historical circumstances. Ideally, it should always come across as timely and new. And on March 20, 1940, when Britain was bracing itself for Hitler's aerial onslaught, Torrance's message must have come across just that way. "The resurrection of Jesus of Nazareth from the dead dynamited the whole world; that is the only light in which to understand the gospel properly, and the light that shines on Easter day. It was the resurrection of the crucified Messiah that constituted the power of God that created the church; it was the resurrection that burst like a flash of lighting plumb down from above, that transformed the disciples and opened their eyes."[9]

The dynamiting of the world begins at the personal, spiritual level. This happens through the "personal touch of the risen Lord" that "transforms everything into living reality," that "turns the world upside down, that dispels darkness."[10] The touch of the risen Lord reveals among other things that our relationship to God is highly personal, "far, far more personal than our relations with one another can ever be."[11] Christ's resurrection is really about the "acute personalization of all our relations with God and all his relations with us."[12]

What accounts for this personal touch? The manhood of the risen Christ. So "what ever happened in the relations of man and God between the incarnation and resurrection" is not invalidated by Easter but, rather, "deepened and extended."[13] A "diffused spirit or ideal projection" could never give us a personal touch.[14] We can have that touch only because Christ Jesus is sits enthroned at the right hand of the Father in heaven.

For Easter 1941, Torrance would preach two sermons on the resurrection; the first based on 1 Cor 15:17–18, the second on 15:20.[15] In these sermons, Christ's resurrection is the *sine qua non* of Christianity. "If Christ is not risen then you have nothing left worth calling a gospel."[16]

---

9. Torrance, Sermon on Luke 24:30ff.

10. Ibid.

11. Ibid.

12. Ibid.

13. Ibid.

14. Ibid.

15. Aside from having to follow the church calendar, Torrance was free to preach from whatever biblical texts he wanted.

16. Torrance, Sermon on 1 Corinthians 15:20.

"On the fact of the resurrection everything is suspended."[17] "Strike it out" and you have nothing left really, he adds.[18] In response to those who believe they can cling to the cross for salvation, he answers: "you must have the resurrection to explain the cross."[19] Without the resurrection, Christ on the cross is, in his view, "dead being alone," and to look for him there is to "seek the living among the dead."[20]

"But now Christ is risen . . ." The Easter story "is essentially the great Christian message."[21] With these words, Torrance launches into his second sermon. It seems that he felt the men and women at Alyth had embraced a truncated version of Christianity, one that did not take seriously that "but" from 1 Cor 15:20. It is not enough for a Christian, he maintains, to have faith in the incarnation and cross of Christ. They "form only half the truth and in themselves mean nothing" apart from Christ's resurrection.[22]

What was the whole truth that Torrance was driving at on that Easter evening? It is this. "The resurrection is the complete movement from God to God that passes through the lowest point of our humanity."[23] He uses a parabola to illustrate the doctrine. God descends to us, down to the pits of human experience—to guilt, death, hell—before he ascends in the resurrection. And the all-important turning point in the parabola is the "but" Paul used. Soteriologically, this turning point is also God's "breakthrough in the realms of human bondage, sin and death."[24] God's victory over these is an objective reality, but it has to become a subjective actuality for Christians. Otherwise, he argues, this great event will be a "mere story" for us. "Until you know the resurrection with power, till you've broken through with the risen Christ, you have not begun to know the real joy and liberty of the Gospel."[25]

No such breakthrough will occur, however, until we are taken to the edge of our thoughts, beyond the limit of what we consider pos-

---

17. Ibid.
18. Ibid.
19. Ibid.
20. Ibid.
21. Torrance, Sermon on 1 Corinthians 15:17–18.
22. Ibid.
23. Ibid.
24. Ibid.
25. Ibid.

sible. That is because the resurrection is "totally incomprehensible by any human standard."[26] We need to "make room for the supernatural," Torrance pleads, so God can "knock a hole in the midst our world" with the force of "Eternity."[27] Easter is a miracle. It is the miracle of miracles. The world is not the same since Jesus rose from the dead. The resurrection is what separates Christianity from all other religions. Indeed, from Torrance's perspective, it is not even proper to call Christianity a religion. Christianity is "a person."[28] The resurrection of Jesus Christ, we must not forget, was the resurrection of a man, who is "bone of our bone . . . flesh of our flesh."[29] Because he is risen, this man Jesus can be the personal presence of God to us. That is why he ends this Easter sermon with the great news that Christ is risen not only "for you, but . . . so that he can be near you."[30]

2. *"Nunc aeternum"*

The resurrection of Christ also opens up an encounter with "Eternity." "Eternity has come plumb down from above and intersected our beggarly time," allowing us to "take to the wings of the spirit."[31] This language too goes back to Auburn, where the incarnation is viewed as the entry of eternity into time.

The best illustration of this type of eschatology is found in Torrance's sermon on 2 Pet 3:8. The entire third chapter from Second Peter is one of the best sources of primitive Christian eschatology. It is a defense of the return of Christ—and its cataclysmic impact—in response to doubts about his return. But Torrance shows no interest in these things. Instead, his message is about meeting the eternal God in the midst of time. "With the Lord one day is as a thousand years, and a thousand years is as one day." The real value of this verse, then, is that it enables us to see the world from God's point of view, which is infinitely different from our view of it. If this is done, we will have wings with which "to soar above

---

26. Ibid.
27. Ibid.
28. Ibid.
29. Ibid.
30. Ibid.
31. Torrance, Sermon on 1 Corinthians 15:20.

tensions and limitations of a temporal world."[32] How is this so? The first part of this verse applies to God's being. "One day in the Divine Mind overrides all finite thinking; for every day has its roots in eternity."[33] It is natural to break time into future, present, and past. But Torrance thinks this distorts the real truth about time, because with God every moment is the eternal moment, the eternal now. This is what is meant, he explains, by the words: "He is the same yesterday, today, and forever" (Heb 13:8). God is indeed the eternal one, but eternity should not be conceived as duration without end. It is better to see eternity as a vertical extension, not a horizontal one. "With God you do not live in the past or the future—but in the eternal now. Each day is as a thousand years; each day is crammed with eternity."[34] Since every moment is of the "utmost importance" to God, it should be of like importance to us. "'Now is the day of Salvation'; each day you make history, for each day is loaded with destiny."[35] If we look upon time from God's perspective, every moment can be a moment in eternity, in the presence of God. "Do not crowd tomorrow into your today; don't divide up your life with yesterday, today and tomorrow. Rather, carry Eternity with your today."[36] Here then we have the first wing needed for our flight.

"A thousand years as one day" refers to the second wing. Torrance is convinced that sin distorts time. It makes the days long. "Sin is sin against the infinite majesty of God and therefore in its guilt; and when God opposes you, your conscience burns and time becomes endless."[37] That is why one day can feel like a thousand years. But when we are justified before God and thus free to remain in his presence, time can fly by without us realizing it. Still, we feel small against the backdrop of history. Perhaps that is why Torrance urges us "get inside Eternity" to find "God's view," for then "you'll see that the whole panorama of history which unfolds before your eyes is all meant for you."[38]

Although we can talk about the two "wings" of time separately, Torrance insists we need both "to fly." In other words, the two parts of

32. Torrance, Sermon on 2 Peter 3:8.
33. Ibid.
34. Ibid.
35. Ibid.
36. Ibid.
37. Ibid.
38. Ibid.

the verse must be "telescoped" together like "twin spectacles" in order get God's view of the world. "It is only in the supreme effort in which we look through both at once that we get a proper perspective which will transfigure this flat world of time into the bold relief of eternity."[39]

Torrance was not just interested in changing attitudes. His real aim was evangelical, to bring people into a life-changing encounter with the living God, with eternity. What is more, we can detect a "theology of crisis" in his words. He tells his church that if they heed his advice they will be brought to a "moment of decision" in which they will be "confronted by God Himself."[40] As such it will be a moment like no other. It will not be fleeting, like the passing moment of illumination created by a bolt of lightning. "This moment is an eternal crisis, an eternal moment; for you find that eternity has become your contemporary; contemporaneous with every instant of your life, impinging on you at every moment. Face to face with God, faith has reached out and in an everlasting decision grasped eternity and thrust it in its bosom– and now a thousand years are as a day and a day a thousand years."[41] In conclusion, he calls them to "seize both these truths in the hand of faith" so that "God will plant eternity in your heart."[42]

This sermon is remarkable for what it lacks, that christocentism that is so typical of Torrance. The experience of eternity is central, but the resurrection of Christ is not the sole condition for this experience.

3. Death and the Afterlife

The *nunc aeternum* is also Torrance's answer to concerns about death and the afterlife. One would expect a heightening of these concerns during a time of war. Christians of all stripes have traditionally viewed death as the gateway to eternal life with God. Later, Torrance would write enthusiastically about Calvin's *Psychopannychia*, which is a defense of that traditional view. For Calvin, death promises a better state than anything in the present. But Torrance tries to show how the future state can be a present possession. Preaching from John 14:19, he argues that these words contain the promise of a new life in the present. Christ's resurrected life can be a "present power in the believer," "not simply a fact

39. Ibid.
40. Ibid.
41. Ibid.
42. Ibid.

outside of us."[43] And this life is no ordinary life but one in which the "Eternal" is a "present possession."[44] It is not necessary, he concludes, "to wait for a great change at the end of life."[45] When "Eternity comes into the soul" the "bitterness of death" is behind and "the power of the endless life becomes our experience."[46]

4. Resurrection and History

In the summer of 1940, Britain was bracing itself for a German invasion. It was a dark time in history, even darker than the summer before, but you would be hard pressed to know this from reading Torrance's sermons. They are primarily concerned with the timeless truths of the gospel and with the soul's relationship with Christ. Here we can gauge the influence of Mackintosh.

The soul's relation to Christ is important, of course. But what does a minister of the Word say during a time of war, when historical events are making a mockery of God's love and justice? What does he or she say about *last things* in the midst of terrible things?

To be sure, Torrance does not ignore the historical situation. It seems to have inspired an early sermon on peace. The world will never give us peace, he says. Its offers of peace are as "as shallow as the German offers of peace."[47] Besides, the source of the "dispeace" in the world is the human heart. "Each man carries a troubled kingdom within him"—in "passions," "conscience," and "desires."[48] The real war is in our hearts, between us and the heavenly Father. The only answer is to "look Christ squarely in the face" and "allow him to be the Sovereign and King."[49] Then we will enjoy true peace and the "calm of eternity."

What about this Nazi menace to Britain? It is the kind of question that must have stirred in the heads of his parishioners. Torrance's answer: "If your hopes and desires are lodged in the altitude of Eternity, you'll be above the clouds and storms" of the world.[50]

43. Torrance, Sermon on John 14:19.

44. Ibid.

45. Ibid.

46. Ibid.

47. Torrance, Sermon on John 14:27.

48. Ibid.

49. Ibid.

50. Ibid.

These last words tell us a lot about Torrance's earliest sermons. They do not have much to do with eschatology in the usual sense—with future things and the afterlife. The eschatology in them can be described as a timeless, presentative eschatology. One could also call it a "radical eschatology."[51] It has its roots in Barth's *The Epistle to the Romans*. This commentary had a strong eschatological orientation, but not the kind Christians were used to. It had nothing to do with the future. Instead, it had to do with an "Eternity-time" dialectic. These two things are absolutely different (as God and man). Yet in the Word of God "Eternity" breaks into time. In Barth's words, the "moment" is the "eschatological moment . . . which is no moment in time."[52] In this sense, every moment in time can be the end-time.

However, Torrance's eschatology is more christocentric than that found in Barth's *Romans* (although this could be an echo of the christological turn that eventually occurred in Barth's eschatology). For Torrance, then, the resurrection of Christ is what allows us (generally) to experience eternity in the present.[53] Although the resurrection is an event in time, it is timeless in the sense that we can participate in it at any time, and no particular time is more propitious than any other time for this.

This kind of eschatology has biblical warrant, especially in the Fourth Gospel. But the Bible, including the Fourth Gospel (cf. 6:39, 40, 54), also relates eschatology to history. To ignore this fact is to condone, in Moltmann's words, a "blinkered disregard of world history and the history of nature."[54]

It would not be long before Torrance began to ponder the relationship between Christ and history. When tons of bombs from the Nazi

---

51. Sauter, *What Dare We Hope?* 97ff.

52. Barth, *The Epistle to the Romans,* 109.

53. We cannot ignore the strong possibility that Torrance's early eschatology was influenced by Emil Brunner, who has a similar view of the resurrection. In *The Mediator* he writes: "At Easter this is what took place: our breaking through into eternal life" (ibid., 582). He does not believe that the benefits of the kingdom of God, including eternal life, are all completely realized or experienced. The point is that nothing more need be done objectively from God's side. "The story of Christ has now reached its end," he adds (ibid., 584). All that remains is our subjective realization of the resurrection through faith. Christ's resurrection is the "turning-point"; although it has happened, is only *ours* if we ourselves turn around" (ibid., 584).

54. Moltmann, *The Coming of God,* 20.

Luftwaffe were raining down on British cities in the summer of 1940, it would not be enough simply to tell people to take the "wings of the spirit" and to soar to the high "altitude of Eternity." Besides, if we recall his Auburn lectures, we should expect more than a time-less eschatology from Torrance. He asserts that Christianity has to do with "God-in-Time, with God-in-Action" in relation to men. Consequently, redemption "has to be actualized in history and must be mediated through history." Indeed, he insists that salvation is not "intelligible or even accessible to us" if it is not "historically conveyed."[55]

We see the change in his Easter sermon from 1941. There is no change in the subject of the message. It is still centered on the resurrection of Christ. "This broken world is living on the wrong side of the Easter day," he declares.[56] In other words, he saw the world stuck in the dark between Good Friday and Easter. Consequently, the world seeks its own "man-made, humanistic" solutions to "evil's tragic dominion."[57] What the world desperately needs, he concludes, is for the miracle of the resurrection "to knock the very bottom out of the world."[58]

However, he is convinced that the resurrection has really "broken through the spokes of history," that eternity has "intersected our beggarly time."[59] Thus not only do we have eternity in our hearts but an "Eternal axle in the wheel of history."[60] Still, Easter means triumph. The axle indicates that we can "take to the wings of the spirit" and "ride triumphant" into the kingdom of God.[61]

The historical implications of the resurrection are more pronounced in the Easter sermon of 1942. He returns to Luke 24, and begins with a metaphor for the resurrection that must have aroused people's attention. "No atomic revolution can compare to the complete transformation that this Easter awakening means for a broken, darkened world."[62] And by 1942 the world was broken and dark indeed, more so than it had been a year or two earlier. It was very likely a time too when men and women

55. Torrance, *The Doctrine of Jesus Christ*, 4.

56. Torrance, Sermon on 1 Corinthians 15:20.

57. Ibid.

58. Ibid.

59. Ibid.

60. Ibid.

61. Ibid.

62. Torrance, Sermon on Luke 24:39–45.

were beginning to suspect that evil is an eradicable part the world, that death is indeed the "final verdict" of history. Yet, in spite of the dire situation, Torrance was not about to give up on the Easter story. It was time to look more deeply into it, for in his mind only this story could provide a real basis for hope in the midst of darkness. "At the death of Jesus the final verdict of history seemed to be: death ends all. Nothing can stop evil and wickedness—the world rolls on and on, inexorably on; not even God can stop it, for the Son of God is destroyed in the maelstrom of evil and death like any common son of man."[63]

But in the bodily resurrection of Christ, he adds, we have an event "that completely shatters the whole frame of history" and "breaks in upon the uniformity of nature."[64] And all this can only mean that "cause and effect" and all "the rigid laws of the universe are snapped and broken forever."[65] Still, however, the resurrection is pictured as an epochal, vertical breakthrough. The only difference is that instead of eternity coming into our world, it is the kingdom of God. It "comes plumb down from above and intersects our world at right angles."[66]

For the folks at Alyth all this must have sounded fantastic, far removed from the "personal touch" of the risen Lord and the "calm of eternity." But Torrance's purpose was to make the gospel the Word for his time. Thus he brings his sermon to a close with these words: "The resurrection of the body of Jesus Christ means the end, the end of our world-this wicked warring world of bloodshed, cruelty and sorrow; it means the end of history, the ruthless triumph of unrighteousness; it means the end of time."[67]

On this view, though, Easter is about the judgment of the world rather than the birth of a new one. Thankfully, he does not end there. He points to a new world, one "ruled by love," where life prevails, and "Jesus is conqueror, king, Lord and God."[68]

Still, there is no escaping the fact that the historical eschatology in these Easter sermons is somewhat triumphalistic. It is hard to believe

63. Ibid.
64. Ibid.
65. Ibid.
66. Ibid.
67. Ibid.
68. Ibid.

that Torrance is taking history seriously when he claims in the middle of a war that the resurrection of Jesus means the "end of history," the "end of time." What we have is really a transposition of his individual eschatology. It is all about the "first fruits" of the new creation, with little thought given to the future resurrection of humankind.[69] It is without the eschatological tension that is so much a part of the New Testament, the tension between the present and future, old creation and new creation. There is reference to a new world on the horizon, but it looks about as substantial as the eternity that we can receive into our hearts.

If one teaches only a timeless, triumphalistic eschatology, then something has got to give in Christian faith. Either one will fall into a docetic view of world history. "The news is not as bad as it sounds." Or one will fall into a docetic view of Jesus and his history. "Jesus did not actually rise from dead." "If he did, then why does history continue as it always has—filled with conflict, war, bloodshed, and every kind of evil?"

Yet Torrance does something to ensure that the believer does not fall one way or the other. The facile solution is to affirm the world's history, its pain, and suffering; and then to affirm Jesus' history in terms of those things. This is not his solution, for that would put into question the great impact of Christ's resurrection. His answer is to look to the humanity of Jesus, to his historical life, his suffering, and his death. Paradoxically, that means looking toward the risen and ascended Christ.

B. Ascension

1. Incarnation and History

We can see this approach in his New Year's sermon of 1941. "Here at the outset of a New Year in these terrible days in which we live . . . asking what the future will bring forth . . . what unknown lies ahead."[70] And the

---

69. It is surprising that Torrance neglects to discuss the future general resurrection. His overriding interest is Christ's resurrection and our present participation in it. His interpretation of this pivotal event stresses the "already" a lot more than the "not yet" aspect of it. On the matter of the resurrection, the contrast between the Torrance of 1942 and the Barth of 1924 is stark. That was the year Barth published his commentary on 1 Corinthians 15. Barth defends the final resurrection of believers, but insists that it is only "grasped as a promise" and that it is not "something that is fulfilled proleptically." Karl Barth, *Resurrection*, 176. If it is realized for Barth, it is so only by being "present in hope" (ibid., 211).

70. Torrance, Sermon on Acts 1:7.

preceding days were the most terrible the country had seen. German air raids on British cities began in September 1940. They continued nightly, and within two months about 11,700 died, most in London.[71] One of the most devastating attacks occurred on December 29th. The attacks left 1,500 fires raging in the city. The event is remembered as the "second fire of London." It is only natural that people wondered what was ahead. Torrance responds with the words from Acts 1:7: "It is not for you to know times or seasons which the Father has put in his own authority."[72] God hides the future from us in order to establish us in faith. Going "out into the blue"; this, he adds, is what faith is about.

More importantly, every year, even the darkest ones, are full of Jesus Christ. Ever since the advent of Christ, he explains, "time is no longer empty, but definitely full of God himself . . . full of Jesus Christ; even 1941 is filled with Jesus Christ . . . with "Bethlehem, the Cross, and Easter as well."[73] Jesus Christ is called the "shape of the future." "Have therefore no tears," he comforts his church, "for the future can only hold Christ for you."[74] There is no need to be troubled by war, mass destruction, or the sight of evil run amok in the world; these are not signs that evil has vanquished good or that Easter is meaningless. On the contrary, this "turmoil, this dispeace" are signs that evil is in its "last death throes," as God comes to grips with it all in the history of this age.[75]

The task of trying to reconcile evil in the world with a good Creator is difficult, but it is far more difficult when the time of the world is reckoned to be full of God himself. But Torrance has an explanation: the incarnation. Jesus Christ provoked conflict from the moment he came into the world. That was to be expected. His advent represents judgment, the assertion of God's holiness.[76] This judgment explains why he came not "to bring peace but a sword" and to "cast fire upon earth."[77] This leads Torrance to interpret the violence between the nations as a violent reaction to God, because the "cross of Christ is flung into their midst."[78]

71. Pelling, *Britain*, 97.

72. Ibid.

73. Ibid.

74. Ibid.

75. Ibid.

76. See Torrance, *The Doctrine of Jesus Christ*, 83.

77. Torrance, Sermon on Acts 1:7.

78. Ibid.

However, the incarnate Christ turns the world against him in order to "triumph over" all the evil in the world. For Torrance, every "dark page" in the history of Europe "augurs the breakthrough of God" and the victory of the Christ.[79] In order to strengthen their faith in this victory he directs his church, for the first time, to the Revelation of Jesus Christ. They are told not to look for a disclosure of times or seasons in this book, but instead for a "glimpse of the final triumph of his love and power."[80] Those hands that were nailed to the cross of Calvary by a sinful world are the same hands of the one who holds the "seven stars," who is the "First and the Last." There is "nothing in the world history to compare" to Jesus' victory.[81] It is he who "dominates the ages." He is the "everlasting mountain" while "man's systems" are the "shadows on the hillside."[82] "It is not for you to know times or seasons which the Father has put in his own authority."[83] On New Year's 1941, with no end to the war in sight, the pastor urges his flock to cling to Christ with all their faith, and then sends them away with the promise that when the "pageantry of history is over . . . Christ the conqueror will come from Edom" and then the darkness will be "turned into day."[84]

This sermon differs substantially from others we have examined. While they have more to do with a realized eschatology, based on the power of the resurrection and the nature of eternity, this one contains an historical eschatology based on the incarnation and the cross. In his sermon on 2 Pet 3, Torrance described the resurrection as God's "breakthrough in the realms of human bondage, sin and death," but in the New Year's sermon he tells us that every "dark page" in the history of Europe "augurs the breakthrough of God." If we can say the eschatology in the first sermon is *realized*, then the one in the second is *realist*.

This historical eschatology, however, is not something entirely new in Torrance. The seeds for it had been sown at Auburn, but historical circumstances and the pastoral needs at Ayth caused it to spring up and bloom.

79. Ibid.
80. Ibid.
81. Ibid.
82. Ibid.
83. Ibid.
84. Ibid.

It hard to know for sure what Torrance means when he says time is full of Christ, full of Bethlehem, the cross, and Easter. From his Auburn lectures we know that he believes Bethlehem is where the eternal God truly entered time, where God truly became a man. Christ then fills time in a real way, but also in a way that is according to his nature: the God-Man-in-saving action. As a man Christ reveals God, for there can be no revelation to us until revelation takes "human form." As God he is our redeemer. For Torrance, there is no way of knowing Christ outside his redeeming action. So to say our time is filled with Christ, must mean that our time is marked by the humanity of the incarnation, the suffering of the cross, the new life of the resurrection and the hope of the advent.

Jesus Christ filled time during his earthly ministry, but his exaltation is our assurance that he continues to fill time. We need to recall what he taught his students at Auburn: "Fundamentally, the function of the ascended and risen Lord Jesus cannot be anything than the dominating purpose of his incarnation and life on earth: the revelation of God to mankind and the redemption of mankind."[85] The risen and ascended Jesus Christ remains the God-Man, the God who entered time and took on human form. Thus time and human relations continue to have substance before God. We can say that the ascension makes possible a *mirifica commutatio*. Since Christ the God-Man has our time before him in heaven, he is thus able to fill our time here on earth. And, as we will discover, the church, the sacraments, and the Holy Spirit are the means by which he does this.

2. Christ and the Individual

Torrance's New Year's sermon of 1941 tells us that he had begun to take the relationship between eschatology and history more seriously. Yet he did not allow individual eschatology to become swallowed by world history. He accents it. That is because the key to this relationship between eschatology and history is the personal history of Jesus. That means the cross, not just the power of the resurrection and the experience of eternity, will have to define individual eschatology.[86] Torrance does not

85. Torrance, *The Doctrine of Jesus Christ*, 192.

86. It is probable that at this stage Torrance saw the individual's journey with God through time as a necessary extension of the existential encounter with God. This is because he preferred to see God in a state of becoming, not a state of being. He may have been guided by Kierkegaard's *Philosophical Fragments*, which for him was "one

forget the lesson he learned from Mackintosh, that it is *at the cross* that
the full significance of God in Christ becomes clear to the human mind.
The cross gives Christians direction in the world, an eschatological
orientation. This is underscored in a communion service from 1942.[87]
Christians today, he says, can easily go off course, like the Christians
at Corinth, especially when the church is in a "muddle," as a result of
the tumult in the world. Therefore he encourages people to come to
the communion table; for this is where they can get re-centered, find
their "spiritual bearings" and "set the course" of their souls toward Jesus
Christ.[88] By what means? The cross. It has been "flung into our midst." It
causes tumult in the world, but it also provides spiritual direction for believers. Using navigation as a metaphor for the Christian life, he writes:
"the Cross is our compass, the Holy Spirit our sextant and the Word of
God our chart."[89] It is only fitting that his final word of advice is to follow
Christ by taking up his cross daily.

But taking up the cross means living more by faith, than by the experience of eternity or the "personal touch" of the risen Christ. It means
following the hidden Christ as well as the revealed Christ. Besides, for
Torrance, these two are found together. Luke 24 is about the experience
of the glorious risen Christ, but it is also about the "shadow Christ," who
dwells in the "dark" and is encountered only through faith. His point is
that the Christian journey through life is a lot like the journey of the disciples on the road to Emmaus. The individual Christian journey is filled
with the "shadow Christ" or the hidden God who inhabits the places of
spiritual darkness. He urges believers not to cower when caught in terrible situations. After all, God dwells in them; though he can be found

---

of the greatest books written in modern times" (Torrance, "Theology in Action," 7 n.
1). "Because the Truth has become event in time thus acquiring particularity, knowledge of the Truth must conform to the historical element in that becoming" (Torrance,
"Kierkegaard," 6). From Kierkegaard he learns also that it is faith that allows us to
conform to this historical element. "Faith, says Kierkegaard, is the . . . correlative of
becoming" (ibid.). Yet Torrance's historical eschatology is not patterned entirely after
Kierkegaard's existentialism. He defines the historical element that the Dane espouses as
the "historical Moment." For Torrance, the cross is the key to historical movement; but in
his view the incarnation was the key to the historical moment for Kierkegaard.

87. Torrance, Sermon on 1 Corinthians 2:2.

88. Ibid.

89. Ibid.

through faith alone. "The truth is that faith can see only in the dark."[90] Yet it does truly see.

Talk about eternity does not suddenly disappear from Torrance's sermons, but it takes on new eschatological meaning. If the shadow Christ tells us that God is hidden as well as revealed, then eternity too must be hidden as much as it is revealed. It is as much a promise as a present experience. This truth comes out in a sermon on Philippians, dealing with the basic tensions in the Christian life, including that between time and eternity. Torrance exhorts believers to "stop having a double mind" and to 'subordinate everything to the kingdom of God."[91] There is no suggestion that the eternal kingdom is now within our grasp. Indeed in the first months of 1942 it probably never looked farther away. Rather, the kingdom is tied up with the future life. There is a call, then, to recover the New Testament "sense of eternity," epitomized in Paul's words to the Philippians. It means reaching out for eternity. "Everywhere in the New Testament . . . human destiny is stretched out beyond our imagination, stretched out to eternity."[92] And "that is what we need to do."[93] But that is naturally going to create an "inescapable tension," he warns, exactly like the kind Paul refers to. "There is a vision of the life Beyond, of Eternity that will always throw us into an inescapable tension—in a straight between the two."[94] This sense of eternity is linked to faith, as faith always contains a "future reference" and is always about "living beyond our range."[95]

Here faith is understood somewhat existentially, as a function of the tension between time and eternity. On the other hand, Torrance sees it as a function of the life between two great times, the ascension and second advent. The whole situation leads Torrance to compare Christians to "arrows" that are shot from God's bow in the direction of their target, the kingdom of God.[96] The second advent adds both substance and hope to faith. It also creates a sense of urgency. The time-between, after all, is a time of grace, a time for spreading the gospel, for hearing and respond-

90. Torrance, Sermon on Luke 20:30f.

91. Torrance, Sermon on Philippians 1:23.

92. Ibid.

93. Ibid.

94. Ibid.

95. Ibid.

96. Torrance, Sermon on Philippians 3:8, 12–14.

ing to it. "The Church must capture again today . . . this note of the ut-most urgency of the Gospel."[97] For the kingdom of God "draweth nigh."

For the many Christians who equated the coming of Christ's kingdom with peace and prosperity, their faith in the coming of this kingdom must have been battered in the 1940s.[98] But Torrance assures them that their hopes will be fulfilled with the final advent of the Judge and Savior. "Come it certainly shall, when the terrible tide of evil now let loose upon the earth will be utterly destroyed by the immediate presence of the majesty and judgement of God."[99] Then there will be "no Hitlers" to terrorize the world. As for salvation, Christians can hope for more than peace, progress, and brotherhood. This is because Jesus will return "with all the fullness of his *perfect manhood*" to establish the new heaven and new earth.[100]

3. Christ and the Church

Concomitant with the new emphasis on Christ and history in Torrance is an emphasis on the church in history. The church is the principle means by which Christ fills time and "gives shape to the future," for individual Christians and for the world at large. How so? Torrance did not discuss the church in his Auburn lectures, but they contain two seminal statements. The church is "the visible 'incarnation' of Christ on earth in lieu of his very Self," and the "ascended and enthroned Lord Jesus" uses her "for his work of redemption . . . on earth and in history."[101] By the 1950s Torrance will have in place a highly developed ecclesiology, and one with a strong eschatological orientation. But the roots of that ecclesiology are found in Auburn, and its development takes place during those tense first years at Alyth.

---

97. Ibid.

98. The observation that many Christians subscribed to an ideology of progress in place of a theology of the kingdom is confirmed in a Church of Scotland report on the war. 'There are indeed very many among us in whose souls the old hope of secular progress still continues to burn brightly, and even to be the master light of all seeing. There are those who still believe that a golden age of human society awaits us "just around the corner," requiring for its realisation no more that the enactment of certain long-delayed reforms' (Church of Scotland, *God's Will In Our Time*, 9).

99. Torrance, Sermon on Philippians 3:8, 12–14.

100. Ibid.

101. Torrance, *The Doctrine of Jesus Christ*, 194.

Torrance's early doctrine of the church is modest. It begins with an exhortation to recover the New Testament model of the church.[102] There is a focus on those four basic features mentioned in Acts 2.42: the teachings of the apostles, fellowship, Holy Communion, and prayer. In his view, the modern church—in particular the Church of Scotland—was barely distinguishable from the state and the prevailing culture. He faults it for having "degenerated" to a point where it was a "bulwark of national order and life."[103] This represented a double tragedy for him. The church was out of touch with the kingdom of God, and she was powerless to make a real difference in the world. She is so deeply "identified with the present shape of the nation that she can't change it . . . can't strike at the heart of contemporary civilization, culture and society. [S]he has substituted public spiritness, philanthropy, good citizenship for what the New Testament calls the Kingdom of God."[104]

How should the church relate to the surrounding society? Taking a lesson from the parable in Matt 13:33, he maintains that the church should be to society as the "leaven" is to the "loaf." The church is not the kingdom of God in visible form. It is instead an "instrument" of the kingdom of God. As such, it should be the "greatest disturbing factor on earth."[105] The church is always tempted to "settle down" in the world but, for Torrance, that is something it must never do. The reason is the kingdom of God "can't be domesticated." He calls the attempt to do so the "greatest sin." Why? It "betrays" Jesus' resurrection. Yet everywhere this sin was apparent to him, and so were the consequences. "Any wonder," he says, "God has raised up utterly ruthless men in Europe to shake us out of our religious self-complacency and self-satisfaction."[106] "If the church won't shake up the world . . . then God will shake the world in another way."[107]

---

102. Torrance, "Marks of the Church?" Sermon on Acts 2:42.

103. Torrance, Sermon on Matthew 13:33. Torrance obviously felt that the message in this sermon was urgent. He delivered it at three other places between 1941 and 1948. It was also the basis for a locally published pamphlet, "The Place and Function of the Church in the World."

104. Torrance, Sermon on Matthew 13:33.

105. Ibid.

106. Ibid.

107. Ibid.

What is the secret of the leaven that enables the church to affect the whole of society, "life at all points"? It is the power of Christ's resurrection. In his Easter sermons this power made the "Eternal a present possession," but here it turns the world upside down. It is the "most revolutionary power" on earth. It is a power of judgment as much as life. Torrance calls it the "living, disturbing, fermenting, revolutionary, recreating word of the living God."[108]

The leavening effect of the church on the society is tied up with the task of evangelism. The church, we recall, lives between two great times, "between the ascension of Christ and his second coming." So there is another reason the church cannot settle down and let "let her roots go down into the soil" of the world.[109] It is an evil-filled world, and no matter how great the church's impact on the world, this world cannot be remade into the kingdom of God. The church can find no "continuing city here," and thus it is incumbent upon her to be a pilgrim church till the advent of Christ.[110]

4. The Lord's Supper

Torrance's doctrine of the church and his new eschatological orientation is reflected in his understanding of the Lord's Supper. Let us go back to his very first sermon for Easter 1940 (Luke 24:30f.). There he draws attention to the fact that the revelation of the risen Christ in Luke is centered on the breaking of bread. It is the basis for a "realized" eschatology, one on a vertical axis, so to speak. Christ's resurrection meant that eternity came "plumb down" and "blew the top of" the disciples' world. Yet Torrance refers also to that other form of eschatology that we have been examining, one that runs on the horizontal axis of time or history (cf. Luke 24:27, 44ff.). Holy Communion, he says, is the "right place to understand the whole movement of history through the Old Testament" as it leads to the death of Christ on Good Friday. From one angle, the vertical, the resurrection discloses the abrupt "end of history" (i.e., man's fallen, corrupt history); but from another angle, the horizontal, it discloses the teleological movement in history towards redemption.

108. Ibid.

109. Torrance, Sermon on Philippians 3:8, 12–14.

110. Ibid.

These two kinds of eschatologies, one on a vertical and the other on a horizontal axis, are found in several early communion sermons. In the first, the Lord's Supper is called a "place of vision," a "tabernacle of eternity."[111] It is a place of vision—much like the first Easter communion—because the "veil of sense is torn aside" and we get a "direct encounter with God."[112] It is not a mystical vision either, because, as 1 John indicates, God "got a footing in history."[113] The bread and wine remind us of God's incarnation, and that a meeting with him is possible only among "worldly things," and that our faith is "anchored in solid fact."[114] Moreover, the elements are not just bare reminders. Through them faith penetrates the "unseen . . . to touch and handle things there."[115]

The most instructive communion sermon is the one titled "The three tenses of communion."[116] Here Torrance explains how the two dimensions of eschatology, the vertical and horizontal, are united in Christ. Relying on three New Testament passages, Torrance shows how the Lord's Supper telescopes Christ's past, present and future work of redemption. Through it the "past becomes alive in the present" and the "future also comes into the present."[117] The central point is that through Holy Communion we get a "real sense of the fulfillment of all the promises of Christ."[118] That is because it stands between—and is conditioned by—two great acts of redemption in time: Christ's sacrificial death and his second advent. For Torrance, the future aspect of communion is underlined in St. Paul's words of institution. "For as often as you eat this bread and drink this cup, you proclaim the Lord's death till He comes."

Just prior to this sermon on communion Torrance devoted a sermon to the second advent.[119] Here his concern is to show how that event

---

111. Torrance, Sermon on 1John 1:1–3.

112. Ibid.

113. Ibid.

114. Ibid.

115. Ibid.

116. Torrance, Sermon on Luke 22:19; John 6; 1 Cor 11.

117. Ibid.

118. Torrance, Sermon on Luke 22:19; John 6; 1 Cor 11. The quarterly Communion services at Alyth made a tremendous impression on Torrance. "It is at Holy Communion," he writes, "that we really understand best the Gospel of salvation by grace alone" (Torrance, "My Parish Ministry," 18).

119. This sermon on the second advent is based on Luke 17:20–37. Christ will thus return in the way the kingdom of God will come, in a way that is "unobservable, silent

bears on the present. His lesson is commensurate with his earlier one on the church in the world. The return of Christ ought to embolden Christians to go into the world to "proclaim the Lord's death." The proclamation begins at the Lord's Table where we "take on the standards of Jesus Christ."[120] That means we are "pledged to fight against the world," as Christ did, until the day when he "shall come in power and take up the reign of government."[121]

Imitating Christ's struggle with the world, becoming the church militant, involves taking up the cross—not the sword. The vision of the Lord's coming, he says, is what inspired Paul and the other disciples to go out and proclaim the Lord's death with such "confidence and daring in spite of persecution."[122] Their minds were fixed, he tells them, as much on the future as on the past.

5. The Ascension

The development of Torrance's eschatology, from a quite triumphalistic one to a cross-centered one, is linked to his increasing focus in this period on the ascension of Christ. The ascension of course is predicated on the resurrection of Christ, but in his earliest sermons he construes the resurrection in terms that obviate the former, in ways that suit a timeless, realized eschatology. The resurrection is "the complete movement from God to God that passes through the lowest point of our humanity." "It means the end of history, the ruthless triumph of unrighteousness. It means the end of time." But when faced with a war-torn world, Torrance knew he had to qualify the triumphalism of the resurrection with the eschatological reserve implicit in the ascension. This meant applying the lesson from Auburn about "the MAN in heaven today" who, because our humanity and our time are real for him, is still graciously carrying out his redeeming work through the church and history. The ascension backs the promise to the distraught that Christ is the "shape of the future"; it backs the promise that he will come again in history to bring an end to all its conflicts. It even explains why the world, notwithstanding the resurrection, is gripped by suffering and spiritual darkness.

---

and sudden." The advent will be a supernatural event in the midst of the natural, "ordinary activities."

120. Torrance, Sermon on Luke 22:19; John 6; 1 Cor 11.

121. Ibid.

122. Ibid.

The importance of the ascension is attested in a sermon Torrance gives on the subject in the spring of 1942, a sermon that harks back to his Auburn lecture. Following John 16:7, he discusses the benefits of it. The ascension ensures that we have a "spiritual" relationship" with Christ, that he is real in our hearts. Second, it forces us to encounter him as "the crucified" one, instead of just the risen and transcendent one. "Jesus Christ refuses to be known, refuses to have any relations with man apart from the cross. He will be known, worshiped and adorned only as the one who went to Bethlehem, Gethsemane and Calvary."[123]

This is the case because the Holy Spirit makes the cross "contemporaneous"—"now confronting us and demanding our faith, trust, and participation."[124] For Torrance, the "secret" of Jesus is "locked up in the experience of the Cross."[125] But if Jesus had not ascended, we would forget about the cross and never learn this *secret*.

The third benefit is that we might know him as the "very right hand of God." The "right hand of God" is a biblical expression for God's authority and power, which, according to Psalm 110, is shared with the Messiah. This is the greatest advantage of the ascension for Torrance. Through it, the divinity of Christ is attested to faith. At Auburn, he put it this way: "What Christ IS, God IS, because Christ IS God's Right Hand." That means there is "no work, no Word, no Will, no Judgement of God other than the act and word and will and judgement of the Lord Jesus Christ."[126] In his view these acts are all manifestations of the power of God (cf. Mark 14.62). "Christ himself IS the 'omni-potence' of God."[127]

There must have been many Christians at Alyth parish in 1942 who longed for a baring of the right hand of God in Old Testament fashion (Pss 2:9; 110:5f.), for a triumphal display of Christ's Lordship, of his wrath against evildoers (cf. Luke 9:54). Yet Torrance controverts this view of God's "right hand." He calls it a "false picture," one that is about "almighty force" and rooted in a very un-Pauline definition of justice.

---

123. Torrance, Sermon on John 16:7.

124. Ibid. This advantage of the ascension, making the cross contemporaneous, is in marked contrast with one of the advantages of the resurrection. For, in the way Torrance describes it in his sermon on John 14:19, the resurrection makes *eternity* contemporaneous.

125. Torrance, Sermon on John 16:7.

126. Torrance, *The Doctrine of Jesus Christ*, 193.

127. Ibid., 193.

God's "sword of justice" has been wielded on the cross.[128] Jesus ascended to the Father, so we could "learn that God's right hand is revealed at Calvary" and to realize that the crucifixion is an "act of God . . . an act of Eternity."[129] God's right hand is Jesus' hand nailed to the cross. In spite of the evil enveloping in the world in 1942, Torrance assures his church that "God is reigning over the world." But what sort of God? What sort of reign? It is the "Lamb of God on the throne," he adds, "the Lamb that bears the sins of the world . . . that can be angry with the wicked," yet whose "holy living will shall be done."[130] And it is precisely because he reigns over the world with a "cross in his heart" that we can be assured he is essentially love.[131]

The "right hand of God" is an anthropomorphism but, in Torrance's view, the scarred hands of Jesus are not. The ascension, then, not only verifies the divinity of Christ; it verifies his humanity too. As Mark 14:62 tells us, it is the Son of Man who now sits at the right hand of God. "The Ruler and King of the Universe is none other than the Man who suffered on the Cross."[132]

But all this, however, puts faith through a trial. Although faith is not sight, it still "sees." In order to see more and better, it seeks understanding: *fides quaerens intellectum*. How, faith will inquire, does Christ from the throne of God rule over the world and redeem it? How, when this world is in shambles, when Christ is not present in the world? Is Christ the true Redeemer? Is God really as Christ is? Or is there a hidden right hand to God?

For Torrance, the revelation of Christ is proof there are "no dark spots" in God.[133] However, if he cannot account for the great dark spots in the world (and in 1942 there were many), if he cannot show how all the evil in the world is working for good, and *is evidence of* Christ's continuous rule and redemption, then Christians will begin to believe there is indeed a hidden hand to God—or worse, no hand and no God at all.

Torrance does meet this demand, and he does so without subordinating Christ to history, metaphysics, or ontology. There is no need to.

128. Torrance, Sermon on John 16:7.
129. Ibid.
130. Ibid.
131. Ibid.
132. Torrance, *The Doctrine of Jesus Christ*, 194.
133. Torrance, Sermon on John 16:7.

Christology is based on the reality of Jesus Christ, as the incarnate, risen, and ascended God-Man, and on the illuminating work of his Spirit.[134] Further, through the study of Christology we can "gain a clear understanding of the risen and ascended Lord Jesus, and all that he means for us in the Church and the world."[135]

This brings us to Torrance's sermons on Revelation.

C. The Apocalypse: Sermons on Revelation I

1. Christ and the Soul

Of all the sermons Torrance preached, the best known and most original are his published collection on Revelation, titled *The Apocalypse Today*. It appeared in 1959, but the sermons within were first delivered during the war and just after it while Torrance was a minister at Alyth parish. Needless to say, *The Apocalypse Today* gives us the best picture of his eschatology in the 1940s. Under sixteen thematic chapters, it covers the whole of Revelation.

Torrance apparently had no intention of ever publishing these sermons but did so "at the request" of many friends and students who longed for "a fresh and straightforward account of the meaning of the Apocalypse for today."[136] "For today" really stood for days that were a throwback to the first century of the church. The 1950s were not as bloody as the 1940s but they were still years of "world distress and conflict," when people experienced the "plagues of war and the tyranny of oppression."[137] There was no shortage of literature on Revelation in this

134. Torrance expatiates on his theological method in a small pamphlet titled "The Modern Theological Debate," which was his first publication. In it he acknowledges that the task of theology is a difficult one, since the mind of every theologian is cluttered with all kinds of worldly knowledge. "But the theologian must try and keep his knowledge of God clear and only theological in content" (ibid., 15). This means he must stay focussed on the object of faith, the historical Jesus Christ. "The whole of dogmatic must link itself with the historical Christ, or it is not Christian theology at all. It may not seek for some eternal truth of reason, or attempt to universalize; it must begin with exegesis, for in the Bible alone we learn of Jesus Christ, the object of faith" (ibid., 16). This, however, does not mean theology is contrary to reason, that it is strictly fideistic. It has to employ reason, but reason must never be allowed to become its own object; it must be made subject to its object, i.e., Christ (ibid., 15).

135. Torrance, *The Doctrine of Jesus Christ*, 190.

136. Torrance, *Apocalypse Today*, 5.

137. Ibid., 6.

period, but it was not very good at relating the contents of this book to the present. Roughly, there were two kinds. First, there were the exegetical commentaries, notably R. H. Charles's monumental two-volume work, which focused on the meaning of the Apocalypse for *yesterday*, for first-century Christians.[138] There were the expository commentaries that tried to make the Apocalypse relevant, but this usually involved extracting the timeless, spiritual truths from the husk of historical and eschatological material.[139] Apart from these, one was left with, in Torrance's words, the "fantastic interpretations of the sects."[140] These interpretations tried to relate the Apocalypse to the modern world, but failed because they took the images and symbols of the book too literally.[141]

However, *The Apocalypse Today* does not contain the whole story of Torrance's engagement with Revelation. Most of the sermons in it originate in 1946, though several originate in 1942.[142] Some sermons underwent significant changes by the time they were published; some early sermons never made it into book form.

His first three sermons are not in *The Apocalypse Today*. This is not surprising, since they are not in line with the historical nature of its eschatology. In the first chapter Torrance defines Apocalypse this way. "[It] is the unveiling of history already invaded and conquered by the Lamb of God. Apocalypse means the tearing aside of the veil of sense and time to reveal the decisive conquest of organic evil by the incarnate Son of God."[143]

Those first three sermons, by contrast, reflect Torrance's early eschatology at Alyth; one that is personal, ahistorical, and rather existentialist. The first one was delivered in 1940 and is about the "Lion and the Lamb"

138. Charles, *A Critical and Exegetical Commentary*. In the class of historical-critical commentaries, this work is still regarded as the gold standard; and for good reason. It is the product of twenty-five years of painstaking scholarly research. Other notable commentaries in this class, and this period, are Bousset's *Die Offenbarung Johannis*, Beckwith's *The Apocalypse of John* and Swete's *The Apocalypse of St. John*.

139. In this category we find Carrington's *The Meaning of Revelation* and Scott's *The Book of Revelation*. Consideration should also be given to Farrer's *The Rebirth of Images*.

140. Torrance, *Apocalypse Today*, 5.

141. See Wilson, "Millennialism and Sect Formation," in Rowland and Barton, *Apocalyptic in History*.

142. Chapters 1 (Rev 1:9, 10), 6 (Rev 7), and part of 16 (Rev 2, 3) are based on sermons from 1942. Chapter 2, which is about the church, is based on two later sermons on Rev 2, 3. They were delivered in 1948 and coincide with Torrance's association with the ecumenical movement.

143. Torrance, *Apocalypse Today*, 12.

in chapter 5:5ff. "What's the meaning of this vision?" he asks. He finds three meanings in it. One, it refers to the "liberation of life . . . the sense of the absolute release."[144] Looking deeper, he understands it as an escape from "the bonds of some narrow obsession that blots out all sunshine."[145] Second, there is "salvation in the vision," salvation for the "hopes you cherished [that were] broken . . . desires of the spirit [that were] broken."[146] Finally, it means "God's judgement of sin."[147]

The sermon is not without historical references, but there is not much in terms of an historical eschatology. He refers to the men who "talk pessimistically about the future" and about the "new dark ages" that are approaching us.[148] Yet he promises his church that the evil in the world will be overcome. "The day is already at hand when arrogant evil and the dictators of the earth shall become dust under the chariot wheels of time; and the Lord will reign."[149]

This pattern stands out when we compare his treatment of those passages in a sermon from 1946, one that was included in *The Apocalypse Today*. Here the starting point is not personal eschatology, but historical eschatology. What does he think now about the sealed scroll and the Lamb? They suggest that we can look behind the process of history into the divine secrets. "And so the apocalyptic drama of world history begins to unfold itself before our eyes."[150]

The early Alyth type of eschatology is even more pronounced in Torrance's second sermon on Revelation. It is on 3:20, which is perfectly suited for this form of eschatology—if the verse is taken out its original historical context. And that is exactly what Torrance confesses to doing, for the sake, he says, of interpreting it in a more "personal sense." What he finds in the verse, as a result, is a "description of the inner relations between man and Christ," for Christ is the "true inhabitant of the soul."[151] Indeed, "Christ is our true self"; he produces a rebirth, a "new man,"

---

144. Torrance, Sermon on Revelation 5:5ff.

145. Ibid.

146. Ibid.

147. Ibid.

148. Ibid.

149. Ibid.

150. Torrance, *Apocalypse Today*, 41.

151. Torrance, Sermon on Revelation 3:20.

when he "enters the heart as the word . . . knocking at the ramparts of the soul."[152]

We must say something about the sermon on Rev 21:1. "*And there shall be no more sea*," which is a "symbol of mysterious, rebellious power, perpetual unrest."[153] No more sea, in one sense, means no more "painful mystery." Thus he calls people to "set Christ before [their] minds," so that they can "climb higher and higher upon the mount of God," till they come to a point where they will know him just as they will be known by him.[154]

The verse also points to the end of all "disquiet and unrest." Torrance describes life as a "voyage over a turbulent sea," one that makes for "wearisome sailing."[155] But we can look forward to a deliverance from this someday, for "on the other side of the shore" is rest in Christ.[156] Where exactly is the unrest? It is in day-to-day living, but it is also in our hearts. There is the deep unrest caused from our "separation from God and our opposition to Him" and there is the acute unrest in the "soul tossed with bodily passion."[157]

Compare his treatment of this verse in *The Apocalypse Today*. The sea remains a symbol. Now, however, it is a symbol of the "masses of the nations in ceaseless unrest, in godless antagonism."[158] "But now there is no sea, there are no tempests and no storms, no hideous forms of evil, no mysterious depths throwing up their nameless terrors upon the shores of history."[159]

So much for stormy seas. Where is the watershed in Torrance's interpretation of Revelation? What convinced him that this book has more to do with salvation in history than with the salvation of individual souls? Walter Lüthi and Karl Ludwig Schmidt, two continental theologians, may have persuaded him. In the preface to *The Apocalypse Today*, he credits them for giving him the "impulse to preach from the Apocalypse." Torrance had heard Lüthi preach in Basel, when he was a

---

152. Ibid.

153. Torrance, Sermon on Revelation 21:1.

154. Ibid.

155. Ibid.

156. Ibid.

157. Ibid.

158. Torrance, *Apocalypse Today*, 177.

159. Ibid.

university student there. Lüthi also put out a collection of sermons on the Book of Daniel. They have a lot in common with Torrance's sermons on Revelation.[160] On Lüthi's view, the prophet's main point is that "he sets forth Christ" amid the trials of history.[161] But Daniel also has a "particular message for our time." This is because Christ is the "same yesterday, to-day, and forever"; but it is also because Luthi interprets Daniel symbolically. "Nebuchadnezzar still lives." He is the "spirit of the Century . . . of this World . . . of the Times."[162]

Schmidt delivered a series of addresses on the Apocalypse over Swiss radio during the Second World War.[163] Inspired by Albrect Durer's woodcuts of the Apocalypse, he showed how the last book of the Bible was connected to the terrible and trying events of his own day. But Torrance must have got the first "impulse" to preach on Revelation from Luthi. His sermons were published in 1939, whereas Schmidt's radio broadcasts did not come out until 1944. These men not only inspired Torrance to preach from the Apocalypse, they also lent a Germanic cast to his sermons. Unlike many English expositions on Revelation, there is nothing anodyne about Torrance's sermons. They do not gloss over the deep conflict between good and evil, Christ and the anti-Christ, the kingdom of Christ and the kingdoms of the world.

2. Christ and World History

Torrance's new approach meant a return to the very first chapter of Revelation. The fruit of that labor is the first chapter of *The Apocalypse Today*. His opening words present a graphic picture of the world in 1942:

> This modern world is even more terrible and tyrannical than the ancient world—like a huge monster that grows every time we look at it—till it assumes immense proportions before our eyes . . . destroying our nerve, threatening to swallow us up and devour us altogether. How can we carry on? A man cries . . . We are in the clutches of the great machine of fate . . . one person after another, one nature after another becomes mangled and battered . . . the whole world is tottering and already crashing down to utter destruction.[164]

160. Lüthi, *The Church to Come*.

161. Ibid., ix.

162. Ibid., 17.

163. Schmidt, "Aus der Johannes Apokalypse," 1941.

164. Torrance, Sermon on Revelation 1:9, 10.

These words are not found in *The Apocalypse Today*. Things were bad in 1960, but unlike 1942 the world was not *crashing down to utter destruction*. The picture of the world in 1942 is frightening, but it is only the picture of those who are "enslaved" by a "false vision." St. John the Divine, on the other hand, was privy to the true vision of the world when he was in the "spirit on the Lord's Day." And Christians today, since they partake with the same Spirit, can share in St. John's vision, which "brings release" from the "evil of the world."[165]

What is in this vision that brings this release? It is the "unveiling of history already invaded and conquered by the Lamb of God . . . the tearing aside of the veil of sense and time to reveal the decisive triumph of organic evil by the incarnate Son of God."[166] This is in fact the meaning of the Revelation for Torrance. It represents a new direction in his eschatology. The triumphalism that marked his first Easter sermon is gone. Instead of the risen Christ who "dynamites" and "shatters" our time, our history, it is the "Lamb of God" who conquers and the "incarnate Son of God" who triumphs. But it is not a completely new direction. It was anticipated strongly in his New Year's sermon in the preceding year, where in order to bolster hope he sends them to the book of Revelation. There we learned that the turmoil in the world was due to the cross in the midst of the nations. We were told that every "dark page" in the history of Europe "augurs the breakthrough of God" and the victory of the advent. So the current world war is really a battle in the war against the lordship of Christ. What is happening in the world is a replay of the passion of Jesus on a world scale, with the "body" of Christ, the church, as the centre of the storm. The evil in the world will mature until Christ can finally "triumph over" it all when he comes again (cf. Ps 92:7).

How is Christ the clue to history? The answer is in the nature and life of Christ. Something utterly devoid of history (e.g., a First Cause, Platonic Forms) could not offer a clue to history; nor could something imminent in history such as an evolutionary principle. In Christ, by contrast, we have something that is both in history and outside it. Christ had a history on earth. Like other histories, his was visible, physical, driven forward by a combination of forces. But the true meaning of his history lies outside history, in the eternal God. Jesus' suffering, trial, and death were not just events in the inexorable march of history. Rather,

165. Ibid.

166. Torrance, *Apocalypse Today*, 12.

they were for the redemption of the world, and the reversal of history itself. Through these events, Jesus bore God's judgment on our sin and canceled our guilt. Likewise, the ongoing violence in history reflects the "guilt and wrath of history." And just as Christ's suffering and death yielded good—the forgiveness of sins and eternal life—the events of history, in spite of all appearances, are also working out for good, "so as to yield holiness and love." By the "power of the Cross," argues Torrance, Christ "even makes the wrath of man praise Him."[167]

But what is really happening in this sermon on Revelation? Is this interest in the "shadow Christ" a clever attempt to save theology in the face of mounting evidence that God has abandoned the world? Is Torrance about to give in to the forces and the "brute facts" of history? Not at all. His sermon on Rev 1 is testimony to his resolve to put Christ first in the face of great temptations to do otherwise. It is common to think of the Revelation as a cryptic description of events past, of events to come, or of things happening now.[168] But for Torrance the book is more about the Last One (*Eschatos*) than last things (*eschata*). The Apocalypse, then, is not just about the second advent, for at the "heart of Revelation" is the "unveiling of Jesus Christ" now.[169] That is the "clue to the whole book," he insists.[170] God's "unveiling" in Christ tells us, however, that he has also been "veiled" in Christ. What is more, this veiling is not an incidental feature of Christ's life, something that took place at Calvary or on his way to Emmaus. It is part of his very nature, "one of the facts of the incarna-

---

167. Ibid., 14.

168. The literature on Revelation is voluminous, and the book has been subject to widely divergent interpretations. Modern scholars, though, have found isolated four main views: 1) There is the "preterist" view, which interprets the book in light of its original first-century context only; 2) the "historicist" view, which interprets it in light of world history through the ages; 3) the "futurist or eschatological" view, which holds that Revelation is mainly a description of last things at the end of history; 4) the "idealist" or "timeless symbolic" approach, which does not link the visions in the book with any specific events in history but sees them as symbolizing God's relationship with history in general. See Mounce, *The Book of Revelation*, 39–44. Torrance's approach is unique. Probably due to the influence of William Milligan's commentary, it is strongly symbolic, though it has characteristics of all four. Yet what really sets Torrance's approach apart is its Christ-centeredness.

169. Torrance, *Apocalypse Today*, 13.

170. Torrance puts a lot of stock in the root definition of the Greek word: *Apo + kalypto* (uncover, to reveal).

tion." "In a very real sense God was concealed in Jesus, veiled behind his flesh and suffering."[171]

And what about that kingdom of God that Jesus had announced, the kingdom that many saw on the horizon only decades earlier? It too is veiled. "[W]e must think of the Kingdom of God as having entered our world in the life and death of Jesus and as veiled in history."[172] How could it be otherwise? "Look out," Torrance tells his church, "upon the history of these two thousand years culminating in two wars of unheard-of magnitude and disaster. It is impossible to say, 'Lo, here is the Kingdom of God! Lo, there!'"[173]

The kingdom is *veiled* in Christ, but it will also be *unveiled* in him. If Christ is the clue to history, he must also be the clue to the kingdom. This means the kingdom is not fundamentally about things, events, or power structures, but creaturely life. This brings us to another meaning of the Revelation. It unveils the new creation that is now hidden behind the "ugly shape of sinful history." We cannot expect the new creation to arrive apart from suffering or conflict. It must follow the pattern of its first-fruits, the resurrection of Jesus, whose triumph was the climax of a cross-centered life. Ultimately, there will be a new creation "which is the outworking of the Cross in the teeth of all the principles and powers of darkness."[174]

From the start, Revelation radiates a theology of glory. "Behold, He is coming with clouds, and every eye will see Him" (Rev 1:7). But in this glory Torrance finds a theology of the cross. The whole book convinces him that "the Cross is in the field."[175] The history of the world revolves around the cross, since no nation can be neutral toward it. It either violently resists or humbly submits to the crucified One.

We must not take the *cross in the field*, the violence and suffering of the world, to mean that Christ has not actually risen. On the contrary, this image is meant to be a sure sign Jesus has risen. We need only recall his Auburn lectures to know that for Torrance the cross of Christ—and even the incarnation—can only be understood in the light of Christ's resurrection. The resurrection unveiled the divinity of Jesus, but it also

171. Torrance, *Apocalypse Today*, 14.
172. Ibid.
173. Ibid.
174. Ibid., 12.
175. Ibid., 13.

unveiled his life and death as divine acts of redemption. The Risen One is also the Ascended One. But we must encounter anew the Risen One in order to see the Jesus of the Gospels aright: as the Son of God, as Savior and Lord.

People may encounter the Risen One because he is still a man and because God's Spirit unveils him to them. The Spirit has to unveil the man Christ Jesus too, for that man is now hidden from us just as he was hidden to the disciples on the road to Emmaus. As St. John reports, he is one "like unto the Son of Man" (1:13). Before the resurrection, Christ's human flesh veiled his divine glory; now after the resurrection his humanity is veiled by his divine glory. "Flesh and blood cannot reveal the transfigured Jesus as the Son of the living God, not even the flesh and blood of Jesus."[176] Only the Holy Spirit can, and unless we see this one "like unto a Son of Man" we are without a clue to history and to the mystery of the kingdom God. For none other than the "incarnate Son of God" has conquered the "organic evil" in the world, and the new creation he brings is the "out-working" of his cross.

Torrance would preach a series of six sermons on the Apocalypse in 1942, an indication of how important this book had become to him. In any event, it seems certain that he wanted to strengthen the hope of his church as it faced a dark period of history; to keep his congregation in the assurance that Christ is risen and that through him God "governs and orders the course of the world."[177] For Torrance, the kingdom of God has come in Jesus Christ—in his incarnation, atonement, and resurrection. "It is not too much to say that *Jesus Christ is himself the Kingdom of God.*"[178] The kingdom encompasses a new order to the world and new life for all creation, but these will remain hidden from us as long as the King of the kingdom is hidden from us, i.e., until the final *parousia.* At times in history, like the nineteenth century, Christians thought they could clearly see the kingdom taking shape in history. In 1942 no Christian in his or her right mind could claim to see outlines of the kingdom in the world.

176. Ibid., 16.

177. For Torrance, the sermons on Revelation "met a real need" (Torrance, "My Parish Ministry," 12). They were intended to "strengthen the faith of the congregation by spelling out the implications of St. John's Apocalyptic visions for people's outlook on the war" (ibid., 11).

178. Torrance, *The Doctrine of Jesus Christ*, 32.

Ironically, Torrance does see the kingdom in his day, but only through the eye of faith, with the help of the Spirit, and through the lens of the Apocalypse. It is easy to interpret the Apocalypse, with its fantastic images, as an escape from history. But if it is part of the Word of God, then it must be a witness to Christ's salvation in history. Redemption has to be "actualized" in history and "mediated" through history.[179] Apocalypse is the link between eschatology and history. Without apocalyptic, the Christian hope becomes sterile. The kingdom of God is viewed as wholly transcendent, beyond time and history. The counter response is to try and construct something like a kingdom of God on earth; and this is something Torrance will observe in his day.

Three years elapse between Torrance's first series of sermons on Revelation and his second, mainly because he was absent from Alyth, serving as a volunteer chaplain in the Royal Army from the spring of 1943 to the summer of 1945. His tour of duty included service in North Africa and Italy.[180] Yet his time on the battlefields of those regions did not cause an undoing of his new approach to Revelation. It reinforced it.

---

179. Ibid., 4.

180. For a short record of Torrance's war service, see McGrath, *T. F. Torrance*, 69–77.

3

Apocalyptic Eschatology, 1942–1950

A. The Chaplaincy Lectures, 1945

Torrance gave three lectures in theology to a group of fellow chaplains in Assisi, Italy just before the guns fell silent across Europe. Two of them are extant, but only one has been published. Neither one is explicitly about eschatology, yet they are essentially of a piece with his sermons on the Apocalypse. What is more, the lectures show how the experience of war shaped Torrance's theology. It reinforced his conviction that salvation is closely bound up with history. As a result, theology and action must go together. More precisely, the war reinforced the point that the cross of Christ is the center of salvation and history. That is the meaning behind "*In Hoc Signo Vinces*," the one that was published.

But as the anecdote that introduces this lecture reveals, the war also challenged Torrance's theological presuppositions.

> I shall never forget the experience of walking along a ridge that outflanks Faenza from the south-west. It was the morning after it was captured and the city fell. Never have I seen such devastation and havoc. The trees were all stripped and battered to unshapely trunks, and there was not a square yard undisturbed by the upheaval, while scores of German bodies all over the place in bits and pieces . . . [A]nd one could not help being aghast with sheer horror and shame. It seemed as if there could never be any beauty again in earth or sky—it seemed as if one could not believe again in the love and goodness of God.[1]

It was the kind of scene that could kill a person's faith in God. But Torrance's faith remained alive, not because he hedged it from the hor-

---

1. Torrance, "In Hoc," 13.

rors of history but because he resolved to anchor it firmly to the cross of Christ in history. He continues: "Then one remembered Golgotha, and, as never before, thanked God that at the heart of the faith there was the terrible tragedy of the Cross which in the astounding will and almighty love of God had become our redemption. One felt deeply that had it not been for the Cross faith would have perished utterly and irremediably from the earth—it could not have survived a day such as that."[2] In short, Torrance's experiences on the battlefield reinforced his belief that there is "no hidden God, no *Deus Absconditus*, no God behind the back of the Lord Jesus."

"*In Hoc Signo Vinces*" is a controversial title. It hearkens back to Constantine the Great's victory at Milvian. But the lecture is anything but a discussion of man's triumphalism. Torrance sees the cross as a "lasting testimony of the failure of men to recognize God."[3] More importantly, it is really a symbol of God's victory over evil. This victory, though, did not come through direct force but only after God submitted himself to evil. "The cross is the point at which God outflanks the whole position of evil in the world at its worst, undoing evil in the only way in which it can be done. Not by sweeping it violently away with the stroke of His hand, but by getting at the back of it, by entering it from within, into the very heart of the blackest evil, and making its sorrow and suffering his own."[4]

God's victory over evil is the "most potent and aggressive deed that heaven and earth have ever known."[5] The cross reminds us that Christ "was here for war: to be baptized with a baptism of fire."[6] This provocative language is more than just a case of Torrance trying to capture his audience through a contextualization of the gospel. It reflects his understanding of the atonement as more than a legal transaction between Christ and God. Although the cross is the summit, atonement involves the entire life and ministry of Christ.[7] Torrance opts for a wider

2. Ibid.

3. Ibid., 15.

4. Ibid., 13.

5. Ibid.

6. Ibid., 17.

7. Torrance's discussion of the cross here evokes the "classic" view of the atonement, revived in the twentieth century by Gustaf Aulen with his *Christus Victor* (1931). On this view, atonement is the objective work of God from first to last. It is also grounded in the incarnation. Despite the similarities, Torrance's doctrine differs in a very important respect. He makes the work of Christ as *man* part and parcel of the atonement. The

understanding of atonement, one that refers to God's reconciliation of all things through Christ. This includes the reversal of history, since the cross "remains an abiding force" in history and the "secret of what is happening in the world" today.[8] Through it God is completing his judgment.

The cross "remains an abiding force" in history. That is the main point in this lecture. If we fail to recognize the cross then world history is nothing more than a frightening mystery, and the gospel story is nothing more than an old tale with little relevance. "Make the cross a story of history, and it has no power on the world of today, but make it something contemporary, and see in the events of our time the same violent intervention on the part of God."[9] In other words, God "cast fire on earth" (Luke 12:49), but the fire still rages and we must see him "in the fire." This means that the "divine purpose of Love" is still at work, that Christ "holds the initiative" even in the most terrible events of human history.[10]

But how does the cross remain an "abiding force" in history? How does the Crucified One become contemporary? We need to point to the church's proclamation of the Word. The world still reacts violently to this Word, just as it did 2,000 years ago. "Why do the nations rage . . . against the Lord and against His Anointed" (Ps 2). This Word continues to provoke the demons in our cultures—"all pagan and anti-Christian ideas"—in order to bring them to judgment. "No one who knows anything about German thought," Torrance writes, "can fail to recognize that behind all the history today we have as a driving and directive force of it all . . . an outlook that is diametrically opposed to the Christian faith."[11] Now, however, it "has been provoked to express at last in true colours the base titanistic forces at work beneath—provoked, that is, by the Christian Gospel."[12]

The other lecture from this period is "Theology and Action," which was the original title of the lecture series. The title suggests the influence of Barth's small book, *God in Action* (1936), but the influence of Kierkegaard is also apparent. For Torrance, theology is essentially about

---

problem with the "classic" view, he writes, is that it is based only one aspect of the hypostatic union, the *anhypostastia*, without any recognition of Christ's "incorporation," the *enhypostasia*. See Torrance, "Atonement and Oneness," 250.

8. Torrance, "In Hoc," 17.

9. Ibid.

10. Ibid., 18.

11. Ibid.

12. Ibid.

the action of God; Christology, thus, has to do with "God-in-action." God is known through the "analogy of becoming, not an analogy of being."[13] And our knowledge takes its rise with the fact that God has entered history. Further, this knowledge is immediately eschatological, since it is faced with the "end" that has "broken into the present where we are."[14]

B. Sermons on the Apocalypse II

The purpose of Torrance's sermons on the Apocalypse was to show that this portion of the Bible was "the very Word of the living God, the Lord of history."[15] That has never been an easy task. Torrance would later say that in preparation for his weekly sermons he often turned to Calvin's commentaries as a resource.[16] But Calvin could not have been much help when he took up the Apocalypse. It was the only book the Reformer did not write a commentary on. He also turned to the modern, critical commentaries on the Apocalypse, but these were of limited help to him. As we pointed out, they failed to speak to the church of today. It is not because they did not take history seriously; their authors were slaves to the historical-critical method. The problem was that these works, reflecting the influence of nineteenth-century liberal theology, separated history from eschatology. The eschatological perspective of the Apocalypse could not be imported into the twentieth century history.[17] It was the product of a former age. Besides, history had shown that parts of this perspective were "false"; Jesus did not come quickly, as he had prom-

---

13. Torrance, "Theology in Action," 7.

14. Ibid., 6.

15. Torrance, *Apocalypse*, 6.

16. McGrath, *T. F. Torrance*, 62.

17. On the question of modern approaches to the Apocalypse, see Beardslee, "New Testament Apocalyptic," 419–35; and Collins, "Reading the Book of Revelation," 229–42. Beardslee points to R. H. Charles' majestic commentary as an example of a deliberate use of an "historical interpretation" of apocalyptic in place of an "eschatological interpretation" (ibid., 420). The latter approach involved the direct application of the symbols in apocalyptic books to events taking place in the present time of the interpreter (ibid., 420). This historical approach, on the other hand, was really an illustration of the "history-of-religions methodology." Thus the form and even the content of the Apocalypse was not so much a revelation (*apocalypse*) from above but a "response to the historical conditions and needs of a certain time" (ibid., 421).

ised.[18] Bultmann and his followers would only reinforce this separation between history and eschatology.[19]

Torrance's fourfold definition of Apocalypse, which comes from a sermon in 1942, highlights the contrast between his approach and that of Charles and his disciples. 1) Apocalypse is the "unveiling of history already invaded and conquered by the Lamb of God"; 2) Apocalypse "means the tearing aside of the veil of the sense of time to reveal the decisive conquest of organic evil by the incarnate Son of God"; 3) Apocalypse "means the unveiling of the new creation as yet hidden from our eyes behind the ugly shape of history"; 4) the Apocalypse reminds us that "there is to be a new creation which is the out-working of the Cross in the teeth of all the principalities and powers of darkness."

Since the 1960s there has been a torrent of literature on the Apocalypse and on apocalyptic literature in general. It may be argued that in this period the pendulum has swung the other way, in favor of the eschatological approach to the Apocalypse. But in some cases this has meant a thoroughgoing or futurist eschatology, which becomes dislocated from present history.[20] Fundamentalists, notably Hal Lindsay, have sought to redress that problem.[21] Unfortunately, the results are "fantastic interpretations" which really only defeat the purpose behind them.

Torrance takes a balanced approach to the Apocalypse, one that incorporates an historical and eschatological perspective. The key is Christology. Christology qualifies the historical approach. History here is defined by *Jesus'* history. For that reason the Apocalypse does not, as Ellul would say, "narrate history."[22] It is in one sense "ahistorical," since

---

18. This view is associated with Albert Schweitzer. We find it as well in H. H. Rowley, a British scholar who also tried to show the contemporary relevance of the Apocalypse. In his view, the apocalyptic writers were "mistaken" in many of their hopes, and that is why the Apocalypse cannot be used to interpret current events or the future. It is only useful for expressing "eternal values." See Rowley, "The Voice of God," 403–18. Cf. also chapter IV of his book *The Relevance of Apocalyptic*.

19. See Rudolph Bultmann, *History and Eschatology*.

20. See Beardslee, "New Testament Apocalyptic," and the short but helpful discussion by Bandstra, "History and Eschatology," 180–83. The author credits Elisabeth Fiorenza especially with recovering the eschatological dimension of the Apocalypse, although he feels she has done so at the expense of the "history of redemption" in the book.

21. Lindsay, *The Late Great*.

22. Ellul, *The Meaning of the City*, 28.

it "concentrates history in a point," and that point is the Lamb, the one who has brought and is bringing history as we know it to an end, a *telos*.[23]

This also explains why the eschatology of the Apocalypse is not an inexplicable future, or an escape from history. Eschatology is centered on Christ, the "first fruits" of the new creation. But he is "the last" as well as the "the first."

This fourfold definition also indicates that Torrance's chaplaincy lectures depended upon his reading of the Apocalypse. This definition underlines the cross, history, evil, and the new creation. The definitions' strong verbs signify its teleological orientation. An approach to the Apocalypse that is both historical and eschatological finds purposeful action in this book. This explains why the Apocalypse is also prophecy. Still Christ is the focus of this action. He is the Alpha and Omega, the source and end of the action.

Torrance's definition also reminds us of an important principle at Auburn: that we must understand the person and work of Christ together. The person of Christ is central, but we only know this person in light of his work: (1) the cross; (2) the incarnation; (3) resurrection; (4) the second advent.

Let us now look at the rest of Torrance's sermons on the Apocalypse in terms of his definition of Apocalypse.

1. "Apocalypse is the unveiling of history already invaded and conquered by the Lamb of God"

a. "The Secret Destiny"

This first part of the definition may be taken as another summary of the Apocalypse. John encounters the Lamb in the throne room of heaven, which signifies that he has "already invaded and conquered history," contrary to all appearances in history. In his incarnation and death

---

23. Ibid., 23, 28. Hans Conzelman notes that there is "a remarkable elimination of time" in Revelation, that there is "no idea of tradition," "no time-line," "no reflection on pre-Christian Israel" (Conzelman, *An Outline of the Theology*, 313). There is not even a reflection on the historical Jesus in the Apocalypse. The only historical event mentioned is his death, although his resurrection and ascension are certainly implied. See Boring, "The Theology of Revelation," 265. However, for Boring, this does not mean Revelation has no sense of history or time. Rather, the book tends to telescope past and future into the present (ibid., 263). In any event, there are more references to the present action of Christ than to his future action. See Boring, "Narrative Christology," 716.

Christ bore the fetters of history, but by the resurrection and ascension he has broken them, and now "lives forever and ever." While chapter 4 unveils the "final outcome of world history," chapter 5 lets us in on the "process of history" and "into its divine secrets."[24] This "process" is really an "apocalyptic drama" of history, which begins to unfold in chapter 6. The drama is about the transformation of the fallen creation into the new creation, the kingdoms of the world into the kingdom of God. It looks chaotic, but for Torrance the scroll in the hand of God indicates that there is a divine order behind it all. The text does not tell us what this scroll is. Some commentators contend that it is the Old Testament; others insist it is the Lamb's Book of Life (cf. 13:8; 21:27). For Torrance, it is the "sealed volume of world-destiny," which includes the destiny of every man.[25]

However, the world's destiny is not the product of the inscrutable will of God. Human sin is a major factor. Our "guilty past" is the "master of our present," a determining force of history's destiny.[26] "Man's life is not just a biological process; it is a history, and indeed history summed up in himself in the present moment."[27] Why does our sinful past haunt us and drive us down the road of chaos, destruction, and death? The judgment of God. The scroll contains an "imprint of the divine *No* on all that lifts itself up in rebellion against Him."[28] It is the "handwriting of God against us" that St. Paul referred to. On our own we are unable to change the course of our nature, to avoid destruction and death. For our evil-filled destiny is the product of the "iron rigidity of the past," of the "laws of guilt and retribution," which "lurk in human history like an insatiable monster relentlessly devouring the present and menacing the future."[29]

However, this terrible destiny has been reversed through the intervention of the Lamb of God. He has wiped out the "handwriting of requirements against us." That is why the scroll of destiny was put into his hands. His atoning death earned him the right to open the seals, to disclose the destiny *after altering it*. The cross is rightfully called the

24. Torrance, *Apocalypse*, 41.
25. Ibid.
26. Ibid., 44.
27. Ibid., 41.
28. Ibid., 44.
29. Ibid.

"Power of God," for through it Christ was able to "break the iron rigidity of the past, to intervene in our chaotic history, to bring order and peace and eternal blessedness out of it all."[30] He alone has conquered history. Because of his work our history now has divine purpose and redemptive order. This scroll in the hand of God reminds us of his sovereignty over history and creation, but the fact that only the Lamb of God is worthy to open it tells us that God's sovereignty has the purpose of redeeming, sacrificial love. "God's almighty power, God as the Lion of the Tribe of Judah, is revealed as the Lamb as it had been slain."[31]

These words are a clue to understanding Torrance's sermons on the Apocalypse. They indicate that there is no hidden God (*Deus Absconditus*) behind Jesus Christ, behind the Lamb that was slain. Barth had planted this idea in him, but—as we already noted—it was reinforced on the battlefield. Indeed in his memoir he relates how after returning from the war he had resolved to effect "theological change throughout the Kirk," by correcting the proclivity to sever the relation between faith in Christ and faith in God.[32]

Many Christians have difficulty accepting the Apocalypse as part of the New Testament canon. Its portrayal of Christ in many places (cf. Rev 19) reminds one of the God of the Old Testament, not the New.[33] For Torrance, though, the Apocalypse is a fitting end to the New Testament and the whole Bible.

b. "The Wrath of the Lamb"

The Old Testament theme of the wrath of God is prominent in the book. Torrance does not dodge this fact. Instead he tries to see it in light of the good news of Christ's forgiveness and love. His approach is eschatological. We see this clearly in his sermons on chapters 15 and 16, where God's wrath is extraordinarily harsh, striking the whole world. Worse,

---

30. Ibid., 46.

31. Ibid., 48.

32. Torrance, "My Parish Ministry," 28. One incident in particular on the front "haunted" and inspired Torrance. This was the dying soldier who asked his chaplain whether God was really like Jesus (ibid.).

33. The contrast between the Christ in Revelation and the rest of the New Testament is more apparent than real. In Revelation we do get a clear picture of Christ as the judge of the world, but that is not the only picture we get. Besides, the image of Christ as judge can be found in other areas of the New Testament (cf. John 5:22; Acts 10:42; 17:31; 2 Thess 1:7–9).

it seems, this wrath does not produce anything good. No repentance comes from it; only blasphemy. Still, Torrance maintains that "no judgement of divine wrath is purely destructive in its intention."[34] Ultimately, it serves God's salvific purpose.[35] The key for him is the prelude to the bowls of judgment, which contains a hymn of praise and thanksgiving from the redeemed. In Torrance's view, this hymn should be ascribed to the totality of God's judgments—those in the past, the present, and the future. That explains why the hymn is the "song of Moses" and the "song of the Lamb." The song of Moses was in response to the judgment of God that permitted Israel to cross the Red Sea, to the right hand of God that pulverized the enemy. The song of Moses, then, should be a song of hope for those who trust in Christ. "That Old Testament story gives us an understanding of what will happen in the great day when at last the Captain of our Salvation shall have led the host of the redeemed in triumph over all that is bestial and unholy."[36]

But the redeemed also sing, as part of the same hymn, the "song of the Lamb." So on that "great day," after the advent of Christ (16:15), there will be a hymn of praise to God for his triumph over the "cruel taskmaster of guilt and sin."[37] There will be a hymn too for the victory of love over wrath. In other words, the hymn will be "the perfect blend of mercy and truth, of love and judgement."[38] Thus we should interpret that "sea of glass mingled with fire" in light of those terms. The glass symbolizes the "crystal clear" judgments of God, which uncover the "dark depths of iniquity."[39] The fire is the "consuming fire" of God. Yet it is a fire that does not destroy, for it expresses God's redeeming love. It is a chastening, sanctifying fire; one that "burns the dross and refines the silver."[40] This

---

34. Torrance, *Apocalypse*, 126.

35. Torrance's view of judgement in the Apocalypse is echoed by other commentators. See John Bollier, "Judgement in the Apocalypse," 14–25. He also argues that the judgements are christocentric, in accord with the New Testament doctrine of salvation in Christ, and that they aim not at destruction but repentance. Cf. also Klassen, "Vengeance in the Apocalypse," 300–311. His point is that vengeance must be understood in terms of the wrath of the Lamb, whose authority was gained through suffering. This means that Christ's acts of vengeance are really defensive and aim at universal repentance.

36. Torrance, *Apocalypse*, 128.

37. Ibid.

38. Ibid.

39. Ibid., 126.

40. Ibid., 127.

unusual sea of glass and unusual hymn are apocalyptic forms of expression. They are unusual because they signify new realities, which need to be interpreted eschatologically, i.e., in light of the consummation of history and God's final judgment.

"Until that day," Torrance maintains, "there must be an inevitable contrast between Sinai and Calvary."[41] In the bowls of wrath poured out on the world we are reminded only of Sinai, of God's awesome holiness and remoteness (Heb 12:18ff). Yet the bowls of wrath should point us to Calvary too; for in Christ mercy and judgment, love and holiness, were perfectly combined.

"But before that day comes" God must shake not only earth but also heaven, as Hebrews predicts (12:27). That is what the seven bowls of wrath are about. The wrath of God should not be confused with the violence of the beast in Rev 12. The wrath of God is "pure and sinless, priestly in function and golden integrity."[42] It comes from the inner shrine of the Holy of Holies in heaven. But Jesus Christ is both the Lamb of sacrifice and the High Priest in this temple. He was offered once to bear the sins of many. In a sense, he is in these bowls of wrath poured out upon earth, in the shaking of heaven and earth. For Torrance, that loud voice from the temple of heaven that follows the seventh bowl can only be an echo of Jesus' final words at Golgotha: "It is done!—surely it is intended that we should understand in all that something of the unmitigated darkness and agony of Golgotha. If God must at last pour out such wrath upon inveterate and defiant godlessness, it is wrath at the cost of infinite agony to Himself."[43] To say then that history is "already conquered" by the Lamb means that history is judged through the Lamb. It means that Calvary is proleptic of the final judgment, a judgment in the "heart of love."[44]

Christ's judgment and conquest of history are highlighted as well towards the end of the eleventh chapter. "The kingdoms of this world are become the Kingdom of our Lord, and of His Christ." We have a revelation of the kingdom of God in its consummation, a picture of the "finished work of Christ," of that which awaits us on the "other side" of

41. Ibid., 128.
42. Ibid., 130.
43. Ibid., 131.
44. Ibid., 129.

the resurrection and final judgment.[45] Yet there is no complete realization of this kingdom on earth. The reconciliation of the world has not been actualized. There is still evil in the world, still violent resistance to the rule of Christ (cf. v.19b). Yet "even now," Torrance writes, Christ's kingdom is "striking at the black heart of this world's evil with invincible might."[46] John refers to God's "great power," his "wrath," and destruction of those who "destroy the earth." They are compatible with other references to Christ's messianic reign, when he puts all things under his feet and makes a "footstool out of his enemies" (1 Cor 15:25; Ps 110:1). But Torrance does not interpret John's words as a vindication of raw power. He reminds us that Christ's kingdom is not of this world (John 18:36). It is a kingdom of "Truth and Love." That means its power is veiled in weakness. "That is the only way the kingdoms of this earth can become the Kingdom of God—by the might of the Lamb, by the Word of the living God and by the blood of Cross in the heart and conscience of men. That is the most potent force in heaven and earth."[47]

2. Apocalypse "means the tearing aside of the veil of the sense of time to reveal the decisive conquest of organic evil by the incarnate Son of God"

a. "The Kingdom of Heaven suffereth violence"

The story of how the kingdoms of the world are transformed into the kingdom of God is really the subject of Rev 12–20. Torrance does not believe that they are transformed by the bare hand of God, but he still takes seriously the world's resistance to this transformation. Indeed, his penetrating grasp of modern forms of evil is one of the outstanding features of his sermons. The title fits: *Apocalypse Today.*

The evil in this world is "organic," because it is embedded in the very foundations and structures of the world. It snares individuals and societies. It is most formidable when it disguises itself as good, as something divine, even Christian. Evil is well equipped to do this, for it has a spiritual home. It may be organic, but its roots are in heaven, not earth.

---

45. Ibid., 91.
46. Ibid., 92.
47. Ibid., 98.

What makes this evil so mysterious and demonic is its god-likeness. It comes down from heaven. It is essentially spiritual evil and it succeeds in dragging down a great train of spiritual forces in rebellious activity.[48]

The existence of evil on earth is really a sign of its final destruction. It has already been defeated in heaven, and cast down (Luke 10:18), through God's action in Christ. Christ's humiliation was an opportunity for Satan's triumph, but Christ's exaltation through the cross resulted in Satan's humiliation, his fall to earth. Satan wrecks havoc in the world as result. He is the spirit of the anti-Christ, though he cannot assail the exalted Christ. Instead, this spirit resists Christ's redeeming work by attacking the church and deceiving the world. It lodges in the "high places," in the consciences of men and in the cultures of nations. "The evil one is entrenched throughout the whole of human life and the whole world is in the grip of it, deceived by it . . . It is false religion, a false order; a false wisdom."[49] Only the Word of God can dislodge evil from these "high places." And Torrance was sure that this was happening in his day; hence the "turmoil and trouble" in the world. "That dragon is cast out of Heaven, out of spiritual regions, and indeed it only because he is cast out that he creates such a din on earth. So long as the devil deceives the world successfully and charms men away from the Word of God, the devil is as quiet as a mouse."[50]

The "din on earth," the warfare and social upheaval around the world, is therefore a "sign of hope," a sign of the "beginning of the end."[51] Of course, the church was in the eye of the storm, for it bears testimony to the mighty Word. But it was not just the church which suffered evil's violent reaction. Torrance was cognizant of the virulent anti-Semitism that marked this era, although at the time of his sermon (January, 1946) he may not have been aware that genocide had taken place in Europe. The "spiteful tyrant . . . works out his wrath against Jews and Christians everywhere, those 'who keep the commandments of God and have the testimony of Jesus.'"[52]

---

48. Ibid., 94.
49. Ibid., 96.
50. Ibid., 97.
51. Ibid.
52. Ibid., 95.

b. "The Mystery of Iniquity"

In his sermon on Rev 13 Torrance looks deeper into this organic evil and at its operation in the world. It is organic not only because it infects the whole world but also because it incarnates in the world. It is not only god-like in having a spiritual home; it tries to be Christ-like, too. This is the goal of the spirit of the anti-Christ. That is the significance of the two beasts. The one that rises from the sea "actually dares to imitate the death and resurrection of Christ" by displaying the restoration of a deadly wound.[53] The one that rises from the land has "two horns like a lamb" of God. This beast tries to disguise its real nature by imitating Christ's signs and wonders.

However, the most disturbing picture to emerge from these monstrous images is the "demonic-trinity." While many commentators see this trinity arising from the dragon and the two beasts, Torrance sees it in the dragon, the beast, and the speaking image of the beast (so the two beasts are really one). The dragon is the devil, the "loathsome power of spiritual evil," as he calls it.[54] The beast is the "entrenchment of that power in the passions of men and its embodiment in the increasing debasement and brutalizing of the world."[55] In the image of the beast he sees the false spirit and the "propaganda power of the anti-Christ in the world."[56] That is the meaning of the 666, "an unholy and unsuccessful trinity of evil." "*This evil trinity 666 apes the Holy Trinity 777, but always fall short and fails.*"[57]

By the twentieth century it was common to treat the imagery in Rev 13 as merely the stuff of a "poet's imagination."[58] Torrance could not follow suit. He saw the imagery as integral to the Word of God, and the terrible events of his day persuaded him that the demonic trinity was "a real and ghastly fact."[59] In clear reference to Hitler he writes: "'And all the world wondered after the beast.' Is that not a perfect description of what has happened in Europe since 1933? Nation after nation was bemused, struck dumb, and rendered quite inactive at the terror of an unearthly

53. Ibid., 102.
54. Ibid., 138.
55. Ibid.
56. Ibid., 105.
57. Ibid.
58. See Dodd, *The Coming of Christ*, 3.
59. Torrance, *Apocalypse*, 106.

monster of evil. And the next verse reads, 'Who is like unto the beast? Who is able to make war with him?' Who has not heard that said in the last few decades?"[60] And in the powerful propaganda machine around Hitler, Torrance could not help but hear the voice of the false prophet. Yet by the time Torrance resumed his exposition of Revelation in 1946, this particular form of the beast had been humiliated; but he warns of others that have emerged in world. There were even more disturbing ones. One was Communism.

It takes little effort today to convince people of the dangers of Communism, but this was not the case six decades ago. In Britain of 1946 Communism was synonymous with the USSR, yet at this time, according to historian Henry Pelling, "enthusiasm for all things Russian was at its peak among the British public."[61] This was especially the case among British intellectuals. A number of them viewed the Soviet system as a "great and inspiring experiment in science and democracy."[62] An example was John Macmurray, a Christian philosopher and an important influence on Torrance.[63] He referred to the Soviet Union as "the nearest approach to the realization of the Christian intention that the world had ever seen."[64] In one sense Torrance would have concurred, but that only helps us understand why he saw Communism as a more sinister danger than Nazism. He explains: "One of the astonishing things about Communism . . . is that it has absorbed so much of Christianity that we can trace what appear to be dim lineaments of the Kingdom of God

---

60. Ibid.

61. Pelling, *Britain*, 306. He notes that "public opinion was so strongly pro-Soviet in 1944 that it was almost impossible to publish a book implying sharp criticism of the Stalinist regime" (Pelling, *Britain*, 306.). T. S. Eliot, for example, blocked the publication of George Orwell's *Animal Farm*, which aimed to debunk Communism through an ingenious allegorization of this social system (ibid.).

62. Addison, *The Road to 1945*, 137.

63. What did Torrance take from Macmurray? It is hard to ascertain. But when you read *The Clue to History*, Macmurray's most important work, you will find many ideas that Torrance would have found congenial at least. For Macmurray, the "clue to history" lies in the Hebraic consciousness. He has in mind modern Western history, where there has been a growing rejection of metaphysical dualism and a stress on action. "Action is the test of ideals." Macmurray also appreciated the apocalyptic element in Jesus' teaching. This element is the "affirmation of the inevitability" of the kingdom of God (Macmurray, *The Clue*, 53).

64. Macmurray, *The Clue*, 202.

upon it."[65] It represented a false kingdom with a false Christ.[66] "The beast has his false image which is an imitation of the Christian Church, an imitation of Christian brotherhood, an imitation of the Christian doctrine of universal humanity, an imitation of Christian hope for a new heaven and new earth."[67]

Yet despite Communism's "collective, communal image that embraces small and great, rich and poor, free and bond," Torrance warns of the bestial, dehumanizing power that lurks behind this image. "Behold, it awakens to life and power, a dread tyrannical might prostituting the social good of all to its bestial aim clamps down upon men with an iron hand. In its communal rule every man is but a number, a number of the same beast and bearing his name alone."[68] More worrisome was the fact that this "iron hand" was extending its grip upon humanity. The Soviet Bloc was carved out after the war, and then when the People's Republic of China was formed in 1949, that put about one-third of humanity under Communist rule.[69]

While Communism extended its grip around the world, there was a counter movement in the West in the 1940s. This movement sought to reorder societies with a mixture of liberal-democratic ideas and Christian principles, in the hope of averting another war and securing

65. Torrance, *Apocalypse*, 145.

66. Later, Torrance will explain "Marxian Socialism" more rationally, as a "secularised eschatology" that thrives on the eschatological void in modern Christianity (Torrance, "The Modern," 49). He obviously took a harder stand on Communism than Karl Barth. Emil Brunner, himself a Christian socialist, chided Barth for taking a soft line on Communism while in Hungary. Barth defended his non-action by saying that a condemnation of Communism would be redundant and that, in any case, the Church in the West was not in any spiritual danger from Communism. See Barth, *Against the Stream*, 139. On the other hand, Charles West in *Communism and the Theologians* argues that Barth provides the best answer to the challenges raised by Marxist ideology (ibid., 216). He confronts Marx's false eschatology with a "genuine eschatology," one centred in Christ (ibid., 281). One could argue, then, that Torrance fills out Barth's answer to Communism.

67. Torrance, *Apocalypse*, 145.

68. Ibid., 104.

69. These events prompted the Church of Scotland to set up its Commission on Communism in 1949. It produced two large reports: *The Challenge of Communism* and the *Church under Communism*. Many of Torrance's concerns are echoed, and even elaborated on, in these reports. The Communist takeover of China, perhaps more than any other event, contributed to Torrance's antipathy toward Marxian ideology. He was born in China to missionary parents who were later evicted by the Maoist forces.

socio-economic order. This led to socially progressive governments and to the creation of the United Nations in 1945. Yet Torrance felt it was necessary to issue warnings about these things as well. "Let us make no mistake. No amount of reshuffling can put a truly Christian shape upon the world. No amount of international discussion, no amount of diplomatic arrangements, and no United Nations policy can really imprint a Christian pattern and character upon the world apart from the Gospel of salvation. If nations do not give Christ pre-eminence, they are bound to fail in their efforts for peace."[70]

This new world order called not only for a consensus in politics but the cooperation of churches as well.[71] A fine example of the latter was the Church of England's Malvern Conference in 1941, chaired by William Temple and attended by fifteen bishops and 400 clergy. The conference was in response to a "crisis of civilization," but its purpose was to consider how "Christian faith and principles" could be a guide to "action in the world of to-day."[72] That conference was the basis for Temple's popular and influential book *Christianity and Social Order* (1942). It has been called "one of the foundation piers of the welfare state" (D. L. Munby). Consider also *The Church and the New Order* (1941) by William Paton, a secretary at the time to the International Missionary Council. Paton's stated aim is to "discuss the remaking of the world order, and the practical steps that may be taken towards it, in the light of Christian faith and from the point of view of the Christian Church regarded as a universal society."[73]

The world crisis also forced the Church of Scotland to ponder anew the relationship between Church and society. From 1940 to 1945 the General Assembly had a special commission in operation for the "Interpretation of God's Will in the Present Crisis," better known as the Baillie Commission, after its Convenor John Baillie.[74]

70. Torrance, *Apocalypse*, 108.

71. Addison, *The Road to 1945*, 187.

72. *The Life of the Church*, vii, 10. For Temple, the key Christian principles are "Freedom, Fellowship and Service." See also his book *The Hope of the New World*.

73. Paton, *The Church and the New Order*, 17.

74. As suggested by the name of the commission, the Church of Scotland took a more theological approach to the socio-political problems facing the church and state. Nonetheless, it shares the social objectives of William Temple and the Malvern Conference. While the Commission sees the present crisis as proof of the failure of the eschatology of progress, its own eschatological orientation is not that much different. It

It is not that Torrance did not share a concern for society and its future. What he did not share was the eschatology of men like Temple and Patton. While they may not have believed that the kingdom of God was something that Christians could establish on earth, nonetheless they believed that the kingdom could be approximated on earth through the application of Christian principles. In that sense their eschatology is a throwback to that of the nineteenth-century liberal Protestants.

For Torrance, the essence of the kingdom of God is the person of Jesus Christ. Christian principles are no substitute for him. This explains why "so-called Christian organizations" raised before Torrance the specter of the "many-headed monster of evil," that demonic trinity with its false spirit and a false incarnation.[75] His congregation is urged to take the 666 of Revelation as a "gale warning," for it is the "number of so-called Christian civilization without Jesus Christ."[76] Or, in the words of Saint Paul, 666 is about "having the form of godliness but denying its power" (2 Tim 3:5).

How then do we go about giving Christ preeminence? First, we have to heed the second commandment. "We must learn . . . not to put our trust in any human image, no matter how Christian it may appear to be."[77] On Torrance's view, Jesus Christ is the only image of God we have. However, we must not confuse this image with a pure spirit. He is also the "true Image of man," and so there will be an earthly kingdom of God in accord with humankind's deepest hopes and aspirations. Giving preeminence to Christ means in fact giving preeminence to his ascension and advent. The man Christ Jesus is in heaven, hidden from us. Therefore, until he returns, the visible kingdom must remain the church's great hope. At the advent of Christ we will behold this kingdom with our eyes. Until then the church can only bear witness to the coming of the kingdom, in word and deed, and wait in patience and suffering for it. "Let us not drag the Kingdom of God down to the patterns of and politics of this strange and evil world. Let us rather hold fast to the Word of God, the Word that promises a new heaven and new earth."[78] These

---

proposes changes that will achieve a "better ordering of society" and the "advancement of the Kingdom of God in the world" (Church of Scotland, *God's Will in Our Time*, 5).

75. Torrance, *Apocalypse*, 108.

76. Ibid., 109.

77. Ibid.

78. Ibid.

promises are not empty. While we are forbidden to build the kingdom on earth or to *drag* it down from heaven, we can however through the Spirit catch a glimpse of this kingdom and become privy to signs of its coming.

c. "The Trinity of Evil"

In the Apocalypse the great sign of the coming of the kingdom is the fall of Babylon the Great. There is no doubt that Babylon stands for first-century Rome; and for those who take a preterist approach to the book, that is all it can refer to. But if one believes that the whole Apocalypse is book for *today*, then it has to refer to more than that. For Luther, and countless Protestants after him, Babylon stood for Papal Rome. For Torrance it stood for something more universal: "world power and the proud attempt of humanity to make itself out to be great and indeed divine."[79] This is the *so-called Christian civilization without Jesus Christ*.[80] He could not help seeing the lineaments of a new Babylon in his own day: some in Nazi Germany, some in Soviet Union, and others in the democratic West. This Babylon is the embodiment of the demonic trinity, the kingdom of the world that is opposed to God. It has three main characteristics.

First, it is about "worship of this world, the deification of economic power and world security."[81] He found in Rev 18 a warning to all those who worship mammon, and it was one he felt the world sorely needed to hear. What he saw in his day was the deification of economic power across political and ideological boundaries (fascist, communist, and democratic), which indicated that a new Babylon was taking shape. "Babylon is the worship of Mammon, the tyrant deity of capitalists and Communists alike."[82] These two were ideological enemies, but for Torrance they were spiritual comrades, and slaves to "the devil's lie" that "man lives by bread alone."[83] The notion that economic factors are responsible for the mass

79. Ibid., 139.

80. For a full scale treatment of the biblical and theological significance of the city, read Jacques Ellul's *The Meaning of the City*. For Ellul, Babylon is "The City in the Bible" (ibid., 48). In her "all of human civilization is symbolized and summed up. She is the sum of man's spiritual effort; she represents not only the city but the condemned power behind the city" (ibid., 49).

81. Torrance, *Apocalypse*, 141.

82. Ibid., 142.

83. Ibid.

of suffering and conflict in the world is "the lie of the beast."[84] Despite their ideological differences, both communists and capitalists trusted economics to solve the world's problems. For the first group the solution was economic justice; for the second it was economic freedom.[85] The explosive growth in trade in the 1940s, thanks to the establishment of international trade agreements, also provoked Torrance. "Babylon is the queen of international trade and luxury, the queen of state capitalists."[86] All these things were signs to some that the whole world was becoming enmeshed in the net of economic evil, that every "man" was being turned into an "economic man."[87]

Second, Babylon represents "human collectivity" (cf. Rev 17:17). This problem was most acute in the Communist world, where great efforts were made to bind people together, largely by incorporating elements of the kingdom of God. But the so-called "free world" was not free from the dangers of human collectivity either. Its economic integration actually encouraged a type of collectivity.

The universal drive toward collectivity sheds light on Torrance's ambivalence toward the United Nations. On the one hand he supported its social mandate: "we must work as hard as we can on behalf of the United Nations . . . We must have these collective organizations."[88] On the other he warns that "even the United Nations can easily occupy the place of God."[89]

> It imitates a unity-in-diversity that is exemplified in the Triune God. We must not put religious faith in collectives and bow down and worship this image. We must not deck it out in moral glory and give it divine sanction. Then it becomes a Babylonian

---

84. Ibid., 141.

85. Consider that by 1946 economics had become the queen of the social sciences. In 1948 Paul Samuelson published his *Economics*, which has become a classic textbook in the field. The year of publication is no coincidence. The author was motivated by the belief that ignorance of economics was a major cause of the wars of the twentieth century.

86. Ibid., 141. It is worth noting that the General Agreement on Tariffs and Trade (GATT) was formed in 1944.

87. The term "economic man" was a buzzword in this era. It formed the title of a popular and provocative book on political economy: Peter Drucker's *The End of Economic Man*.

88. Torrance, *Apocalypse*, 143.

89. This sentence does not appear in the original sermon from 1946. That it was inserted in the published form in 1960 suggests that Torrance's view of the United Nations had not changed a lot in the interval.

idol. And yet this is one of the subtlest temptations of the modern world—to worship the common mind, to worship the community, to worship society, to believe that men belong to a society of people where all think alike and believe alike.[90]

It is hard today to sympathize with Torrance's political views; they sound reactionary and out of step with the principles of a liberal democracy. Torrance probably had many sympathizers in his day, however. In any event, his real concern is theological, not political. He draws attention to a neglected aspect of the doctrine of sin. Christians rarely focus on sin's corporate side, which is often cleverly disguised. "In the last resort sin is a social magnitude, and it loves to maneuver in the form of moral magnitudes and of the communal good because it is thus that it gains its great and cohesive might."[91] Now the implication is that cities, states, corporations, and organizations can become objects of God's judgment too.

Not many years after these sermons, Torrance would find himself working on behalf of the World Council of Churches, but not even the ecumenical movement at this point is above reproach. While he confesses that the church is the only "true community" in the world, he fears the church may be inadvertently "doing homage to the beast" when—in response her "internal spiritual bankruptcy" and the "menace of Communism and nationalism"—she desperately tries to bind herself together.[92] Not even the walls of an earthly church are sure refuge, then, against the beast of Babylon. The only refuge is our faith in things above and beyond this world, in the eschatological promises. "A Christian may be a citizen of no earthly 'Babylon.' He is a citizen of heaven and belongs to a new heaven and a new earth, the city of God."[93]

We should not assume that Babylon is anti-religious. The third feature of Babylon is "pride." "Ostensibly Babylon is a world-wide civilization and culture, magnificent in her science and arts and commerce, but it is drugged with pride and intoxicated with her own success."[94] However, nothing increases Babylon's pride more than the "religious

90. Torrance, *Apocalypse*, 143.
91. Ibid., 144.
92. Ibid., 145.
93. Ibid., 146.
94. Ibid., 140.

sanctions and religious pretences" that overlay her success.[95] In this way Babylon pretends to be the New Jerusalem.

Pride is the greatest evil. It is sin separated from all guilt and shame. It is the deification of the individual and collective ego. It attacks the very nature of God by turning his glory into the "image of sinful man and what is worse, the image of the beast."[96] In 1946 it was the collective ego of nation states that sparked Torrance's prophetic warnings. Nazi Germany had been an unmistakable instance of this. He remarks on the "terrible unity" there that was forged by Rosenberg and Goebbels by "playing upon the German pride." However, Nazi Germany should also be understood as a case of the beast that plunders and destroys the Babylon that rode precariously upon it (17:16). In the nineteenth century Germany represented the rebirth of classical Greece, but by the end of WWII the Nazis had reduced the country literally to a heap of smoldering ruins. Torrance's warning is that every society—even a democratic one—is vulnerable to the sins of Babylon. "Babylon is fallen! Babylon the great is fallen!" This is still a warning to every nation, to every culture and every economic power on earth. "Such is the judgement of God upon the defiant pride and culture of man that tries to storm the way back into Utopia, into the Garden of Eden. That way is barred by an angel with a flaming sword. But there is a way, through the Garden of Gethsemane and the Garden of Arimathea."[97]

d. "The Marriage of the Lamb"

No part of the Apocalypse illustrates Christ's conquest of organic evil as well as Rev 19:11–21, the Battle of Armageddon. For Torrance, the visions therein pertain to the "final outcome of history." Here we witness the advent of Christ and the final destruction of the "beast" and the "false prophet" which become manifest in history. Yet this part of the Apocalypse throws up formidable challenges to a commentator like Torrance, who wants to make the cross the paradigm with which to understand God's final judgments. It is a section brimming with Old Testament imagery. "He Himself will rule them with a rod of iron. He Himself treads the winepress of the fierceness and the wrath of God"

---

95. Ibid., 146.
96. Ibid., 148.
97. Ibid., 149.

(19:15). Yet Torrance would have us believe that God will judge the world only by the Lamb of God. True, a "fire" of suffering, conflict and judgment "rages" in the world, but still God is "in" this fire.

Torrance does not soft-pedal the Day of Judgment. He sees the final advent of Christ as a day of judgment upon wickedness, a day of the "manifest power of God," a day when the Word in "righteousness judges and makes war."[98] It is a day "when the Kingdom of God is violent and the armies of heaven are completely victorious."[99] Yet the cross will be in the foreground even on judgment day.

The advent will also be the day of the "The Marriage of the Lamb." This refers to the "entry of the earthly Church into her heavenly estate."[100] The Marriage is also a trope for the union of "two times," the "Word of Pardon, and the Word of Eternal Power."[101] For many commentators the blood on Christ's vesture in 19:13 points forward to the winepress of the final wrath of God in 19:15. For Torrance, though, the blood is not from the enemies of Christ, but from Christ himself. It points back to the cross, to the time of pardon and the "Invisible Power" of God.

He finds an anticipation of this union of two times in the story of the paralytic in Matt 9. He sees a "moment of forgiveness and of invisible power" but, at the same time, a "moment of healing and manifest power."[102] Now, however, the church lives between these two moments, "between the First Advent and Second Advent, between the Word of Forgiveness and the Word of Judgement, between the Last Supper and the Marriage Supper."[103] The invisible power of the Word is at work in the church and in the world. It is invisible, yet it is still the greatest disturbing force in the world. It rouses the anti-Christ; causes tumult among the nations; it presses the whole world to a decision about Christ (cf. Rev 10:9–10).

There is much concern today with the misuse of power in the church. On one hand, Torrance legitimizes power within it; but on the other, he warns against the misuse of it. The "false Church" is one that tries to establish an illegitimate marriage of "temporal and spiritual power," in order to establish a kingdom of God on earth. It bargains away the

98. Ibid., 158–59.
99. Ibid., 160.
100. Ibid., 158.
101. Ibid., 159.
102. Ibid., 158.
103. Ibid., 160.

invisible power of the cross for the manifest power of world. The church cannot forget that by itself it has no spiritual power. All spiritual power comes from the Word of God. "The Word of God empowers itself, enacts itself, for the Word of God and the Power of God are one. No man can fulfil the Word of God . . . No church has control over" it.[104] It means that the visible might of God at the end of history, the power that comes with the advent of Christ, is none other than the Word of God itself. It is not a raw physical power. The Word of God is the "sharp sword" that uncovers the "lies and hypocrisies of men" (cf. Heb 4.12) that strikes down the ungodly power of nations.[105] It is the Word incarnate, who is "King of Kings and Lord of Lords." And by this name, Torrance adds, the "whole world is given to know that Christ Crucified is indeed the Power of God."[106]

In his reading of Rev 19, Torrance once again tries to understand eschatology in terms of the cross of Christ. He also tries to preserve the unity of the Word and its action; or, as he expressed it at Auburn, the unity of the Person and Work of Christ. This principle of unity means that the second advent is closely tied to the first advent. Torrance does not think about the *parousia* in the usual way, i.e., as the return of Christ. Strictly speaking, he believes in only one *parousia* (a coming and a presence) with two moments (just as he will later think about the "one sacrament" with "two moments"). Christ is the Alpha and Omega. In one sense, the Marriage of the Lamb will be the joining of the Word of Pardon and the Word of Power; in another sense, it will be a matter of the full unveiling of a union that already exists. "Christ crucified is indeed the *Power of God*."[107] The church that lives under the cross also lives by that *power*. Even now, it presses in upon the church, and the world. Through the Word, the Sacrament, and the Holy Spirit, Christians gain a foretaste of the final resurrection. Through the disturbing and fermenting word of the cross the Babylons of the earth are shaken and brought low, in an anticipation of that final judgment on all evil.

104. Ibid.
105. Ibid.
106. Ibid.
107. Ibid.

3. Apocalypse "means the unveiling of the new creation as yet hidden from our eyes behind the ugly shape of history"

If we want a glimpse of the new creation we naturally gravitate to Rev 21 and 22, but Torrance first draws our attention to the obscure vision of the new creation in Rev 4. He finds important lessons here. First, this chapter shows God enthroned in the middle of his creation. The vision is not of the One in isolation but, rather, of the One in union with the Many. The "sea of glass" before him signifies the "everlasting covenant" between them. The four creatures represent the fullness of creation. They are fantastic, but for Torrance that fact signifies the "hidden ways of God in nature and history."[108] Less strange are the twenty-four elders. They stand for the church, the people of God. They are the centerpiece of the new creation.

We must bear in mind that we have a vision of a *new* creation. It is not the Platonic form of the creation below, but a "glimpse of what shall be," the fruit of redemption and the "final outcome of world history."[109] Yet it is a kingdom already realized through Christ's resurrection and ascension; one that is pressing in upon us. "Lift up your eyes and see already the kingdom of peace and new creation enthroned above the world and about to break into our troubled world."[110]

1. "Ordeal by History"

We have already seen the "ugly shape of history," and the "trinity of evil" and "Babylon the Great" are the climax of that history. But the four horsemen of Rev 6 preview that history. World history is "ugly" because it suffers from the "laws of guilt and retribution." It is man "caught in the cords of his own sin." As Torrance puts it: "these four evil powers make it quite plain that the course of world history is also the course of the world's judgement."[111] It was plain to him too that the world in

---

108. Ibid., 32.

109. Ibid., 41, 32.

110. Ibid., 38.

111. Ibid., 54. The idea that world history is world judgment was made famous by F. W. J. Schelling. But his conception is neither christocentric nor teleological. History and judgment are part of an immanent process without resolution.

the 1940s was suffering the scourges of judgment. "He who does not see these horsemen abroad in the world today must be blind."[112]

This includes the first horse. Torrance is not among those who believe this horse symbolizes Christ.[113] It obviously bears no relation to Christ crucified, which is the key motif for Torrance. Another explanation for his view is his sense of the nature of evil in his day. Contrary to appearances, he thinks this horse is the most terrible. It augurs the beast of Rev 13. It is a "vision of the anti-Christ," of "spiritual wickedness disguised in Christian dress."[114] That is why the first seal is the source of the other three. The upshot is the cry of the martyrs under the fifth seal. This cry, Torrance exclaims, is more terrible than all the warfare, famine, and widespread death. At the heart of the "apocalypse of evil" in world history is the "malignant evil that hates God and is bitterly opposed to the servants of God and of His Word."[115]

We tend to associate Christian martyrdom with the first centuries of the church, but the twentieth century is also filled with martyrs. Many were made in the 1940s, [116] at the hands of Communists and Nazis. For Torrance, this was no surprise. In his view, these forces were not just enemies of human rights and democracy; they were essentially anti-Christian, bent upon the destruction of the church and the people of God. On the other hand, martyrdom was a sign to him of the church's witness to the cross of Christ, its loyalty to the Lamb.[117] The word of the cross, after all, is the greatest disturbing force in the world. Nothing provokes a stronger reaction from the forces of evil.

Even more disturbing than this vision of history's dark destiny, is the suggestion that God has a direct hand in it all—even in the most terrible violence. "And there was given to him a great sword" (Rev 6:4).

112. Torrance, *Apocalypse*, 54.

113. This means seeing the horse as a portent of Christ the conqueror in Rev 19. Among those who take this position are Hendriksen, *More than Conquerors*; Considine, "The Rider on the White Horse"; and Ellul, *The Meaning of the City*.

114. Torrance, *Apocalypse*, 54.

115 Ibid.

116. See the extensive collection of statements and reports on this tragedy in Carmer, *The War against God*. Cf. also Keller, *Christian Europe Today*.

117. One should not neglect the importance of martyrdom in the Apocalypse. See Reddish, "Martyr Theology," 85–95. The author argues that martyrdom is "the primary motif" of Revelation. This may be an exaggeration, but he certainly deserves credit for highlighting an important theme in Revelation, one which accounts for the popularity of this part of the Bible during times of great suffering and distress.

This is no justification for holy wars, but it does tell us that God may permit wars that are "history's own chastisement and judgement."[118] These events are not always the direct result of human guilt, however, but the result of "spiritual wickedness in high places" (Eph 6:12), which leads captive people and whole nations. Moreover, as we learned, divine judgment is never wholly destructive. If the scourges of history are signs that world history is world judgment, then we have to believe that these things serve somehow God's plan of cosmic redemption.

The last two seals remind us of the patience of God in the face evil. While the sixth tells us that a final judgment on evil is imminent, the fifth tells us that God suspends this judgment. But where is the justice or holiness of God in all this? The explanation for Torrance is more complex than the one suggested by the text (to complete the number of martyrs). The real explanation is again in the act of God in Christ. The Scripture tells us that God has committed all judgment to the Son (John 5:22), but for Torrance all judgment essentially took place *in* the Son also. "At last on the Cross God pronounced His final and irrevocable No against all that is contradictory of His holy love."[119] And just as the world was judged in the man of Calvary, so God "will only judge the world by the Man of Calvary."[120] This means that Christ "died for all men" and that as a consequence "all men are apprehended by God's love in Christ."[121]

The persistence of evil in the world overruled by God baffles even the most ardent believer. One can only look to the cross for an explanation. The cross is proof that God does not tolerate evil, but it is also the revelation of God's holy love. It is not easy to understand what Torrance means when he says God "will only judge the world by the man of Calvary." All that can be said is that Calvary reveals the fact that God's judgment is redemptive, and that his judgment is an expression of his holiness and his redemption is an expression of his love. His love is of the kind that "uproots all evil . . . destroys sin . . . and blots out all darkness."[122] This redemptive judgment also extends into the spiritual places. That is the significance of the sixth seal. "This is an upheaval among the cosmic powers . . . a cosmic event in which the whole world of spirit is shaken to

118. Torrance, *Apocalypse*, 53.

119. Ibid., 56.

120. Ibid.

121. Ibid.

122. Ibid.

its depths, in which principalities and powers and spiritual wickedness in high places become dislodged."[123]

By this spiritual shake-up God puts everyone on trial. All "the spiritual secrets of men" have to be made plain to them, tried by fire (1 Cor 3:13), so that "you and I may know where we stand before the day of the Lord comes upon us."[124]

The universal application of the work of Christ, however, does not lead inexorably to universalism.[125] Grace is not a disqualification of human freedom. God "pleads" with all people to turn toward him, but that means there is the possibility that some will refuse the grace of God. God does not save through coercion, only through holy love. That is the message behind the phrase, "wrath of the Lamb." This phrase has baffled commentators. For Torrance, it means that "even in wrath God remains love."[126] Even those who purposely choose evil cannot escape completely from the love of God. Its light uncovers their intentions and convicts them of their evil.

b. "The Lord God Omnipotent Reigned"

The "great day" of the "wrath of the Lamb" in Rev 6 is an anticipation of the judgment that brings the downfall of Babylon and the defeat of the beast in Rev 18 and 19. In between these judgments there is another "unveiling of the new creation" in 19:1–6. "Now these visions carry us forward to see how that great day of the Lord will dawn, when all the holy aspirations and yearnings of God's creatures, when all the snatches of triumphant singing, shall reach their fulfillment in a magnificent paean of victory as history breaks into eternity and the *Word of God rides forth in complete sovereignty over all*."[127]

In fact, it is an unveiling of the church triumphant (19:4–7), the heart of the new creation. The vision here is related to the ones in Rev 4 and 14, but here we "begin to see the final outcome of history."[128] The church is very much involved in this history. Torrance calls the music in

123. Torrance, *Apocalypse*, 57.

124. Ibid., 58.

125. Again, see Torrance's debate with J. A. T. Robinson on the question of universalism (Torrance, "Universalism," 310–18).

126. Torrance, *Apocalypse*, 58–59.

127. Ibid., 153.

128. Ibid., 152.

this chapter the "wedding march of the Church," since here is depicted the "marriage supper of the Lamb and the entry of the Church as the bride of Christ into the family above."[129] Here too is the contrast between the "false Babylonian church" that received its due for rejecting the Word of God and the "true Church" that triumphs because of its obedience to the Word of God.

It is a vision that carries us "forward," that reveals the future. Yet Torrance believes this is a vision also of the church now. How could it not be? After all, "she belongs to the City of God and is supremely the church from above," where Christ is.[130]

The Church is a unique entity in that she spans two worlds. She is caught up in the "ugly shape of history," since, like Jesus, she has roots in the world; but she also belongs "to the heavenly assembly of the redeemed who are already triumphant."[131] This is because the risen Christ "dwells in the midst" of her. Yet her dual existence calls for continuous repentance. "She must ever be shedding her outward garments, putting off the old and putting on the new."[132]

Torrance tells us that his reading of the Apocalypse was shaped by the book's liturgical nature, which can be traced to the Old Testament and also to the life of the early church.[133] The prayers, hymns, and eucharistic language all attest to this liturgical nature. But so do those words from Rev 1:19. "I was in the Spirit on the Lord's Day." It suggests that the liturgy of the Apocalypse is a participation in a heavenly liturgy. It also indicates that the church spans two worlds, so that from within the church we can get a glimpse of the new creation, penetrate into the drama of history, and uncover the mystery of inequity. Yet the church is also a subject of apocalyptic. She is the heart of that new creation even while she is still caught up in the old creation.

---

129. Ibid.

130. Ibid., 155.

131. Ibid., 152. Cf. Heb 12.

132. Ibid., 155.

133. Ibid., 5. For more on liturgical character of The Apocalypse, see Piper, "The Apocalypse of John," 10–22; Allen Cabaniss, "A Note on the Liturgy," 78–86; Prigent, *Apocalypse et Liturgie*; and Shepherd, *The Paschal Liturgy*.

c. "The Silver Lining"

Without doubt, more ink has been spilled over Rev 20 than on any other part of the book. Based on what we know, we would expect Torrance to be a millennialist, on the side of church fathers such as Irenaeus and Tertullian. Did he not insist on taking history "seriously"? He would not allow us to "de-mythologize" Christ's resurrection, ascension, or advent. They are events that intersect history, that happen in time. Yet Torrance stands in line with Augustine. He is an *a*millennialist. There is not a little irony here. Torrance will later deplore the church's neglect of the Apocalypse through the centuries, and there can be no question that Augustine has to bear much of the blame for this situation. Much of the historic church's eschatology can be traced back to the Augustine's *City of God*, which overlooks all but one chapter (Rev 20) in the Apocalypse.

Torrance refuses to take the thousand years in Rev 20 literally for the same reason he does not take the multi-headed monsters in Rev 13 literally. However, he holds fast to the idea that through Christ the kingdom of God is present with us now. However, unlike the typical amillennialist, Torrance believes the thousand years represents a new time. While the monsters in Rev 13 are symbolic of something that occurs on the plane of our history and time, the thousand years is symbolic of something outside our time and history. He calls the millennial vision the "silver lining behind history" and the "Kingdom-of-God time."[134]

What is the nature of this kingdom of God time? It has to do first with the fact that God is the "Wholly Other." This is the axiom underlying Barth's early eschatology. It was the basis for his "Eternity/time" dialectic, which also plays a role in Torrance's early eschatology. This makes God's time unlike our time. This is where the Apocalypse comes in. It is an unveiling of God's time. But first, how does Torrance understand *our time*?

> It is (a) time that has a beginning and a time that has an end, but not a time that fulfils itself. It is a time that is empty, haunted by lost mystery, time that aches with restlessness, reaching out beyond itself but only to fall back to futility. Between the beginning and ending it is subjected to vanity, day following night, and night following day in unmeaning circularity. This is the time of sinful history, of deeds that cannot be undone, of words that cannot be plucked back, of opportunities lost like water spilt on the

134. Torrance, *Apocalypse*, 165.

ground. It is time that knows nothing new for all is devoured by the insatiable dragon of guilt.[135]

Indeed Torrance's understanding of fallen time informs his understanding of hell. Hell is basically a perpetuation and intensification of this time. "It is time that has denied itself fulfillment in Christ, and time therefore which has a dreary lastingness about it, for it can only double back upon itself forever in sulky, sullen memory of past sins."[136]

Now if God's time is unlike ours, then it is a time that defies description. All Torrance will say is "somehow present, past, and future are in one another, and do not simply follow one another in God's eternal time."[137]

This sermon on the millennium is not without ambiguity, which is to be expected given the nature of the subject matter. At first we are reminded of his early sermons on the resurrection. In them God's time was really eternity, in contrast to our time. The resurrection of Christ meant "Eternity has come plumb down from above and intersected our beggarly time." In this sermon, however, Torrance does not equate God and eternity or even make use of the eternity/time contrast. He has moved beyond this dualism to an exploration of the new time that Christ brings. This is "Kingdom of God time" or "millennium-time. It is not simply eternity; rather it is created time in "union with Eternity."[138] When we think of God's time we ought to think in terms of Christ, for in him God's time has "broken into our sinful time."[139]

This was a necessary development. If our understanding of God's nature is to be determined by God's revelation in Jesus Christ, then the same principle has to apply to God's time. We cannot operate with an a priori understanding of it. The Apocalypse makes this plain. Christ is the "Alpha and Omega, the Beginning and the End . . . who is who was and who is to come." And through him the new time of the kingdom is a present reality. "Already the Kingdom of God time runs throughout

135. Ibid., 163.

136. Ibid., 171.

137. Ibid., 163. While Revelation does not give us a definition of God's time, the structure of the book, which is aptly summarized in verse 1:19, gives credence to Torrance's definition. On the significance of this verse for the whole of Revelation, see Mounce, *The Book of Revelation*, 82; also Moffatt, "The Revelation of St. John," 279–494.

138. Torrance, *Apocalypse*, 166.

139. Ibid., 164.

time, and presses to its manifestation in the Advent of Christ. Behind the course of sinful history the reign of Christ is actually taking place."[140]

Millennium time is a new time, a creaturely time redeemed through Christ. The "thousand" signifies the "completeness and perfection" of this kingdom "in the midst of time" while the "years" convey the important fact that life in this kingdom is not a "timeless life of the spirit."[141] This is what it means to take the millennium seriously. "It is the time of life abundant, of fulfillment, the time of the end that is also the beginning, the time that gathers up in itself all things visible and invisible in perfection of communion with the living God."[142] Putting it more mundanely, the millennium is about full life in the body, so that there is time "to think and act and feel, time to know and speak and sing, time to worship and time to love."[143]

How does God secure this new time for us through Christ? First, by removing sin from it. Millennium time cannot begin until the "dragon of guilt is bound."[144] Guilt is that "insatiable monster" he referred to, one that "*devours* the present and *menaces* the future." This shows that Torrance has not completely abandoned his earlier personal, existential eschatology. In an early sermon, he explained how guilt makes time feel terribly long.[145] Yet this guilt has been objectively bound through the Christ-event, through his incarnation, cross and resurrection. That is the point of Rev 20:2.

According to Rev 20:4–6, the millennium begins with the resurrection of the saints. For Torrance, though, it begins with the resurrection of Christ. It is "the power of the resurrection that really rules."[146] Christians, however, partake of this power when they are baptized into Christ. Baptism represents the "first resurrection." The first resurrection, then, is not something reserved for a future age. It is enjoyed by all Christians in this age. In baptism the Christian dies with Christ, but also

140. Ibid., 165.

141. Ibid., 166.

142. Ibid., 164.

143. Ibid., 166.

144. Ibid., 164.

145. In this case, Torrance thinks about time in subjective terms. While sin and its attendant guilt make time feel long, pardon for sin and life in the presence of God brings a forgetfulness of time. See his sermons on 2 Pet 3:8 and 2 Cor 4:17–18.

146. Torrance, *Apocalypse*, 166.

rises with Christ to become a new creature. Through the seal of baptism the Christian has the "power of endless life lodged within him."[147]

Of course, the Apocalypse makes it clear that this "first resurrection" is not a shield against suffering. The baptized partake of Christ's sufferings as much as they partake of his resurrection. This is actually a sign of their union with Christ. That is why it is a "joy and a privilege" for the believer to suffer with Christ. The baptismal seal is also tested through suffering.

Torrance does not tell us much about the second resurrection, but neither does Rev 20. Besides, his theological method does not permit speculation. The important thing for Torrance is that the final resurrection will be a natural succession to the "first resurrection." "So the Christian with Christ alive in his heart cannot be holden to death. He will rise again and the second death is powerless to keep him in captivity."[148]

4. "There is to be a new creation which is the out-working of the Cross in the teeth of all the principalities and powers of darkness"

However, the millennium stands for more than a personal, realized eschatology. It is about the "reversal of world history."[149] The basis for this is the person of Christ who is the union of God's time with created time. The reversal of history means time is undergoing redemption. Though individual faith can never fully comprehend this, it perceives that events in history serve God's redemptive purpose. The reversal of history also suggests the millennium is about teleology, as do the words "fulfillment" and "gathers up" in the definition above.

The millennium tells us that the "end-time" has come upon us through Christ, that the kingdom of God is present in the "midst of our time." It is a thoroughly eschatological event that Christians participate in by means of baptism. This explains why Torrance will later define this sacrament as the "primary eschatological act."[150] On the contrary, the millennium indicates that the "Kingdom-of-God time moves beneath our time until it is fully unveiled in the Advent of Christ."[151] The span of

---

147. Ibid., 168.

148. Ibid., 169.

149. Ibid., 167.

150. Torrance, "Eschatology and Eucharist," 314.

151. Torrance, Apocalypse, 165.

a millennium reminds us that the "things concerning Jesus have an end, a fulfillment."[152] Now we are able to see why the millennium, though presentative, is identified at the *end* of the Scriptures. Since the first advent of Jesus Christ "all things move towards a climax, which will be the day of harvest both of good and of evil."[153] All these things are the outworking of the cross. Everything is put "to the test" of Christ's sacrificial love. Even the church is put to the test. It has a *"telos"* that is governed by the cross. Throughout history God is "fashioning His Church by the Word of the Gospel, by the power of the Cross."[154]

The church is plainly grounded in the world. She is caught in between God's judgments on the world and the world's assault on God's rule. She "lives on" in the middle of the tumults of world history, in the "turgid cataract" of evil, under the menace of the "image of the beast."[155] This gives her a "tainted worldly form."[156] She bears the marks of human civilization and, as we have seen, she may even pay homage to "the beast." The Church is fashioned through the cross in order to "seal" its members with "the image of God."[157] This entails repentance for the church. The church "must ever be shedding her outward garments, putting off the old and putting on the new, refusing to be built into the fabric of orders fashioned to suit human selfishness or some naturalistic ideology."[158] "Repent" is the message to the churches in Rev 2–3, and it will also be Torrance's message to the churches of the ecumenical movement in the 1950s.

a. "The Master Powers of History"

What really propels history forward? Where does its teleological orientation come from? One may find the explanation in the human will, the "cunning of reason" (Hegel), or the "élan vital" (Bergson). After reading Torrance's sermons on Rev 13 and 14, one might think that the spirit of the anti-Christ is the clue to history, until this spirit is driven back by the hand of God. Yet it would be a mistake to attribute too much power

152. Ibid., 170.
153. Ibid. Cf. Rev 14:14–20; 20:7–15.
154. Ibid., 152.
155. Ibid., 156.
156. Ibid., 155.
157. Ibid., 156.
158. Ibid., 155.

to evil. The demonic trinity is a "ghastly fact" of history. Still, it is only semi-real; it has no independent existence or purpose. Torrance does not overlook the contrast between Christ and the demonic trinity. While Christ is the one that "was and is and is to come," the demonic trinity "was and is not . . . and shall go into perdition."[159]

The real driving force of history is "the prayer of the Church and the fire of God."[160] This is a point he gathers from Rev 8:3–5. Few in 1946 would have denied that Hitler and his allies were the greatest aggressors in the world. Torrance was one who would have denied this, because in his view the cross of Christ is the "supreme aggressor" in the world.[161] We have heard this view of the cross before. Now what is said about the cross must be said about the church. The church is actually the reason Torrance can say the "cross is still in the field." It is the most "revolutionary force" on earth when it is true to its prophetic role. When the church preaches the word of the cross it makes some hearts as bitter as wormwood (Rev 8:11); it opens the "bottomless pit of human nature."[162]

Just as important as the church's prophetic role in world-history is its priestly role. "The prayers of the saints and the fire of God move the whole course of the world."[163] Through prayer the church participates in the priestly office of Christ, whose prayers while on earth made "Satan fall from heaven like lightening." Through prayer the church participates in Christ's decisive conquest of organic evil. A "fire rages in the world" and God is "in the fire." But prayer ignites this fire.

Rev 8:3–5 does not tell us what kind of prayers comes from the saints, but they would not need to be more elaborate than the Lord's Prayer. The Apocalypse could very well be an answer to its first two petitions: "Thy kingdom come, thy will be done one earth, as it is in heaven."

In conclusion, it can be maintained that God satisfies the human desire to master the course of the world, but only on condition that humanity becomes part of the kingdom of Christ and then priests to the God and Father of all (Rev 1:5).

---

159. Ibid., 105.

160. Ibid., 73.

161. Ibid.

162. Ibid., 75. See Rev 9:2.

163. Ibid., 73.

b. "The New Heaven and New Earth"

Amillennialism can foster an imperial eschatology. This problem is rooted in Augustine's notion that the millennium stands for the time of the church. For Augustine this meant that the visible church manifested the city of God or the kingdom of God. But down the road, some Augustinians would equate the church with the kingdom of God. The most notorious case is Charlemagne and his "Holy Roman Empire."

From Torrance we learn that through Christ the kingdom of God is here among us even now. Yet almost in the same breath, he tells us that the millennium indicates we enjoy only a "prelude" to the eternal kingdom. Still, this *prelude* is teleologically related to this future, eternal kingdom. Here there is no stark contrast between time and eternity. The millennium is the "firstfruits" of the kingdom. The full harvest is described in Rev 21–22.

The word apocalypse has accumulated negative connotations over the centuries. It makes us think of a violent, cataclysmic end to the world. It arouses fear and anxiety. For Torrance, though, the Apocalypse should foremost inspire hope, since it is fixed on the advent of Christ and a new, far better, world. Indeed, if we want to understand quickly the significance of the Apocalypse, we should start at the very end. "That is *apocalypse*, the final revelation or unveiling of God's eternal purpose in the form of the New Jerusalem."[164]

The new creation is also teleologically related to the original creation. The passing away of the first heaven and earth (Rev 21:1) signifies the redemption of the original creation, not the destruction of it. It will be a "homely kingdom with earth in it . . . and time in the heart of it."[165] But eschatology is not all protology. The original creation will also be brought to perfection and fulfillment. The glory of the new creation will far exceed the glory of the original creation.

Yet this does not mean the original creation is pregnant with the new creation. The last chapters of the Apocalypse reveal the Lamb of God at the center of the new creation. This has far reaching significance. It signifies that the "purpose of the original creation" and its fulfillment are achieved through Christ crucified.[166] It signifies too that the new

164. Ibid., 180.
165. Ibid., 176.
166. Ibid.

creation is closely tied the presence (parousia) of Christ. Yes, in one sense, the kingdom of God has already come in Jesus Christ. In him "the union between things visible and things invisible, things temporal and things eternal, the new creation, is a perfect reality."[167] The ascension, though, reminds us that the "form and pattern" of this kingdom, this new creation, is hidden from us until Christ comes again (cf. Luke 17:20). "Then, I saw the holy city, the New Jerusalem, coming down out of heaven from God" (Rev 21:2). These words remind us that the new creation represents an eschatological end as much as a teleological end.

In the meantime the sacraments keep us in touch with this kingdom, and give us a glimpse into it. Through baptism, we know, men and women receive eternal life. Moreover, the concrete reality of this kingdom is sacramentally confirmed in the Lord's Supper. The bread and wine symbolize a "holy sacramental union of things invisible and visible, of body and spirit, of heaven and earth."[168] They carry faith upward to Christ, but also forward in hope to the new creation.

What role will Jesus Christ have in this kingdom? First Corinthians 5:24–28 implies that he will have a minor role in it. On the other hand, Rev 21–22 indicates that he will be the "light" of the New Jerusalem, and the light by which we will see God. Moreover, it will be the light of the "heavenly Man." The Son may give up his kingdom, but Torrance maintains that he will never give up his humanity. "For it is unto His likeness that the redeemed are transformed when they see Him as he is."[169] They will thus have spiritual bodies, bodies in the image of Christ with which to worship and serve God.

Torrance reiterates that there will be no church in the New Jerusalem. Here he defines the church instrumentally, in much the same way Calvin does in his introduction to Book 4 of his *Institutes*. "As long as we are on this side of eternity we need artifices and edifices to keep the heavenly flame alive in our soul, but in the new creation all artificiality disappears."[170] Then there will be no need for ministry or sacraments. These things are for the time between, between the ascension and *parousia*. In the new heaven and earth, God will be in the midst of all his creatures and his children will have an unmediated knowledge of him.

167. Ibid., 179.
168. Ibid.
169. Ibid., 182.
170. Ibid., 180.

Of course, in another sense, the church will be central to the new creation. Revelation 4:4 suggests that even the eldership will have a place in the new world. More fundamental, though, is the fact that the church is the Body of Christ, the people of God, the communion of love. The sacrament of the Lord's Supper will cease, but only because it will be superseded by the Marriage Supper of the Lamb.

Conclusion

Where does *Apocalypse Today* fit within modern studies of Revelation? We must bear in mind that this book is a popular work, not a scholarly one. There is no evidence it had much of an impact on biblical scholars. Even citations of it are scarce. Yet the original sermons marked a resurgence of academic interest in apocalyptic, and their publication was part of the first wave in a flood of literature on the subject.[171] More importantly, these sermons foreshadowed a renewed interest in the theological significance of the Apocalypse. This was spurred by Ernst Kasemann's 1960 essay that argued that "apocalypticism is the mother of Christian theology."[172] While Torrance would not have agreed with this proposition (the resurrection of Christ is the mother of theology), he held that apocalyptic was an indispensable part of theology. Contrary to the opinion of those who seek refuge in an old orthodoxy or a modern liberalism, "there is no unapocalyptic Jesus."[173] Then there are the studies by Jacques Ellul and Richard Bauckham, who began their works on the same premise that Torrance did, that the Apocalypse is first and foremost a theological book, a revelation from above. Although *Apocalypse Today* is not a complete theology of history, it is a development of the seminal idea that God's redemption is something "actualized in history" and "mediated through history." However, redemption is at the same the transformation or "reversal" of history.

This work must also be viewed in the light of Torrance's relationship with Karl Barth. Torrance was an enthusiastic student of Barth's

171. See Jeske and Barr, "The Study of the Apocalypse," 337–44. Jeske believes that Andre Feuillet's *L'Apocalypse*, which was published in 1963, gave "impetus to the modern study" on the Apocalypse (ibid., 337).

172. Kasemann, "The Beginnings of Christian Theology," 40. On the recovery of apocalyptic in systematic theology during the 1960s by Pannenberg, Moltmann, and Sauter, see Klaus Koch, *The Rediscovery of Apocalyptic*, 101–11.

173. These words are from Strobel, *Kerygma und Apokalyptik*, but the idea goes back to Schweitzer.

theology, but this theology (including its eschatology) has been criticized for its lack of connection with history and temporality.[174] In reaction to Barth (although more so, perhaps, to Bultmann) we have *Christ and Time* (1951) from Oscar Cullmann; *God the Meaning of History* (1966) from Henrikus Berkhof[175]; and from Wolfhart Pannenberg, *Revelation as History* (1969). *Apocalypse Today* is, however, less a correction of Barth's theology than a development of it (in combination with a Mackintoshian emphasis on the cross). For Torrance, the historical nature of this theology has to do with the fact that it is grounded in the incarnation. This means that God has entered time; and through the cross and resurrection, history is reversed, the old guilt-ridden, sin-infested time is put to death and a new time, kingdom of God time is born. "The key to ages, the clue to history, is Christ crucified, the Lamb of God." This is a staple theme in *Apocalypse Today*. It means that eschatology in the Apocalypse involves the atonement—the reconciliation of the world—through the outworking of the cross in time and history. "The cross is still in the field," Torrance insists. The cross is borne by the church and the followers of the Lamb. Thus we cannot help being reminded of how much it cost God to forgive us. But the cross also stands for the in-breaking of the kingdom of God, the unveiling of God's holiness and his love, or in other words his desire to establish "dominion over us" and "communion with us."

We need to know too that, for Torrance, apocalyptic is not confined to the scriptures, any more than the Word of God is. Apocalyptic is, or should be, an integral part of the liturgical life of the church. In that way, apocalypse is always an *apocalypse today*. In the next chapter we will see how apocalyptic functions in the church.

C. Civilization, the Jews, and the Universal Church.

The majority of Torrance's sermons on the Apocalypse were delivered at Alyth in 1946, just after the end of the war. This is telling. He saw WWII as one battle in a much larger war between Christ and the anti-Christ spirit in the world, a spirit that was incarnating itself also in the spread of

174. Barth in one place defines history as transcendence in time (CD III/2, 189; 158). See Jenson's discussion in *Alpha and Omega*, 74f.

175. See Berkhof's interview with Baumann in Baumann, *Roundtable: Conversations with European Theologians*. He reports that his book was a response to Barth's hesitancy to speak about God's "footprints in history."

communism, international capitalism, and in the thrust towards a new world order. In *"In Hoc Signo Vinces"* Torrance described his era as "the greatest epoch in the history of the nations whose destiny was in the melting pot."[176] This helps to explain why he was still preaching from the Apocalypse at Beechgrove in 1948, even composing a few new sermons on it. But after a few weeks he laid the book aside, not because he no longer thought it was relevant, but because his new congregation had no appetite for its message after the war had ended.[177] This only proves that there is more than a grain of truth to Churchill's quip that the "maxim of the British people is 'business as usual.'"[178]

While Torrance believed he was living through an apocalyptic age, other Christian thinkers believed they were living amidst a crisis of civilization. This led to a spate of books on the subject. Most notable are John Baillie's *What is Civilization?* (1945), Emil Brunner's *Christianity and Civilization* (1947), and Arnold Toynbee's *Civilization on Trial* (1948).[179]

These men, along with others, mourned the decline of Western civilization and, in varying degrees, ascribed its decline to the erosion of its Christian foundation. Torrance did not side with them; that would be like mourning the fall of Babylon. While he recognized the Christian contribution to Western civilization, especially in science, he was not

---

176. Torrance, "In Hoc," 17.

177. From "Aberdeen, 1947–1950," 9. The end of the war, however, was succeeded by the threat of nuclear holocaust, which raised for many the apocalyptic barometer to new heights. This was evident especially on the other side of the Atlantic. In 1946 a series of articles in *The Christian Century* addressed the matter. It began with one titled "Atomic Apocalypse." The author, Wesner Fallaw, envisions an atomic war "within a few years" a "complete global dissolution" (ibid., 146–48). Torrance, though, did not share this pessimism. He does not even mention the nuclear threat in any of his sermons. While Fallaw and others saw nuclear war as the thing that would bring about the end of the world, Torrance would have seen the nuclear threat as one more illustration that the horsemen of the Apocalypse were on the loose in the world. It was one more scourge. The atom bomb though posed a formidable challenge to biblical eschatology, as the Fallow article makes clear. For it suggested that end of the world would come about not through the advent of Christ but through man's destructive genius. It would be a destructive end only, not a redemptive end.

178. Cahill, *The Quotable Churchill*, 68.

179. Fears over the collapse of western civilization go back further than this. They emerged in Germany decades earlier, and were given philosophical sanction in Spengler's *Decline of the West*. See also Schweitzer's *The Philosophy of Civilization*. For an English example of this pessimism, see the small book by Demant, *What's Happening to Us?*

interested in promoting a "Christian civilization."[180] His sermons on the Apocalypse clearly reveal a suspicion towards such a civilization. "The Kingdom of God does not come with observation" (Luke 17:20). This was one of his favorite New Testament passages. For Torrance, the primary task of the church is not to civilize the world or to supply it with a religious foundation. It is evangelical. It has to "shake up" the world with the gospel, to be the greatest disturbing force in the world, in order to push everyone in it to a decision for Christ crucified.

The outward form of the kingdom of God is hidden from us. One of the weaknesses of Torrance's interpretation of the Apocalypse is that it lacks a clear sense of a resolution to the suffering and evil in the world. However, in a sermon he gave on the "parable of the fig tree" he starts to make up for this. The outward form of the kingdom may be hidden from us, but Torrance saw signs in his day that the kingdoms of the world were about to become the Kingdom of Christ and God.

One was the so-called "crisis of civilization." For Torrance, as we have learned, the tumult in the world was not evidence of the decline of Christianity but evidence that the message of the cross was at work in the world, that the prayers of the saints were being heard in heaven. So instead of mourning over what he calls the "catastrophic cracking up of the world structure," he derives hope from it.[181] Finding direction in the Little Apocalypse (Mark 13), he tells listeners in his church that they should not expect the world to get "better and better" before Christ returns, but instead "worse and worse"; and that the last times will be the "most terrible" of all.[182] In view of the state of the world, he says to them: "was there any time in the whole history of tribulation when the coming of the kingdom . . . when the second advent of Christ, was more likely than it is at this moment?"[183]

The second sign was the predicament of world Jewry. Torrance first brought attention to the Jews in his sermons on the Apocalypse. He saw

---

180. In earlier sermons, Torrance evinces a distrust of Christian civilization. In his sermon on Matt 13:33, "The Leaven and the Loaf," he says that a Christian civilization amounts to a kingdom of God in outward form. A Christian civilization confuses the "loaf" with the "leaven." In a sermon on Jer 17:5, "Cursed is the Man who Trusts in Man," he sees a silver-lining in the destruction of civilization. The destruction is a "God-given opportunity to discover again what Christianity really is."

181. Torrance, "Ascension and Second Advent."

182. Ibid.

183. Ibid.

their persecution, along with that of Christians, as a sign the demonic trinity was at work in the world. This time, 1947, he draws attention to the Zionist movement. For him, this event pointed to the imminent redemption of the world.[184] One of Torrance's most important writings on the Jews is an essay that first appeared in the Beechgrove church magazine in 1949. Titled "Salvation is of the Jews," the essay resurfaced again the following year in the *Evangelical Quarterly*.[185] It looks at the role of the Jews in salvation-history. For Torrance, John 4:22 reveals that the Jews are "God's finger-post pointing to the future."[186] And while the "Christian Church is our only clue to the knowledge of the Saviour," the Jews are "our only clue to history."[187] "Have you ever wondered whether we are not all heading for another great war, more terrible than ever before, the complete devastation of civilization and all mankind? What is going to happen? Will God not do anything? *Watch the Jews*."[188]

But did not Torrance teach us that "Christ crucified" is the "clue to history"? He did, and that is precisely what leads him to say the Jews are our "only clue to history." His interest in modern Jews starts with his devotion to the Jew of Nazareth of yesterday and today; the one who came "out of the womb of Israel."[189] "Christ-crucified" is the basis for the historical realism in his eschatology, and his focus on the Jews is a development of that realism. The Jews are a red thread running through history. Anti-Christ "beasts" arise and are laid low; Babylons rise and fall. They point to the Lamb's conquest of "organic evil," but they do not point to the mercy of God, to the consummation of redemption, the way the Jews do. Torrance calls them an "incontestable witness" of God's

184. Jewish immigration to Palestine began modestly in the late nineteenth century, but the virulent anti-Semitism in Europe during the 1930s and 1940s led to massive immigration. In the year Torrance gave this sermon, the United Nations voted to partition Palestine into a Jewish and Arab state. In the following year, Israel declared itself an independent state. Her Arab neighbors responded immediately by attacking her.

185. See also his essay "The divine vocation and destiny of Israel." Here T. F. Torrance refers to the role of modern Israel "in the eschatological and teleological gathering up of God's interaction with mankind" (ibid., 95). "The Christian Church and the Jewish Church are now harnessed together in the mysterious judgements of God for witness, service and mission in the accelerating rush of world events toward the end-time, when Christ himself will come to take up his reign and make all things new" (ibid., 96).

186. Torrance, "Salvation is of the Jews," 171.

187. Ibid.

188. Ibid.

189. Ibid., 167.

faithfulness and grace."[190] Despite the fact they were made "the scape-goat" of the whole world and almost made extinct, they have returned to their promised land after nearly 2,000 years. The Jews "tell us that God will act, and act in history, act among the nations."[191]

However, Torrance believes that even as a victim of persecution the Jew bears witness to the living God of the Bible. The history of the Jew is actually one of "two lines of witness" to the cross in the world. On the "resurrection side of the Cross," there is the Christian church that speaks of the life eternal in the body. "On the shadow side" there is the Jewish synagogue "bearing mute and unwilling witness of the antagonism of man to God."[192]

While today it is the norm to understand anti-Semitism as a form of racism or intolerance, Torrance understood it in terms of the cross. That means our hatred of the Jews reveals an even darker fact about us: our hatred of the "Jew of Calvary." Anti-Semitism is another form of the anti-Christ. "Let the offence of the Jew point to the offence of the Cross."[193] The offence of the Jew is a sign that God is pressing the gospel in your face, that he is demanding a decision about Christ.

All that Torrance says in this small article is a development of a theology and eschatology that was in place in his Auburn lectures. There he called for a "new and important emphasis on history" in theology, to the God who acts in history. He was not calling for more historicism. He was pleading for a renewed understanding of biblical history. "It is only in relation to the historical people of Israel, in relation to the OT . . . that the NT may be understood—thus in relation to the continuous activity of God in the history of mankind."[194]

The third sign of the advent of Christ is the universal church. This belief contributed to Torrance's ecumenical-mindedness, but also to the development of his eschatology. In the 1950s his eschatology takes shape in response to the international drive toward church unity.

190. Ibid., 172.
191. Ibid.
192. Ibid., 171.
193. Ibid., 170.
194. Torrance, *The Doctrine of Jesus Christ*, 6.

4

Eschatology and the Church, Part I

The World Council of Churches and the Commission on Faith and Order, 1948–1954

A. The Ecumenical Movement and T. F. Torrance

MANY CHRISTIANS MIGHT BE SURPRISED TO LEARN THAT THE ROOTS of modern ecumenism lie in evangelical Christianity. Protestant missionaries who were hampered by church divisions on the mission fields spearheaded the ecumenical movement about a century ago. The World Missionary Conference in Edinburgh in 1910 is regarded as the birthplace of the movement. At a conference in Geneva in 1920, the movement split into two branches: Faith and Order, with a mandate to work for unity in matters of doctrine and polity, and Life and Work, which was committed to church co-operation on social issues. The events of 1910 and 1920 were great milestones in the modern ecumenical movement. They also paved the way for things we now take for granted: cooperation and dialogue between churches.

Torrance was not alone in attaching great eschatological import to the ecumenical movement. At the first world conference of Faith and Order, held in Lausanne in 1927, there was a palpable sense that a "new age was about to begin"; a sense that gave to the conference "something of the atmosphere of apocalypse."[1] The high-water mark of the modern ecumenical movement was the formation of the World Council of Churches (WCC) in 1948, which formally united the Life and Work movement and the Continuation Committee of Faith and Order. The WCC is not a super church and it was never meant to be one. It is an organization comprised of representative churches (mainly Protestant),

1. Rouse and Neill, *History*, 439.

which are devoted to the establishment of unity (not uniformity) among churches in doctrine and practice. In the beginning the only condition for membership in the WCC was the confession of the "Lord Jesus Christ as God and Savior."

As we have seen, Torrance's apocalyptic eschatology is colored and shaped by momentous events of the day: the war, the spread of Communism, and a general crisis of civilization. These events had an impact also on the fledgling WCC. In fact its formation was delayed by WW II. As the churches came together in 1948, an aura of "apocalypse" surrounded them again. This time, however, it was not so bright. "The World Council of Churches has come into being at a moment of peril for all mankind which is without precedent in the whole of human history."[2] It was not just the aftermath of the war that caused this concern. It was the "sickness of civilization" that has "far advanced," coupled with a new threat—nuclear holocaust. [3] But in this dark period the church stood out like the bright city on a hill. "In the hopeless world of our time, the one hope lies in the Church of Christ."[4]

However, while churches at the assembly looked to the church of Christ as the "greatest reality on earth" and as a beacon of hope for the world, they had to confess humbly that the church on earth reflected the disorder of world, and that the unity of the church was as much a hope as a reality, a hope grounded in the purpose of God. Appropriately, the main theme for the assembly was "Man's Disorder and God's Design."

Torrance got officially involved with the ecumenical movement in the late 1940s. Though his involvement may have interfered with his academic career, he was eminently qualified for ecumenical work. His sermons reveal both a commitment to the one church and a deep concern for the world. His church, the Church of Scotland, was a leader in the ecumenical movement.[5] Edinburgh had hosted the Missionary Conference

2. World Council of Churches, *The Universal Church*, 9.

3. Symptoms of the "sickness" include "the disappearance of common standards, the denial of a law of God above the wills of men and states, the disintegration of family life, the dissolution of community, loss of faith save the false faith in human wisdom and goodness, emptiness and meaningless in the souls of men." World Council of Churches, *The Universal Church*, General Introduction.

4. World Council of Churches, *The Universal Church*, 13.

5. Also, the Church of Scotland has always attached great importance to the unity of the Church. See MacPherson, *The Doctrine of the Church*. Moreover, there were personal factors that made Torrance an ideal ecumenical theologian. Both his wife and mother

of 1910 and the second Faith and Order conference in 1937. As well, there was the leadership of John Baillie, Moderator of the Church of Scotland in 1943 and Professor of Divinity at Edinburgh from 1934–56. He was the Steward at the Missionary Conference in 1910, and he would later go on to become president of the WCC. He was also the convener of the Church of Scotland Committee on Church and Nation (1940–45). In its 1943 report the committee declared that the church was "essential to the Gospel" and the only answer to the social and spiritual dangers facing the world.[6] The Baillie Commission, as it was called, wrapped up in 1945 on a strong ecumenical note. "We desire, therefore, to record in the strongest possible terms our sense of duty now laid upon our own church to throw itself with single-minded zeal into the convergent efforts now being made towards the development of a true ecumenical consciousness throughout the whole Body of Christ."[7]

That ecumenical spirit was in evidence again in 1949 when the Church of Scotland set up its Commission on Communism. In the face of the worldwide threat of Communism, which is described in "one sense" as "the most vital and dynamic ecumenical movement in the world at present," the Commission calls for a "new Catholicity of outlook and of action throughout the entire Church."[8] In its judgment, the "only answer to Communism is a reborn Church."[9] Torrance echoed this judgment in his address to the Presbyterian Church in Canada in 1951.[10]

Torrance helped to advance church unity through his membership in the Faith and Order Commission from 1948 to 1962. The depth of his involvement can be gauged by the mass of articles, essays, and reviews he published on the theme of church unity in this period. Most were

---

were Anglicans, and two of his children were confirmed in both the Church of England and the Church of Scotland. See Hesselink, "A Pilgrimage," 49–64.

6. The Church of Scotland, *God's Will*, 64.

7. Ibid., 182.

8. Ibid., 5.

9. Ibid., 74.

10. Torrance, "Answer to God," 3–16. He calls the attempt by Marxian Socialism and Communism to "re-socialize mankind" another "false answer to God" (ibid., 6). Jesus Christ is the "double answer to God," and it is only through him and his Church that man is able to find true community. "The Christian Church alone is the medium by which society is transmuted into community" (ibid., 13). Even here Torrance hits the eschatological key. He urges everyone to "think seriously again about the coming of Jesus Christ," for that is what forces us to think about our answer to God (ibid., 15). That answer, though, is Jesus Christ himself (ibid., 16).

printed in the *Scottish Journal of Theology*, which he co-founded with J. K. S. Reid in 1948. These papers were then republished together, along with a few new papers, as a two volume set titled *Conflict and Agreement in the Church* (1959).

Torrance's most famous works from this period are *Royal Priesthood* (1955) and *Kingdom and Church* (1956), and these were also dedicated to the cause of church unity. Nor can we fail to mention his published collection of sermons, *When Christ Comes and Comes Again* (1957). They were dedicated to "Tell Scotland," the missionary wing of the ecumenical movement in Scotland. As the title suggests, eschatology figures prominently in these sermons. But eschatology is a prominent theme in the majority of Torrance's writings from this era. There is a good explanation for this, as disclosed in a letter to his Doktorvater at Basel in 1948.

> Dear Professor Barth, For my sins I have thrust upon me by the Faith and Order Commission of the British Council of Churches their studies in eschatology. At their last meeting they felt that in many respects it was in eschatology that the great differences between Catholic and Reformed positions were at their acutest; and it was decided to concentrate on the study of this in order to elucidate the positions of both communions in regards to such doctrines as the Church, its continuity, sacraments, ministry, justification . . . As this is a pretty heavy task . . . I feel I need some guidance upon the main issues which should engage our attention.[11]

It looks as if Torrance's only sin was bringing up the subject. According to minutes from the British Council of Churches (BCC)[12], a regional branch of the WCC, it was Torrance himself who recommended this study of eschatology.[13] There is an indication Barth responded to the request, but no reply letter has yet been found. In any event, Torrance carried out the task he had earned. This led to a report for the BCC on the topic in 1950.[14] Alas, this is also missing. However, Torrance's ideas

---

11. Torrance to Karl Barth, 30 March 1949.

12. For a brief history of the British Council of Churches, see Payne, *Thirty years.*

13. Minutes from the British Council of Churches, 3.3.49—5.10.50, pp. 4–13, 20–21. In an unpublished essay, Torrance notes that British Christians, in contrast to Continental ones, have tended to disregard the Church's "basic eschatological tension" that helps us see the Church in terms of "new creation . . . election . . . and justification" (Torrance, "The Sacraments," 1.).

14. Minutes from the British Council of Churches, 3.3.49—5.10.50, pp. 4–13, 20–21.

can be gathered from several essay reviews he produced around this time.

The first is a twelve-page response to *The Apostolic Ministry* (1948).[15] The book is a collection of essays by prominent Anglo-Catholics on the subject of Christian ministry.[16] It is a monumental and erudite work of over five hundred pages, and is one of the most significant contributions to the subject in the twentieth century. More importantly, *The Apostolic Ministry* purports to be an ecumenical work. However, for the authors, the key to church re-union is to be found in the historic episcopate. More precisely, the solution is in the reinvigoration of the apostolic ministry, which for the authors has been transmitted through the ages through the office of the bishop. Yet the authors are not interested simply in defending the status quo in the Anglican Church. They want to reform the episcopate on the basis of its foundations in the early church. For these reasons, Torrance describes *The Apostolic Ministry* as a "volume of outstanding importance." He also commends their biblical, dogmatic, and historical approach to the whole subject of ministry. Nonetheless, Torrance is highly critical of the volume. Of course, one would expect this from a Presbyterian. Yet Torrance is not opposed to the office of bishop *per se*. What he remonstrates against is the notion that a bishop stands for the very person of Christ, that there is a "mystical identity, personal identity between the Bishop-Apostle and Christ Himself."[17] He argues that this concept of identity "turns eschatology into temporal succession."[18] True eschatology depends on the Holy Ghost working through the Word of God. After all, this "Word-Spirit" relation created the church and perpetuates it through history. Instead of recognizing this, the Anglo-Catholic doctrine of apostolic ministry mistakenly uses a "human institution," succession through the laying on of hands, to "perpetuate in continuity of space and time the risen Jesus Christ."[19] Instead of temporal succession, Torrance speaks of "eschatological repetition," which is "enshrined" in the Lord's Supper but is really the work of the Holy Spirit.[20]

15. It is worth noting that Torrance's review of this work comes on the heels of the re-publication of his dissertation, *The Doctrine of Grace* (1948).

16. Torrance, "Concerning the Ministry," 190–201.

17. Ibid., 199.

18. Ibid.

19. Ibid.

20. Ibid., 196–97.

In this review one cannot help hearing the voice of Karl Barth in the background. At this time in fact Barth submitted papers on the church for the WCC and the *Scottish Journal of Theology* (SJT) that defended the work of the Word and Spirit in creating and sustaining the church.[21] However, Torrance will move beyond the stance he takes in these reviews. He will try to find a place for the temporal element in the ministry and in the church as a whole, although he will do this on the basis of Barth's Chalcedonian Christology. He does this thoroughly in *Royal Priesthood* (1955), which we will canvass in the next chapter. This work is Torrance's ecumenical contribution to the doctrine of ministry, but it may also be seen as a response to *The Apostolic Ministry*.[22] After all, he saw this publication as a "real challenge" to the Reformed churches and one that had to be reckoned with.[23]

Royal Priesthood should also be read beside his other essay review in the late 1940s. It deals with a pair of books on catholicity by representatives of the Church of England. The first was by a group of prominent Anglo-Catholics.[24] For them, "the problem of reunion is that of recovery of the wholeness of tradition," a wholeness that encompasses both creation and the supernatural realm of the church.[25] Torrance has good things to say about this book. He agrees that "wholeness" is the basis of catholicity, but disagrees with the book's definition of this "wholeness." It is not to be confused with the church's historical tradition, for that would reduce eschatology to "temporal continuity." True wholeness is the "eschatological fulfillment" found in Christ alone.[26]

He gave a more favorable review of the book by the evangelicals.[27] They defined church unity in terms of "growth into the fulness of Christ."

---

21. Barth, "The Church," 67–69; Barth, "The Real Church," 337–51.

22. The preface to it begins thus: "This little work is offered as a contribution to the discussions initiated by the World Conference of Faith and Order, held at Lund in August 1952, on the Biblical doctrine of the Church and Ministry. It also represents an attempt to relate that to the Church of England and the Church of Scotland, now engaged in talks of reunion, in the belief that the time has arrived for them to unite in a plenitude of faith and order in which neither will be the poorer but both be the richer" (Torrance, *Royal Priesthood*, vii).

23. Torrance, "Concerning the Ministry," 190.

24. Torrance, "Catholicity," 85–93.

25. Ibid., 85.

26. Ibid., 86.

27. Torrance, "The Fulness of Christ," 90–100.

While Torrance was pleased with the authors' christocentric focus, he took exception to their understanding of growth. It was understood as "biological fulfillment" instead of "eschatological fulfillment."[28] Torrance will incorporate the themes of "growth" and "wholeness," along with the temporal element, in his doctrine of ministry. Yet he will put a christological and eschatological stamp on them.

While serving as a substitute member at a regional Faith and Order meeting in Chichester, England in 1949, Torrance was invited to take part in the Faith and Order Commission of the WCC. His ecumenical duties mounted thereafter. He was selected to be a consultant for the Third World Conference of Faith and Order at Lund in 1952. Then he was elected a member of Faith and Order. The Commission made a place for him, then, on its working committees. These were the theological think tanks of the WCC, and it was here precisely that Torrance made his most important contributions to church unity.

We will study the papers that came out of these committees, but first it is important to acknowledge some of the theological influences on his eschatology at this time.

B. Theological Influences on Torrance's Eschatology

1. Reformation Theology

Eschatology does not spring to mind when we hear about the Reformation age. Yet for Torrance it was an age rich in eschatology. Torrance was not always a keen student of the Reformers. His admiration for modern theology antedates his admiration for the Reformers. While his Auburn lectures are studded with references to, and quotes from, Barth, Mackintosh, Forsyth, Brunner, *et al.*, they scarcely refer to Calvin or Luther. Nor do his earliest sermons show a great debt to these theologians. But by the late 1940s Torrance had established himself as authority on Calvin. In 1949 he published *Calvin's Doctrine of Man*, which was his response to the acrimonious debate between Barth and Brunner over natural theology. Then his appointment in 1950 to the chair in Ecclesiastical History at New College, University of Edinburgh, gave him the opportunity to plumb the depths of Reformation theology.

Church history, however, was not his *Hauptfach*. It was Christian dogmatics, but there were no openings in this area. Besides, according

28. Ibid., 94.

McGrath, any effort by Torrance to teach in this field would have generated some static.[29] John Baillie was the Principle of the College and the Dean of Faculty of Divinity. Baillie obviously regarded Torrance as an able scholar, in spite of the fact that Torrance was a leading proponent of Barth's theology and he was, in Torrance words, "bitterly and aggressively opposed" to this theology.[30] Baillie got him his first job at Auburn, and now he approved his appointment to New College. The Chair in Christian Dogmatics became vacant in 1952. Despite some opposition from Baillie, Torrance got the appointment and would hold the chair until his retirement in 1979.[31]

Yet some of his most important contributions to eschatology come from the two years he spent in the department of Church History. During this time he gave a series of lectures on the history of eschatology that became the basis for a number of publications. These include a series of monographs on modern eschatology ("The Modern Eschatological Debate," 1953), which we will deal with shortly. This was followed by an essay on Reformation eschatology.[32] Next there was a paper on the eschatology of Martin Bucer in 1955 ("Kingdom and Church in the Thought of Martin Bucer"). This paper along with ones on Luther and Calvin would comprise his great work on historical eschatology: *Kingdom and Church: A Study in the Theology of the Reformation* (Edinburgh, 1956).[33] As the title suggests, Reformation eschatology on Torrance's view is tied up with ecclesiology. That makes it germane to the ecumenical movement. Still, there is an irony in turning to the Reformation to solve the problem of church disunity. Notwithstanding all its benefits, there is no mistaking that it marked the beginning of endless schisms in the church. Of course, Torrance does not think this problem is traceable to the Reformers themselves but to misinterpretations of them. He understands the Reformation as a renewal movement within the one church of Christ, and he saw its eschatology as a mark of this renewal.

What accounts for the eschatological aspect of the Reformation? It began when the Reformers rediscovered the "living God of the Bible,

29. McGrath, *T. F. Torrance*, 88–90.

30. Torrance, "Student Years," 5

31. McGrath, *T. F. Torrance*, 90.

32. Torrance, *Eschatology*.

33. His lectures on eschatology in those years are the basis also for "Christ the First and the Last," a sub-chapter in *Conflict and Agreement*, vol. 1, 304–15.

who actively intervenes in the affairs of men, the Lord and Judge of history."[34] This would certainly account for the historical side of its eschatology. As for the strong ecclesial element, that is attributable to the Reformers' "emphasis upon the humanity of Christ and the Church as His Body in history."[35]

For Torrance, the eschatological orientation of the Reformation explains the dynamic nature of the movement. Dynamism is a mark of his own doctrine of the church. Early in his ministry, he warned the church of the danger of "settling down" into civil society. The dynamic character of the Reformation naturally entailed protest, but it was a legitimate protest against the "fusion of form and content" in history and in the Church."[36] The Reformers knew that the church had to use worldly forms to communicate the gospel, but they also knew that these forms were temporal and imperfect. Thus they had to be "criticized by being placed under divine judgement."[37] A good illustration would be Calvin's critique of the medieval doctrine of transubstantiation.

It was Luther in particular who stressed divine judgment. His is an "eschatology of judgement" and an "eschatology of faith."[38] For Luther, "all forms of Church life and order on earth are *adiaphora*, and will come under judgement at the Advent of Christ as part of the *schema mundi*."[39] The reason is that the church is constituted by the Word of God, i.e., Jesus Christ himself. And the church becomes incarnate again in "a spiritual way—i.e., through faith" whenever the gospel is preached and believed.[40] In other words, the church for Luther was "essentially an eschatological community," a reality "hid with Christ in God" until the advent of Christ.[41]

This meant that the church is still under the cross. This explains Luther's dialectical understanding of the church. It is "at once *justa et peccatrix*." Visibly, it is sinful; invisibly, it is "forgiven and justified and

---

34. Torrance, "The Israel of God," 3.

35. Ibid., 4.

36. Torrance, "History and Reformation," 282.

37. Ibid., 286.

38. Torrance, *Kingdom and Church*, 5, 7.

39. Ibid., 63.

40. Ibid., 56.

41. Ibid., 55.

formed in Christ."[42] This means "the *forma* . . . of the Church has to be interpreted in terms of the eschatological *reputatio*."[43]

Visibly, not only is the church sinful but "weak and deserted and without sign of power or worth."[44] But that is why the true life of the church is measured by the presence of the "pure Word" and the "pure administration of the sacraments, where there are men who love the Word and confess it" to the world.[45] The church, thus, has its "treasure" in "earthen vessels."

Not only does the church appear "weak and deserted," it even appears afflicted by God. Like Jesus' own experience in the world, the church "suffers continuous abuse and vilification, is confounded and rejected by men, is mortified and dies."[46] It is a church "*sub cruce*," but that is because it "lives in Christ" by faith in Christ.[47] Yet this church under the cross—this weak, sinful, afflicted thing—conquers the kingdoms of the world through the invisible power of the Word. Its weakness is its power.

This dialectical view of the church has its correlative in a "dialectical eschatology," that "tension between having and not-having."[48] In Luther this was so acute that he saw himself caught in the middle of "the apocalyptic strife of the Kingdom of God."[49] Yet this tension exposed a weakness in Luther's eschatology. It suffered, according to Torrance, from a tenuous grasp of the new creation in Christ as an "already accomplished fact, as a *perfectum praesens*."[50] Luther of course believed in the promise of a new creation; however, "his weak stress on the renewal of the whole creation tended to rob it of temporal relevance and force."[51]

When one reads Torrance's description of Luther's "eschatology of faith," it is hard not to be reminded of his own eschatology in the forties. It too was characterized by an emphasis on the church under the

42. Ibid., 66.

43. Ibid.

44. Ibid.

45. Ibid.

46. Ibid., 67.

47. Ibid.

48. Ibid., 71–72.

49. Ibid., 72.

50. Ibid.

51. Ibid.

cross, on judgment and on apocalyptic strife; although in his case this is counterbalanced by an acute sense that the new creation has broken into the present with the resurrection of Christ. If Torrance was not directly influenced by Luther in this decade, his own experiences as a war-time pastor and chaplain would have helped him to understand Luther's eschatology better, both its strengths and weaknesses.

But at the point where Luther is weak, Calvin is strong. At first blush, though, Calvin looks like a poorer source for eschatology than Luther. Not only did he not produce a commentary on the Apocalypse, his *Institutes* is not capped off by a chapter dealing with last things. However, for Torrance, the real clue to Calvin's eschatology is his declaration that "Christ is our clothing."[52] That means his eschatology is all about the "doctrine of the new humanity in Jesus Christ."[53] This, in Torrance's view, is what makes Calvin's understanding of last things an "eschatology of hope." He traces this doctrine in Calvin as far back as his *Psychopannychia* (1534, 1536). In this work Calvin refutes the Anabaptist, and Lutheran, claim that the soul sleeps after death. For Torrance, the "central argument" of the *Psychopannychia* is that Christian souls will be awake and active after death, since they participate now in the resurrection and life of Christ.

One may contest Torrance's reading of the *Psychopannychia*. While the resurrection of Christ is certainly an important part of Calvin's argument, the treatise is basically a defense of the immortality of the soul and depends as much (or more) on a Platonic distinction between the body and the soul as on Christ's bodily resurrection.[54] As for this participation in Christ, Torrance underlines that it is a participation in his new humanity. For Calvin, it is "as Man that Jesus Christ is given to have life in Himself."[55] But that means the new Christian life will entail "time-relations," and thus a life of development and growth. It is the kind of life

---

52. Ibid., 93.

53. Ibid., 94.

54. Calvin writes: "For I come to the second head, which I propose to discuss, viz. that the soul, after death still survives, endued with sense and intellect. And it is a mistake to suppose that I am here affirming anything else than the immortality of the soul" (Calvin, "Psychopannychia," 427). It is natural to assume that there is little difference between the immortality of the soul and the resurrection of the body. Yet the Bible suggests there are clear differences between these. Oscar Cullmann exposed them (and perhaps exaggerated them) in his famous essay "The Immortality of the Soul."

55. Torrance, *Kingdom and Church*, 94.

described by St. Paul in Eph 4, a growth into the "perfect manhood of Christ."[56] Yet this growth is eschatological, not organic. This new life in Christ is "hidden and veiled from sight" and can be articulated only in "terms of eschatology."[57]

It is natural to assume that this hidden life in Christ refers to individual life, but Torrance maintains that when Calvin thought about the growth in Christ he had in mind the growth of the church as the Body of Christ. It is growth into Christ, and thus needs to be understood in "terms of the reign of His Kingdom as it is manifested in the growth and extension of the Church."[58] This explains why Torrance would lean upon Calvin's eschatology as he became immersed in the Commission on Faith and Order.

The kingdom of God is hidden with the ascended Christ until his advent, when it will reveal itself as the new heaven and earth. Yet for Calvin the church is "correlative" of this kingdom, and thus the kingdom can in "some measure" be seen in the church, through its increase and growth.[59] This happens through the preaching of the Word and the work of the Spirit. "'Both must be joined together in order that the Kingdom of God may be established.'"[60]

Torrance also underscores the fact that for Calvin the growth of the church is a kind that takes place through history. The new life entails "time relations." This is why Calvin appeals not only to the New Testament model of the church but to that of the church fathers. This last factor accounts for the strong tincture of optimism in Calvin's eschatology, according to Torrance. He ascribes this to the influence of the Greek Fathers. By contrast, the Latin Fathers held greater sway over Luther, lending a pessimistic overtone to his eschatology.[61]

---

56. Ibid., 95.

57. Ibid., 94. In a later paper Torrance writes: "Nowhere is the eschatological element more in evidence than in Calvin's stress upon the ascension of the risen Christ, and therefore upon the *sursum corda* in the celebration of the Eucharist itself" (Torrance, "Toward a Doctrine of the Lord's Supper" in *Conflict and Agreement*, vol. 2, 138).

58. Torrance, *Kingdom and Church*, 95.

59. Ibid., 134, 95.

60. Ibid., 98.

61. Torrance, "New College Lectures on Eschatology," January–March, 1952.

On the question of visible church unity, Torrance found Calvin a better guide than Luther.[62] "In contrast to Luther," for whom the "real church was wholly concealed under the *larva dei*," "Calvin laid greater emphasis upon the *ecclesia externa sive visibilis*."[63] And while Luther was willing to understand the doctrine of the church in terms of a "dialectical relation between the Word and historical forms," Calvin understood the church as the "Body of Christ continuously actualized within history." [64] He saw the church growing up into the "mature manhood of Christ," but he also envisaged it spreading to all corners of the earth through the power of the Word and Spirit.[65]

Contrary to appearances, Torrance finds eschatology imbedded in the *Institutes,* in the doctrine of the Holy Spirit (book 3) and in the doctrine of the church (book 4). Christ is made "our clothing" through the work of the Holy Spirit. As Torrance sees it, the *Institutes* show us that "eschatology is the doctrine of the Spirit and all that union with Christ through the Spirit involves."[66] This involves a faith that grasps the ascended and risen Christ, and "merges with hope" to take hold of the advent Christ.[67]

Calvin's doctrine of the church, for Torrance, is really about the deepening of that union with Christ through "external means." For example, in the third book union is expressed in terms of justification and sanctification, but in the fourth these have their sacramental counterparts in baptism and the Eucharist respectively. In fact, Torrance maintains that Calvin's eschatology is really the "analogical transposition of Christology to the whole understanding of the Church."[68] This, in his view, is the main thing that differentiates Calvin's eschatology from Luther's. "In His birth, life, death, resurrection and ascension Christ is our only way to understanding the celestial mystery of the last things. He is the Alpha and the Omega, the Elect One and the Final Goal of the Kingdom, but through union with Christ the Church becomes the Body

62. For a wider examination of Torrance's use of Calvin's ecclesiology, see MacLean, "*Regnum Christi,*" 185–202.

63. Torrance, *Kingdom and Church,* 148.

64. Ibid., 147.

65. Ibid., 117.

66. Ibid., 101.

67. Ibid., 102–103.

68. Ibid., 101.

of which He is the Head, so that whatever happens to the Head happens also to the members."[69]

On the one hand, then, Calvin's eschatology is a fully realized one. The kingdom has truly come in Jesus Christ, in his person and work. On the other hand, if the kingdom is regarded in terms of the whole people of God, then it is not fully realized. What has been accomplished in Christ "must be transferred to the whole body of the Church."[70]

Kingdom and Church was written in an ecumenical spirit, not a polemical one. Torrance was bent on demonstrating that the Reformers had much in common and that their differences were more complementary than contradictory. With Luther, for example, the eschatological relation was understood in terms of *"justa et peccatrix,"* while in Calvin this is "a relation between the heavenly and the earthly here and now, and the relation between the present and the future."[71] In Luther the eschatological tension stems from the dialectical relationships: the sense of "having and not having." For Calvin, on the other hand, the tension stems from the "time-lag" between what is already secretly accomplished in Christ and what is transferred outwardly to the whole Body.[72] But this time lag is really the time for the growth of the church before the final advent. In other words, Calvin understood the kingdom of God "in terms of two great eschatological moments," the *"initium,"* and the *"complementum."*[73] The church is the *initium,* and the consummation of the kingdom is the *complementum.* That is because the church and the kingdom must be understood in terms of the "analogy of Christ," in relation to his death and resurrection.[74]

Like Luther, Calvin believed that the church lived *sub cruce.*[75] This means it is a church militant, in war against the demonic powers of the world.[76] However, Torrance believes that Calvin had more confidence than Luther in the complete triumph of the church in the world. Calvin's eschatology accords more with a theology of resurrection than a theol-

---

69. Ibid.

70. Ibid., 116.

71. Ibid., 109.

72. Ibid., 142.

73. Ibid., 113.

74. Ibid.

75. Ibid., 125.

76. Ibid., 161.

ogy of the cross. Yet in this eschatology the cross is essential to the realization of the glory of the resurrection. The "road to the establishment of the Kingdom was that of suffering witness."[77]

Torrance points out that for Calvin the church and the kingdom of God are "essentially correlative."[78] If that is the case, this raises hard questions about the form and structure of the church. What forms are requisite? Which ones are not? But the relation between the church and kingdom is not straightforward. There is also an eschatological reserve that separates them, and which needs to be observed. The church is correlative with the kingdom of God, but not to the extent that it "transcribes the perfect form of the Kingdom in earthly existence."[79] For Calvin, the order of the church in history is marked by ambiguity. Torrance explains how Calvin, on the one hand, insisted on a "fixed form" for the church yet, on the other hand, argued that this form should not be so "rigid" that it militates against "growth and development."[80] This is a lesson Torrance would keep in mind as a member of Faith and Order.

Summing up, Torrance identifies the three signs for Calvin that the "eschatological impulse" was at work in the church. The first is the missionary activity, which involves the "gathering" of the church into one. The second is in the continuous reform of the church, in order to restore its "true face." Finally, the eschatological impulse should manifest itself in the church's ecumenical work. And in order to stimulate ecumenical discussions in his day, Torrance ends *Kingdom and Church* with a quote from Calvin's Commentary on Hebrews (10:25) "For to what end did Christ come except to collect us all into one body from that dispersion in which we are all wandering? Therefore the nearer His coming is, the more we ought to labour that the scattered may be assembled and united together, that there may be one fold and one shepherd."[81]

Luther and Calvin occupy the bulk of *Kingdom and Church*. But in between these giants, Torrance has a short but significant treatise on Martin Butzer's eschatology. Torrance notes the deep similarity between Calvin and Butzer, attributable to their mutual influence and common confession. Butzer also understood the kingdom as a reality both hid-

77. Ibid., 160.

78. Ibid., 134.

79. Ibid.

80. Ibid., 135.

81. Ibid., 164.

den with Christ and progressively realized through the growth of the church. Like Calvin, he had a well-developed doctrine of the church and he worked tirelessly for the unity of the church. Yet it was his interest in the work of the Holy Spirit that warrants his inclusion in *Kingdom and Church*. Torrance makes note of the "strong charismatic element" in his eschatology—an element that begins to accrue in his own eschatology in the 1950s. It is why Torrance calls his eschatology the "eschatology of love." "It is this amazingly eschatological conception of love that is the most moving and characteristic element in Butzer's theology."[82]

In closing, he observes that while Calvin relied on a "powerful Christology" and a "precise doctrine of the Church," Butzer relied more on the idea of a "communion of love by the Word and Spirit."[83] This communion of love is also expansive, so that the kingdom of Christ overflows the church to the world outside it.

Kingdom and Church is an important contribution to Reformation studies. Torrance brings to light a subject of Reformation theology that had been left in the dark by scholars.[84] However, the book is also somewhat tendentious. While Torrance tries to do justice to those eschatological elements that are often implicit in the Reformers, he is not interested in merely adding to our historical knowledge. His reading of Reformation eschatology is shaped by the clamant demands of the ecumenical movement.[85] Hence there is his propensity to highlight the relation between eschatology and ecclesiology in the Reformers as well as the agreements between them in these areas. And while it is undoubtedly true that Torrance was influenced by Reformation eschatology, it seems equally true that his understanding of this eschatology is shaped by his own definition of eschatology as an application of Christology.[86]

---

82. Ibid., 82.

83. Ibid., 89.

84. Luther's eschatology, in particular, has been woefully neglected. This point is made in Forell's article "Justification and Eschatology." According to the author, *Kingdom and Church* is the only study in English on Luther's eschatology.

85. The book is even dedicated to two German scholars for their efforts at bringing the Lutheran and Reformed Churches closer together, Ernst Wolf and Otto Weber.

86. It is worth comparing Quistorp's careful study of Calvin's eschatology (which Torrance endorses with a preface). One the one hand, the author concludes that eschatology was not a strong element in the Reformers; but on the other, he concludes that their "whole theology" was "eschatologically orientated" (Quistorp, *Calvin's Doctrine*, 11). In agreement with Torrance, he states that Calvin's eschatology is "essentially Christology"

2. Biblical Theology

Torrance's work in this period also bears the stamp of the modern biblical theology movement, which began in the 1920s. His frequent use of the term "biblical" in book reviews is telltale. The reach of the biblical theology movement extended into the work of that major movement we are focusing on. Torrance even attributes the great strides toward church unity to the "rising tide of biblical theology."[87] The reason was not just a better understanding of the Bible. In his view, it had laid the basis for a better knowledge of the theology of the church Fathers and of the Reformation period.[88]

It is better, though, to see Torrance at the forefront of this movement, rather than simply as someone shaped by it. Brevard Childs, the leading authority on the movement, lists the *Scottish Journal of Theology* (1948) as one of those biblical theology journals that suddenly arrived on the scene after World War II.[89] Of course, all theology claims to be biblical to one degree or another. However, the biblical theology movement caused theologians to think more deeply about the significance of "biblical." Childs notes five leading features of the movement, although only four are pertinent here. These are the "rediscovery of the theological dimension" of the Bible; "unity of the whole Bible"; the "revelation of God in history"; the "distinctiveness of the biblical mentality."[90]

The landmark accomplishment of the biblical theology movement was Gerhard Kittel's *Theologisches Worterbuch zum Neuen Testament* (TWNT) (1933–79). It is a work Torrance treasured.[91] His comments about it show that Childs knew what he was talking about. He heaps

---

(ibid., 192). However, he faults Calvin's eschatology for being overly spiritual and individualistic. Torrance sees Calvin's eschatology as the transposition of Christology to the church, but in Quistrop's view the church has only a minor place in Calvin's eschatology. And in contrast to Torrance's breakdown of Calvin's eschatology, he describes it in terms of "hope," "the immortality of the soul" and "the general resurrection."

87. Torrance, "Where do we go from Lund?," 54.

88. Indeed for Torrance the biblical theology movement has its genesis in the Reformation. "Among the great figures in the history of the Christian theology Calvin stands out as above all a 'Biblical Theologian'" (Quistorp, *Calvin's Doctrine*, 7).

89. Childs, *Biblical Theology*, 15.

90. Ibid., 32–50.

91. For examples, see "Concerning the Ministry," 190, 193; and "History and Reformation," 284f. In the latter he finds evidence for the interpenetration of history and eschatology on the basis of a TWNT entry on *dabhar* (Heb. "Word").

praises on Kittel's dictionary. He regards it as the "best Biblical scholar-ship" of his day and is confident it holds the keys to a broad recovery of the eschatological element in Christianity.[92]

> No one can read the first four volumes of the *Theologisches Worterbuch* without being profoundly impressed with the fact that scholars from all sides and of many varieties have this in common, that their lexicographical and lexicological studies have forced them back into an exposition of the faith that bears something of the eschatological cast that characterizes all the Scriptures. Undoubtedly the renewed understanding of the Old Testament and its relation to the thought of the New Testament has a great deal to do with this, which would seem to justify the historian in the judgement that whenever the Church has been tempted to tear Christianity from its God-given roots in Hebraic soil, it has destroyed something so essential that its effects bear strange fruit for centuries afterwards.[93]

There is no question that the "unity of the whole Bible" is a cor-nerstone of Torrance's eschatology. While he recognizes different factors in biblical eschatology, he sees them as constituting a whole. For ex-ample, there is the integration of the future and the present. "In the Old Testament the main accent lay upon the future; in the New Testament the main accent lies upon the present, but here the accent on the present has no meaning apart from the future when the kingdom of God now realized intensively in temporal and historical encounter will be real-ized extensively in a new heaven and a new earth."[94] There is also the integration of creation and redemption, of *telos* and *eschaton*. "The roots of the teleological end go back to the prophetic view of the Kingdom, and the roots of the eschatological end go back to the apocalyptic view of the Kingdom. In using both terms the New Testament clearly refuses to teach an eschatology of judgement and new creation that is divorced from a teleological conception of creation and history."[95]

Torrance's essay "The Israel of God" (1956) is perhaps the best single illustration of the influence of biblical theology on him.[96] In it he argues

92. Torrance, "The Modern," 1.

93. Ibid.

94. Ibid., 101.

95. Ibid., 102.

96. Another good example of the influence of biblical theology is his essay "A Study in New Testament Communication." He takes issue with C. H. Dodd's interpretation

that the Christian church is organically related to "old Israel" through the incarnation of Jesus Christ. It is the new "Israel of God." The church is not merely an "offshoot of Israel"; rather, it is Israel "gathered up" in Jesus Christ.[97] Christ has recapitulated in himself "the historico-redemptive service of Israel and who, after fulfilling and transcending all its hopes, launches it out again in its servant-mission laden with the Word of reconciliation for all mankind."[98] This means the "historic-redemptive movement" in both testaments are "essentially one."[99] Although the church is the New Israel, it cannot afford to forget about the old one. For Israel "bears the Church." The church, therefore, "cannot be perfect, cannot reach its fulness apart from Israel."[100] Thus it is necessary for the church to be "schooled" in the "Hebraic" ways of thinking.[101] This will help the church to grasp fully the saving work of God in Jesus Christ. It will also help the church to recapture its essentially eschatological nature. [102]

Not surprisingly, Torrance singled out biblical scholars for their contributions to eschatology. Two in particular were important for him, Oscar Cullmann and William Manson. He calls Cullmann's *Christ and*

---

of Jesus' parables, while using a study by R. S. Wallace to make his own case. Hence the meaning of a parable is theologically—or, better, christologically—determined. Its meaning does not depend, contrary to Dodd, on a natural relation between gospel and the world. New Testament communication necessarily involves use of analogies, but the parable is proof that this communication involves "analogy with a difference," analogy which has at its heart "an eschatological event" (Torrance, "A Study," 300). Dodd's thesis is that the parables are proof that the kingdom of God arrived completely in the ministry of Jesus. Torrance, on the other hand, argues that the parables indicate that there is still an eschatological reserve, owing to the fact that Jesus is himself the great "Parable" of the kingdom. He cannot be put into words, since he is the Word. The Word made flesh is the key, but the parables both reveal this Word and conceal it. They conceal it so that men may have time to repent, so that the eschaton does not come openly upon people and condemn them for their sins. "It is precisely that lapse of time or eschatological reserve between the Word of the Kingdom and the power of the Kingdom that Jesus is concerned to preserve in the Parable where the Word is spoken in such a way that full Action is still suspended" (Torrance, "A Study," 307).

97. Torrance, "The Israel of God," 306.

98. Ibid.

99. Ibid.

100. Ibid., 317.

101. Ibid., 319.

102. See Torrance's paper, "Christ the First and the Last." Here he argues that Christian eschatology has its roots in Hebrew thought, not in Greek thought. Whereas Greek thought focuses on abstract concepts and logic, Hebrew thought is concerned primarily with action and time (ibid., 304–5).

Time (ET, 1951), which has become a classic in biblical theology, the most "exciting work on eschatology since the epoch making work of Albert Schweitzer."[103] What impressed him was Cullmann's attempt to develop an eschatology that brings together both "creation and redemption" and the "teleological and eschatological ends," and all in a way that captures the "deeply biblical tension between present and future."[104]

Still, Torrance, following Barth, could not fully endorse Cullmann's eschatology. He thought it relied too heavily on a linear conception of time (*chronos*). In his view, time in the Bible was more complex than this. Besides, time itself is implicated in the falleness of creation. This means it too has to be interpreted in light of the cross and resurrection. The story of Jesus' forty-day sojourn on earth between the resurrection and ascension suggests that the "reality of the new creation is temporal fact now though its reality is veiled since the ascended Lord is yet to be unveiled in the *parousia*."[105] Thus the eschatological tension is not simply between a present *chronos* and a future *chronos*, but between the "time of a present but hidden reality and the time of the same reality manifest in the future."[106]

Torrance held William Manson's work in even higher regard.[107] In a review of one of his books he refers to Manson as "the authoritative guide" on New Testament theology.[108] Manson was an authoritative guide, of course, not just because he was an able biblical scholar but also because he, like Cullmann, helped to substantiate traditional theological claims.

Manson produced two books that garnered the attention of Torrance. The first was *Jesus the Messiah* (1943), which argues that the messianic claims about Jesus in the Gospels are original—not later ad-

103. Torrance, "The Earliest Christian," 87.

104. Torrance, "The Modern,"175–76.

105. Ibid., 178.

106. Ibid.

107. It is hard not to suspect that there is some personal bias too in these reviews. Torrance had a friendly relationship with both men. Cullmann was a Professor of New Testament at Basel during the time Torrance was there, and it was he who recommended Torrance as the theologian to succeed Barth at Basel. Manson held the chair in New Testament at New College until 1952, and Torrance attended his lectures when he was a divinity student there. He recalls that Manson had a "profound devotional and liturgical impact on him" (Torrance, "Student Years," 6.).

108. Torrance, "The Epistle to the Hebrews," 313.

ditions, as some modern scholars had claimed. The second was *The Epistle to the Hebrews: An Historical and Theological Reconsideration* (1951). This one was especially valuable to Torrance, for he would make the Christology in The Epistle to the Hebrews a cornerstone of *Royal Priesthood*. Manson's commentary got a rave review. It is described as an "epoch-making book" in New Testament scholarship for the way it "cuts cleanly and decisively through the Platonic misinterpretation of Hebrews, and against the trend of modern criticism puts the Epistle back in its theological and historical setting in the Biblical *Heilsgeschichte* and in the world-mission of the Church."[109] Manson convinced Torrance that the writer of Hebrews is fundamentally an "eschatologist," rather than a ""Platonic idealist."[110]

The biblical theology movement started to collapse in the 1960s after many of its assumptions were undermined by critical biblical scholarship. James Barr in particular, with his book *The Semantics of Biblical Language* (1961), dealt a severe blow to the movement. He showed that biblical theologians such as Torrance were jumping to theological conclusions on the basis of words alone.[111] Theological thought in the New Testament, he argued, is not concentrated in individual words but in word combinations (i.e., sentences). He also debunked the myth that certain biblical words signify a real difference between Hebrew thought and Greek thought. Torrance may have initially bristled at Barr's criticisms, but it is probably no coincidence that not long after them detailed biblical word studies disappear from Torrance's writings.

3. Modern Eschatology

Torrance's contribution to eschatology needs to be understood not only in light of the ecumenical movement but also in light of his critical understanding of modern eschatology. As we know, he saw his era as one of three periods in history "rich in eschatology." Few would dispute that claim. James Orr was right when he predicted that the twentieth century would be the "age of eschatology." Torrance's only comprehensive treatment of modern eschatology is found in a forty-one page es-

109. Ibid., 310.

110. Ibid., 312.

111. Torrance's linguistic arguments in *Royal Priesthood*, in particular, come under Barr's withering attack. See Barr, *The Semantics*, 129–35; 151–56.

say series titled the "Modern Eschatological Debate" (1953), which is largely based on his New College lectures. In his view all the current talk about eschatology was a sign of repentance in the church. After neglecting eschatology for long periods, the church was now frantically trying to compensate. When it was not neglected, it was hardly more than an appendix to the faith, rather than the "fibre of the living strand," as Mackintosh had taught him.[112] As we know, Torrance saw the leading Reformers as an exception. Yet they are not above criticism. He feels they must bear some of the blame for the neglect of eschatology in mainstream Protestantism. The problem started when the Reformers began to combat the Anabaptists (*der Schwarmer*), "who conceived of the Kingdom too literally in terms of history and apocalyptic, and salvation too much in terms of the future."[113] Their radicalism caused the Reformers to "recoil from apocalyptic," with the result that eschatology became detached from history, and consequently from its biblical foundations. When that happened, the "logic of ideas" gradually supplanted the "logic of action" in Protestantism.[114] Torrance detects a shift to the "logic of ideas" with the appearance of Calvin's systematic theology. [115] This explains why in order to get to the heart of the reformer's eschatology he goes to his sermons and commentaries.

Torrance sees the divorce between eschatology and history persisting into the twentieth century, but for additional reasons.[116] He credits the German scholars Weiss and Schweitzer for proving that eschatology is part of the kernel of the gospel. For Schweitzer this eschatology was "consistent," which meant that it was essentially futuristic and "abruptly supernatural." Torrance believes, however, that Schweitzer gravely misunderstood the earliest Christian eschatology because he saw it only

---

112. Torrance, "The Modern," 45.

113. Ibid., 48.

114. Ibid.

115. See his review of the English translation of Heppe's *Reformed Dogmatics.* Though he has many fine things to say about this work, he does not like the way it handles eschatology. It has been "transmuted into the federal idea, and all that remains is a harmless chapter at the end on glorification" (Torrance, Review of *Reformed Dogmatics,* 83).

116. He believes that the ramifications of this "recoil" from apocalyptic eschatology in the sixteenth and seventeenth centuries extend into the twentieth century. To illustrate he points to the "secularisation of eschatology" in Communism (Torrance, "The Modern," 49.).

in terms of the "primitive cosmology" of Jewish thinkers.[117] Instead, it should be seen as the *inner form* of the Christian faith, with its own time element.[118] For Schweitzer, then, (and his followers, Buri and Werner) the Christian religion has been shaped less by the event Christ than that great non-event, *die ausgebliebenen Parusie* (the delay of the *parousia*).

This interpretation of early Christianity spawned a *"timeless eschatology"* among scholars who were still determined to take the faith of the New Testament seriously. However, this approach was really just a way to avoid facing up to the question of the advent of Christ.[119] Torrance links this approach with Rudolph Bultmann, C. H. Dodd, and Edwyn Hoskyns, but states that it originates in Karl Barth's *Epistle to the Romans*, which he calls the "great turning point" in eschatology after Schweitzer.[120] In contrast to the "thorough-going" eschatology of Schweitzer, Barth's early eschatology is one where the "stress is as much upon the past and present as it is upon the future."[121] "The end of history is not to be interpreted as an end within time, for no end within time can be a real or complete end. The end is also the beginning, and so the nearness of the end is interpreted as the transcendental relation of the present to its origin in the eternal."[122]

However, Torrance underlines the fact that Barth soon disowned this timeless eschatology when he realized it did not "square with the New Testament emphasis on time."[123] He found the clue to New Testament eschatology, he writes, in Christology—in terms of the incarnation, crucifixion, resurrection, and ascension. "This meant the real eschatological tension was not interpreted in terms of an eternity/ time dialectic, which always means in the end a refusal to take time seriously, but rather in terms of the new and the old, of a new time in reconciliation and union with the eternal and old time which is the time of this fallen world which through sin exists in mysterious contradiction to God."[124]

---

117. Torrance, "The Modern," 52.

118. Ibid., 52–53.

119. Ibid., 53.

120. Ibid., 94.

121. Ibid.

122. Ibid.

123. Ibid.

124. Ibid., 95. Torrance observes the change in Barth's eschatology in *Die Auferstehung de Toten* (1924).

Sadly, according to Torrance, many have remained blind to this seismic shift that occurred in Barth. In his view, Bultmann, Hoskyns, Dodd, and Reinhold Niebuhr still operate within Barth's old eternity/time dialectic. Salvation is in Christ alone, but this is conceived in an "anti-evolutionary and non-teleological" sense.[125]

Torrance's earliest sermons showed that he also operated with a time/eternity model (though even then it was controlled by Christology). However, he was quick, as his sermons on the Apocalypse show, to follow in Barth's new direction by integrating eschatology and teleology in terms of Christology.[126] As we have noted above, he saw this new approach as more biblical also.

For Torrance, then, the way forward in eschatology is not just a matter of devising a proper concept of time. He does not believe New Testament eschatology rests upon a distinct notion of time. Yet he believes that a Christian eschatology must acknowledge the time element, otherwise it defies the witness of Scripture and, more seriously, defies the incarnation. This is why Torrance calls for a "time-concept on the analogy of the incarnation."[127] "Must we not say with Karl Barth that because the Word has become flesh it has also become time?"[128] This suggests that the eschatological tension is actually between "new time in the new creation, and old time as we know it in the continuation of this fallen world."[129] This would explain why the new time is still veiled to our perception and understanding.

But Torrance feels we cannot stop here, otherwise we would be left with the impression that the eternity has been converted into time. That is why he believes it is necessary to think about this new time using the

---

125. Torrance, "The Modern," 95.

126. Torrance did not seeing himself standing alone with Barth. He also saw Brunner, Althaus and Karl Heim working beside him. He thinks Heim, with the help of Bergson and the new physics, has made the greatest advance. He credits him for "thinking eschatology and soteriology into each other" and for supplanting "a static (*stabil*) view of time in favour of a dynamic (*labil*) view" (Torrance, "The Modern," 98). What is more, he admires the way that Heim thinks about eschatology in relation to the church. "Our Christian view of time must inevitably be bound up with God's action in history through the Church as the place which is, so to speak, within time" (ibid.).

127. Ibid., 224.

128. Ibid. Here he turns to the Barth of the *Kirchliche Dogmatik* I/2, p. 55; II/1, pp. 50f. and III/2, pp. 524 ff.

129. Torrance, "The Modern," 224.

analogy of the Chalcedonian doctrine of the hypostatic union, so that we avoid a fusion of the eternal and temporal without creating a separation between them. Yet our understanding of this new time cannot terminate with the incarnation, if we want it to be faithful to the full implications of the incarnation and the whole story of Christ. Hence he stresses the need to "go a step beyond Chalcedon," in order to carry this union forward "through the cross to its perfection in the resurrection."[130] In the cross the new time and the old time collide. Although it resists, the old time is judged and condemned by the new time. Torrance's sermons on the Apocalypse are really a witness to the fact that the new time is made perfect through the cross and resurrection. The new time in Christ has "entered into the heart of our alienation from God, into the heart of the conflicts of history, and in the teeth of all the contradictions of sin and all the abstractions of fallen time."[131] Yet this new time achieves its end, and its glory, in the new creation.

The entire Christ event—the incarnation, cross and resurrection—creates one great eschatological tension between the "new creation" and the "fallen world." However, this tension is usually interpreted in a dual manner, one that has its basis in the Old Testament. Thus there is the tension between the "eternal and the temporal," which brings together the "apocalyptic and prophetic views of the Kingdom," and the tension between the "holy and the sinful."[132]

In Torrance's view, the two major eschatological heresies in his day were a consequence of focusing only on one or the other of these two tensions. In "realized eschatology," represented by men like Dodd and Hoskyns, the focus is on "the relation between the eternal and the temporal in terms of the tension between the new and the old."[133] In other words, "all horizontal relations are transmuted into a vertical relation."[134] All teleological development is eliminated. The belief is that the kingdom of God has been secured through the events of the cross and resurrection. However, since it downplays the incarnation it misses the tension between the eternal and temporal.

130. Ibid., 225.
131. Ibid.
132. Ibid.
133. Ibid.
134. Ibid., 103.

In "realized teleology," which Torrance associates with George MacLeod and other "incarnationists," the focus is on "the relation between the new creation and the old as if it were the perfected union of the eternal and the temporal."[135] In this case it is thought that the incarnation alone has ushered in the kingdom of God. The church tends to be viewed as an extension of the incarnation. In fact, as a result of the incarnation, the whole creation is believed to be renewed already. God is believed to be "earthed"(MacLeod)."[136] This renewal or redemption only needs to be actualized through the ministry of the church.

However, since "realized teleology" downplays the cross and resurrection, it forgets the tension between the "holy and sinful." Torrance bemoans the fact that MacLeod does not take seriously the New Testament idea that redemption is both already in our possession and yet something we must hope for.

In both these expressions of eschatology, the eschatological tension is actually nullified. In the first, the "eschatological end" is thought of as realized "here and now"; in the second, the "teleological end" is "realized here and now."[137]

An eschatology grounded in a proper Christology would force us to interpret the "teleological end" eschatologically, which would prevent one from conceiving the kingdom of God in terms of moral and cultural progress.[138] Conversely, it would make us interpret the "eschatological end" teleologically, so that there will be no justification for arguing that the parousia is behind us and that the kingdom has been realized on the grounds of Jesus' resurrection and ascension.[139]

Likewise, the new creation must be understood strictly in terms of the Christ event. Thus it involves "eschatological fulfillment or development through history."[140] Again, we are reminded of Torrance's sermons

---

135. Ibid. G. F. MacLeod was the founder and leader of a monastic community on the island of Iona in Scotland's Hebrides. The Iona Community restored the once famous abbey of St. Columba. It is debatable whether MacLeod's theology represents a form of "realized teleology." Certainly the incarnation is central to his theology, and there is an emphasis on "God as Now." Yet the high priesthood of Christ is not left out of this theology. The best source for his theology is *Only One Way Left* (1956).

136. Torrance, "The Modern," 171.

137. Ibid., 225.

138. Ibid., 226.

139. Ibid.

140. Ibid.

on the Apocalypse. There we observed a two-fold tension and the integration of the eschatological end and the teleological end. In Torrance's view, this explains why the Apocalypse completes the New Testament. Torrance interpreted the millennium in the Apocalypse as the new time, which is a union of the eternal and temporal. It means the kingdom of God has arrived already with power. But there is also that two-fold tension which inevitably leads to conflict. So the "new creation is here and now breaking up the old . . . until the Kingdom of God will come at last with observation in the new heaven and new earth."[141]

The church signifies that this "two-fold" tension has been injected into the world and "enshrined" in the two sacraments. Baptism is a sign especially of that "once-and-for-all union of God and man, of the eternal and the temporal."[142] It is also a sign of the new creation, the "perfect body of Christ" into which we have been incorporated. The Lord's Supper, on the other hand, is a sign of the "continuation" of that union in space and time. Subjectively speaking, the two sacraments correspond to the two-fold experience of possessing the kingdom and of reaching towards in faith and hope. Objectively, they signify the two-fold character of the *parousia*, as both a "real presence here and now and yet as an advent presence still to come."[143]

This is not all Torrance has to has to say on the sacraments and eschatology in the "Modern Eschatological Debate." But we must not get ahead of ourselves, for much of what he says summarizes what he wrote a few years earlier for the Commission of Faith and Order. The important point is that Torrance's applies his eschatological principles in this essay to his doctrine of the church as the Body of Christ.

C. The Faith and Order Movement

1. Towards Lund, 1948–52

Torrance got involved with the international Commission of Faith and Order just as it was gearing up for its Third World Conference at Lund, Sweden in 1952. However, the agenda for Lund was basically set at the Second World Conference at Edinburgh in 1937. There it was agreed that the focus of the next conference should be on the key issues di-

141. Ibid.
142. Ibid., 227.
143. Ibid., 228.

viding churches from one another. Hence between 1938 and 1939 three international study commissions were appointed for that purpose: 1) *The Nature of the Church*, 2) *Ways of Worship*, and 3) *Intercommunion*. In the years that followed, the commission members met regularly and circulated papers. Torrance was not a member of Faith and Order at this time, but was a substitute for a meeting at Chichester, England in 1949. This is where he was asked to contribute an essay for the commission on Intercommunion on behalf of the Reformed churches. The result was "Eschatology and Eucharist," a forty-seven page essay which was circulated within Faith and Order in 1950. It was published in *Intercommunion* (1952), a volume of reports and essays intended as a basis for discussion at the Lund conference. Of the nineteen essays included in *Intercommunion*, the one by Torrance is the only one that deals with eschatology. It is very likely that his report on eschatology for the British Council of Churches was the nucleus for this essay. We will examine "Eschatology and Eucharist" shortly.

However, by the time of the Third World Conference at Lund substantial changes were afoot within Faith and Order. In fact, historians of the ecumenical movement regard Lund as a major turning point in the history of the movement.[144] It is natural to attribute these changes to the formation of the WCC in 1948, but these were theological changes that can be traced back to the second world conference of Faith and Order held at Edinburgh in 1937. Edinburgh was a great achievement. People spoke of a "real discovery of the churches of one another," of a real coming together of the churches as never before.[145] The feeling of unity overshadowed the sight of division. A frisson of optimism pervaded the conference. Many in attendance thought they were about to enter "the promised land"—a reunified church.

That did not happen. And by 1952 the optimism was gone. Doubtless, historical factors are to blame. After all, the war had delayed the formation of the WCC. The main reason, though, is that the first meeting of the newly formed WCC at Amsterdam exposed a serious fault in the church. It called attention to "our deepest difference," which "we find irreconcilable."[146]

144. See Skoglund and Nelson, *Fifty Years*.
145. See ibid., 65.
146. See ibid., 70.

This was the difference, roughly described, between "catholic" and "protestant" (or "evangelical") definitions of the church.[147] The "catholic" stresses the visible unity of the church, marked especially by the historical succession of bishops; while the "protestant" defines the church in terms of the proclamation of the Word and the faithful response to this Word. More important, the churches on both sides of the divide viewed the Christian faith as a "self-consistent whole." This meant that the many similarities between "catholics" and "protestants" were more superficial than first believed. For instance, the "catholic" understanding of the sacraments had to be understood in light of the "catholic" understanding of the whole faith, but this "catholic" understanding is not compatible with the "protestant" understanding of the faith. The Amsterdam Assembly was a high-water mark in the history of church unity, but it was also wake up call to the commission on Faith and Order.

2. The Amsterdam Assembly, 1948— "The Nature and Mission of the Church"

It is necessary to identify this "turning point" at Lund, for it is really Torrance's entry point into Faith and Order. He addresses that "fundamental division" in a thirty-page response to volumes I & II of the preparatory studies for the Assembly: "Concerning Amsterdam I, The Nature and Mission of the Church." For many, the deep difference between "catholic" and "evangelical" churches was a roadblock to unity, but not for Torrance. Instead he saw a bridge to unity, an eschatological bridge. The crisis at Amsterdam reminded him that the church's unity in Jesus Christ is an "eschatological reality that both interpenetrates history and transcends it."[148] Putting it more plainly, it was a "given unity even in the midst of disorder" which had allowed the churches to come together at Amsterdam, while it was the promised unity transcending the disorder that "prevented them from snatching too hastily at a visible reality."[149]

---

147. "Catholic" in this case does not refer to the Roman Catholic Church, which at this time forbade its members from even attending ecumenical conferences. It refers to churches, though, which have an affinity with the Roman Church such at the Church of England, the Orthodox Churches and Old Catholic Churches. In Europe the term "evangelical" was used instead of "protestant" and this was the term Torrance preferred to use as well.

148. Torrance, "Concerning Amsterdam," 242.

149. Ibid., 242.

Because the unity of the church is an eschatological reality, doctrinal differences are to be expected, since traditional doctrinal formulations cannot fully comprehend this reality.

What did all this mean for the deep divisions in the church? If there is robust faith in the God-given church unity then you will have an "eschatological suspension of the confessionalism" behind these diverse conceptions of Christianity and "a shattering of theological relativism."[150] It means that the "validity" of the outward form of a church has to be qualified by the advent of Christ. Torrance repudiates a "self-consistent whole" in any church tradition, whether it is Roman, Reformed, Orthodox, etc. Churches are obliged to hear the voices of other churches. Finally, churches engaged in ecumenical dialogue need to "think out every doctrine into every other doctrine"—beginning with eschatology.[151] The neglect of this doctrine, he believes, has had a deleterious effect on all church doctrines, but especially Christology and ecclesiology.

Of course, any discussion about the unity of the church should include a clear sense of the nature of the church. Yet it was apparent at Amsterdam that there was no agreement on this matter.[152] Early in his career, Torrance accented the functional nature of the church. It was the "leaven" in society, the greatest disturbing force in the world. He does not abandon this idea, but when he joined Faith and Order he began to think about the church in more substantive, ecumenical terms. This outlook was imperative, since one of the goals of the commission was a confessional unity. In the rest of his essay he tackles some of those confessional agreements and disagreements as they pertain to the nature and mission of the church.

At Amsterdam there was recognition of the divine and human nature of the church, but Torrance is disappointed that more attention was not given to this idea. For him, this dual nature of the church can only be understood through its "analogy" to Christ, i.e., in terms of the "hypostatic union." He adds a word of caution, though, since he knows the union of God and Man in Christ is "absolutely unique." "The analogy runs not 'as God and Man are related in Christ so the divine and the hu-

---

150. Ibid., 243.

151. Ibid., 246.

152. See The World Council of Churches, *The Universal Church*, 17.

man are related in the Church,'" but rather as "God and Man are related in Christ so Christ and the Church are related."[153]

He believes that many faulty doctrines of the church are due to an ignorance of this analogy. For example, there are Anglicans who think of the church as a "pre-existent ontological reality," and Orthodox Christians who think of it as an "invisible Platonic magnitude." Further, this ignorance has bred a lack of respect for the relation between church and creation/re-creation. "In other words the eschatological tension tends to be conceived in terms of eternity and time or transmuted into a mystical relation, instead of being thought of in terms of the new creation and the old."[154] In agreement with Edmund Schlink, Torrance insists that the church in the New Testament is conceived only in terms of an earthly actuality.[155] This is one reason Torrance calls for deeper study of St. Paul's view of the church as the Body of Christ.

Constructing a doctrine of the church on the analogy of Christ will also require a study of the "time-relations" of the church, beginning with its "historical particularity." That will compel the church to incorporate the "time relations" suggested by the incarnation and the cross of Christ. "To cut the link between the church and historical particularity is not only to transubstantiate the Church into some docetic *corpus mysticum* but to sever her from any saving act by God in our actual existence."[156]

153. Torrance, "Concerning Amsterdam," 248.

154. Ibid., 249.

155. Schlink, "Church," 159.

156. Torrance, "Concerning Amsterdam," 252. Torrance frequently throws out the term *corpus mysticum* without reference or definition. Anglo-Catholics have used *corpus mysticum* to describe the church, but Presbyterian churches have also employed the term. It is found, for example, in the Westminster Confession (31.1). The term became popular in the Roman Catholic Church in the twentieth century. Pope Pius XII gave it official sanction and dogmatic justification with his encyclical *Mystici Corporis Christi* in 1943. The encyclical actually aims to counter docetic images of the church. "Hence they err in a matter of divine truth, who imagine the Church to be invisible, intangible, a something merely 'pneumatological' as they, by which many Christian communities, though they differ from each other in their profession of faith, are united by an invisible bond" (ibid., 15). Yet one could still call this Roman model of the church docetic, since the Mystical Body is really "another Christ," with the Pope as the head of this Body (ibid., 94). It is used to distinguish the Body of the church from Christ's physical body which sits at the right hand of God (ibid., 115). The fundamental difference between this model and Torrance's comes down to the relation between the church and Christ. Torrance defines this relation in terms of the hypostatic union, so that the church is neither separated from nor confused with Christ. The church's relation to Christ is analogous

To give attention to the "time relations" of the church is really to give attention to the dynamic aspect of the church. Torrance stressed this aspect of the church in his own ministry, and he continued to do so even after he arrived at a more ontological conception of the church. The nature and mission of the church are closely related, and it is the dynamic nature of the church that accounts for the ministry and mission of the church. In Barth's words, the true church is an "event." It "is . . . in so far as it dares to live by the act of its living Lord"[157] But what accounts for this dynamic nature? It would not be wrong to say the "hypostatic union," but only if this union is understood dynamically, viz. as having its origin in the living Word. In the beginning "was the Word," not the hypostatic union. "[J]ust as in the Incarnation the Word is made flesh, so in the *Kerygma* that same Word continues to be made flesh" through baptism and Eucharist.[158]

On the "catholic" view, the church is often portrayed as a sacramental reality. For Torrance, though, sacramental action depends on a proclamation of the Gospel. Apart from the "Word," the sacrament is ineffectual. This emphasis on the Word is a hallmark of the "evangelical" view of the church, and certainly of Barth's view of it.[159]

This living Word always seeks an end. The ultimate end is the new heaven and earth, but until then we need the sacrament as a sign of that fulfillment. "Although considered in terms of temporal sequence (cf. Mark 2:5ff) there is a teleological suspension of the union of the Word and Act, that union is given to us here and now in the Word and Sacrament as a finished work."[160]

For Torrance, the *kerygma* must never be subordinated to anything, since it is really Christ Himself. He defines *kerygma* as "both the *thing*

---

to the relation between the human and divine in Christ. The church is the Body, then, of the "crucified, risen, ascended and advent Christ." This suggests too, however, that the church is separated from Christ the Head. It is still a body of sinners. This body is justified and sanctified in Christ, yet still must await the day when it will fully *become* the Body of Christ.

157. Barth, "The Church," 67–69. Italics are mine.

158. Torrance, "Concerning Amsterdam," 254.

159. For Barth, the "congregation is the event in which the witness of apostles and prophets to Jesus Christ, deposited in Scripture, as such, becomes present, effective and fruitful; and its authority visible and intelligible in a continual process of research, exposition and preaching" (Barth, "The Church," 68).

160. Torrance, "Concerning Amsterdam," 255.

preached and the *preaching* of it."[161] Christ is the head of the church, which is his Body, but the Body is "gathered up" into Christ through the preaching of the Word *(Kerygma)*. The final goal is "incorporation" into Christ, and the sacrament is the sign of this. The terms "gathering" and "incorporation" are taken from Barth's essay for the Amsterdam Assembly, although Barth actually uses the term "gathering together" *(congregatio)* instead of "gathering up."[162]

This brings us to a point of divergence between Torrance and his master at Basel. For Barth, the accent is on the "gathering together" of the church through the Word. Torrance moves the accent onto "incorporation"; hence his preference for the term "gathering up." There is, he writes, a "mutual involution" between the "gathering up" and the "incorporation," "for it is Christ who by Word and Sacrament does both."[163] This notion of "incorporation" is central to the "catholic" idea of the church. Barth also speaks about "incorporation." Torrance feels this notion is fundamental to Barth's understanding of the church as an "event" and as a unity, but he thinks he ought to have given more weight to "incorporation."[164]

Torrance will give more weight to "incorporation," and this explains why his doctrine of the church appears more ontological and more sacramental than Barth's. This is why Torrance insists on seeing the church as the Body of Christ, whose union with Christ is analogous to the "hypostatic union." It also explains why he will emphasize the teleological growth of the church, rather than just the renewal of it through the Word.[165]

161. Ibid., 254.

162. Barth, "The Church," 68–69, 72

163. Torrance, "Concerning Amsterdam," 256.

164. Baptism, writes Barth, "incorporates" people into a "special relation" to Christ and the Lord's Supper "keeps them . . . belonging to him" (Barth, "The Church," 69). Indeed the sacraments constitute the church as an "event," which marks the unity of the church (ibid.). However, that event and that unity are maintained through a constant renewal of these things, and that happens through a "renewal of her 'gathering' as a congregation" *(Gemeinde)* (ibid., 72).

165. There is a fine point of difference between Barth and Torrance in regards to the church. For Barth, the church depends not only on the Word that "gathers together" but on a free human response to that Word, the "perfect freedom of obedience" to it (Barth, "The Church," 68). The Congregation is one that "dares to live by that act of its living Lord" (ibid., 67). Torrance, on the other hand, rarely thinks of the church in terms of its obedience to God. Rather, he defines the church in terms of *Christ's substitutionary*

This idea of "gathering up" and "incorporation" informs Torrance's understanding of the continuity of the church. With these terms he tries to bring together the "prophetic" and "episcopal" ministry of the church. He was not concerned do this in his review of *The Apostolic Ministry.* There the "prophetic" ministry was used simply to refute Anglo-Catholic claims for the "episcopal" ministry. For those Anglo-Catholics, the episcopal ministry is essential because it preserves and perpetuates the apostolic ministry. For Torrance, the Apostolate is "unrepeatable," in the sense that "it cannot be extended in time on the stage of the world."[166] To claim that it can be is to ignore the nature of time and history. The apostolic ministry is perpetuated through the church's "prophetic ministry," which actually testifies to the continuous ministry of the risen Christ.

However, Torrance now recognizes a kernel of truth in the apostolic succession. It signifies an attempt to honor the church's historical nature, its penetration of space and time. However, "catholics" fail to appreciate the fact that the church, since it is the Body of Christ, represents a new time. The church is an "eschatological reality" that "penetrates history," but it is also one that "transcends it." Thus the continuity of the church cannot be defined in terms of history as we know it. The church is not simply continuous with the Israel of old. It begins with the birth of Israel's Messiah. But this was a virgin birth, which means there was an "invasion from above" that intersects vertically the history of Israel. This also makes the church discontinuous with the Israel of old. "The Birth, Life and Death of Jesus Christ all speak of the most complete interpenetration of history, and indeed of a desperate struggle with the terrible continuity of its sin and guilt, but they receive their truth and validity in the Resurrection where the continuity of sin is decidedly broken and yet where there emerges the new continuity in time."[167]

Underlying this notion of apostolic succession should be a clear sense of the "complete" Body of Christ. This Body must not be understood as something that is completed or fulfilled through the time stream

---

obedience to God. See Torrance, "The Atonement." This difference between Barth and Torrance is mirrored in the way each views the sacraments. Both regard them as actions or events; both tie them closely to the Word. For Torrance they "enshrine" the action of the Word and are "charged" with the power of the resurrection. For Barth, on the other hand, they will come to stand for human responses to the Word. For further comparison, see Hunsinger, "The Dimension of Depth," 15.

166. Torrance, "Concerning Amsterdam," 261.

167. Ibid., 259.

of history. "Rather is it the continuing wholeness of Christ's Body into which from age to age we are sacramentally incorporated, and which can no more be a phenomenon within the time series than the *parousia* itself."[168] The church, as the Body of Christ, is really an "all-inclusive eschatological magnitude."

Now these definitions certainly make us think that the church as something that transcends history, but they can also leave the impression that the church is really a sand castle in the air. One has to recognize, then, that the church has a real connection with time. Hence, apostolic succession bears witness to an important fact. Torrance's answer depends on an understanding of apostolic succession in terms of teleological growth, which has a basis in Colossians and Ephesians and, it would seem, in the Calvin's view of the church. While the church is "already complete as the fullness of Him that filleth all in all," it is at the same time yet "multiplied." [169] This happens through operation of the Word in the world, with the result that the entire visible church increases through time and in space.

What then is the relevance of the church? This is one of the great theological questions of our age. For many the church's relevance is to be gauged by its ability to meet society's deepest and most urgent needs. For Torrance, though, the "relevance" of the church to the world is "precisely her eschatological relevance."[170] The church, in effect, represents more than we can ever imagine. On the narrowest scale, she is "already the new humanity" in "concentrated form"; on a much wider scale, she "possesses proleptically in Christ all things, even the new heaven and the new earth."[171]

"The Nature and Mission of the Church" is Torrance's first substantial contribution to the ecumenical process. It is really a critical overview of the main issues at stake. Dense and desultory, it is not easy reading. Yet it introduces themes and concepts Torrance will develop and press into service in the coming months and years.

---

168. Ibid., 262. This explains why Torrance does not see any delay of the *parousia* (the central problem for Schweitzer). The *parousia* "is strictly one inclusive coming-and-presence operating with different modes of revelation." See Torrance, "Christ the First," 309.

169. Torrance, "Concerning Amsterdam," 263.

170. Ibid., 268.

171. Ibid.

3. Intercommunion: "Eschatology and Eucharist"

Torrance's paper for Intercommunion takes up two of those themes. "Ecumenical thinking," he wrote there, "might well be described as Eucharistic thinking, not that primarily in which we offer our own traditions and efforts toward a common pool, but an ever-new and thankful *receiving together* of the Body of Christ."[172] He also stressed the need to connect eschatology with every other doctrine and to integrate it into the "whole."

This "receiving together" happens in the Eucharist but its full reception is reserved for the eschaton, for the marriage supper of the Lamb. The Eucharist reminds the churches that their unity is in Christ, but that it is also hidden in Christ. It is no less real because it is hidden. Indeed, its hiddeness in Christ means that it is more real than anything here below, for here there is the old creation that is passing away. The church's unity is grounded upon the wholeness of Christ and his work of salvation. For Torrance, this is the only "self-consistent whole," not any church tradition. And unless "catholics" and "evangelicals" understand this, they can never overcome their deepest difference.

This wholeness of Christ, as we learned, is signified by the *kerygma* and the sacrament. In *kerygma* it is the "*Word* made flesh"; while in the sacrament it is the "Word made *flesh*."[173] The first part stresses the "gathering up" and "gathering together" of the Body of Christ; the second the "incorporation" into the Body. In this essay Torrance focuses on the latter.

"Eschatology and Eucharist" certainly reflects the goal and strategy of the Commission of Intercommunion, which was the child of the Second World Conference (1937) on Faith and Order. There it was declared that sacramental intercommunion was a "necessary part" of any kind of church unity. But it soon became apparent that many obstacles stood in the way of intercommunion. Thus in 1947 the Commission decided that instead of merely describing church practices, it would "penetrate to the theological grounds underlying the practices," in order to foster "mutual understanding" and a solution to its main problem.[174]

---

172. Ibid., 243

173. Ibid., 255.

174. World Conference on Faith and Order. The 1947 Meeting of the Continuation Committee, Clarens, Switzerland, August 28–September 1, 1947. Series 1, no. 102: 49.

The problem is that the Eucharist, in spite of its witness to unity in the New Testament, has become a source of deep division between churches. First, there is that basic division between "catholic" and "protestant" churches. For Orthodox and Anglo-Catholics, the Eucharist reflects the visible, organic unity of the church, a fact that they never fail to underscore. And for them intercommunion hinges on more than consensus on the meaning of the Eucharist *per se.* That is because, on their view, the Eucharist is organically connected to the order of ministry. The celebration of the Eucharist must be led by episcopally ordained priests, which most Protestant churches do not have. Indeed for most Orthodox the term "intercommunion" hardly makes sense. There is only Holy Communion, which is an "act of the Church as One Body."[175] And that church, that Body is the Orthodox Church.[176]

Then there are the doctrinal differences between "catholics" and "protestants." The Orthodox and many Anglicans view the Eucharist as an altar sacrifice that is in union with Christ's once-for-all sacrifice on the cross. For Protestants, the Eucharist is a memorial of Christ's sacrifice at Calvary that is meant to elicit a sacrifice of praise and thanksgiving.

The Eucharist has become a source of division even among Protestants. Many Lutherans, for example, will not practice intercommunion unless there is clear doctrinal agreement on the meaning of the Lord's Supper. But this would normally mean consensus on the Lutheran doctrine of the Eucharist, i.e., that the presence of Christ is "in, with and under" the elements of bread and wine.

Torrance's approach to the problem of intercommunion stands out. While it is clear that the Eucharist in the New Testament contains eschatological elements, churches have generally not made much of them; nor have they seen them as holding a solution to the problem of intercommunion.[177] Moreover, modern scholarship on the Eucharist has in general only reflected this neglect of the churches.[178]

175. Tomkins, *The Third World*, 49.

176. What applies to the Anglo-Catholics and Orthodox would apply a fortiori to the Roman Catholic Church, which did not even participate in the assemblies of the WCC.

177. On the central place of eschatology in the Eucharistic worship of the early church, see Cullmann, *Early Christian Worship*. Cullmann makes the point too that the Eucharist was an indispensable part and the "natural climax" of early Christian worship services (ibid., 34).

178. To get an indication of the neglect of the relationship between the Eucharist and eschatology, read the survey of modern scholarship by Wainwright, *Eucharist and Eschatology*, 2–5

a. The Sacraments

However, Torrance's eschatological approach to the Eucharist is—as we have learned to expect—christological. This is obvious from the outset, by the way he defines a sacrament. He follows Barth in setting aside the Augustinian definition of the sacrament.[179] This definition holds that a *signum* (sign) corresponds to a *res* (thing), so that in the Eucharist you have the visible form of an invisible grace. This way, he says, is "unhebraic and unbiblical" because it depicts the sacrament as a "static matter."[180] Instead, he defines the sacrament on the basis of Jesus' whole life and ministry. Thus for him the sign is "essentially an event." It is "the Christ-Event" in history, his "miraculous activity."[181] And instead of two sacraments he would rather talk about "one sacramental relation between Christ and the church" with "two particular 'moments,'" baptism and the Lord's Supper.[182] Baptism and the Lord's Supper refer to the "Christ-event." Yet this is a unique event. It is "once and for all" but also "abiding and enduring."[183] The Word becomes flesh.

The sacraments are not mere symbols, however. They do not just refer to the "Christ-event." Torrance affirms the real presence of Christ in the sacraments. However, since a sacrament is about an event, not a thing, the real presence of Christ is qualified. The sacraments "enshrine" or are "charged with" the presence of the crucified and risen Christ.[184] The problem with long standing debates over the real presence of Christ in the Eucharist is that presence is conceived statically, thus in a way that is neither eschatological nor teleological. For Torrance, the presence of Christ in the sacrament is an active presence in history. The sacrament,

179. Cf. Barth, *The Heidelberg Catechism*, 95–96

180. Torrance, "Eschatology and Eucharist," 309. "Unhebraic and unbiblical" mean not only that this definition is static but that it also reflects a Platonic spirit/matter dualism. In rejecting this Augustinian definition, Torrance is rejecting also a characteristic feature of the Reformed tradition. Calvin inherited Augustine's definition (Cf. *Inst.* IV.14.1) and the metaphysical framework that went with it. For a thorough discussion of Torrance's definition of the sacrament vis-a-vis the Augustinian tradition, see Stamps, "The Sacrament."

181. Torrance, "Eschatology and Eucharist," 309.

182. Ibid., 312.

183. Ibid., 311.

184. Ibid., 309–10. Torrance thinks it is better to speak of a "Real Action" in the Eucharist than a "Real Presence," in order to highlight the eschatological dimension (Torrance, "Sacrament," 8).

though, cannot fully capture this presence. There is an eschatological reserve in the sacrament. It is a presence "which is also yet to come . . . yet to be unveiled."[185] We should bear in mind Torrance's view of the *parousia,* as a coming-and-presence, for this helps to make sense of his understanding of the real presence in the sacraments.

But it is really the ascension and advent of Christ that determines his understanding of the real presence. The sacraments cannot be identical with the full presence of Christ, for they are given to the church precisely because of the ascension of Christ. "When Christ comes again and the Marriage Supper of the Lamb is consummated, the sacraments will give way to literal reality."[186]

The sacraments thus "enshrine" a two-fold tension that has to do with the new creation. There is the tension created by the "present but hidden reality" and the one deriving from the promise of its future full manifestation. Therefore, they must be understood both in terms of "mystery" and "eschatology." Eschatology, then, is not simply linear or futurist. The eschatological reality is partially unveiled to us now. Like baptism and the Lord's Supper, mystery and eschatology cannot be separated. This adds another layer of depth to Torrance's sacramental theology.[187]

The two-fold tension of the sacraments explains why it is important to understand baptism and the Lord's Supper together, as one "sacramental relation" with "two particular moments." Yet these moments are not identical. Both stand for "incorporation" in Christ, but in baptism the accent is more on the "once-and-for-all incorporation," which, broadly speaking, refers the union between the church and the new creation. This is the reason Baptism is unrepeatable. The Lord's Supper is repeatable, for good reason. The accent here is on the incorporation-union as an "enduring" reality and as a "temporal fact." It renews the once-and-for-all-union between the church and Christ, the new creation. "It is just because, in the sign of Baptism, the complete event recedes into the mystery of the Eternal that we are given in the Eucharist continual participation and renewal in that complete event."[188]

185. Torrance, "Eschatology and Eucharist," 310.

186. Ibid., 311.

187. For an appreciation of the profound nature of Torrance's sacramental theology, see Hunsinger, "The Dimension of Depth."

188. Torrance, "Eschatology and Eucharist," 313.

b. Baptism

Whence comes the power of the sacrament to incorporate us into Christ? They have no power of their own. We could say this power comes from the Word preached, for without that the sacraments would be empty signs. But we must bear in mind that the Word that is preached is the *Word made flesh*. The sacraments are signs of the Word made flesh, wherein lies the power of incorporation.

As for baptism, its real basis is in Jesus' baptism. This is the real point of the believer's incorporation into Christ. "Jesus' baptism was substitutionary and was completed in His Baptism of blood on the cross when he died for all men."[189] The sacrament of baptism thus represents the actualization in time of the "Christ event," of the "absolutely decisive event of the Cross and the resurrection of Christ."[190]

The church, through the summoning power of the Word, is the means by which the Christ-event is actualized in time. But it is through baptism that the church becomes a "bodily Church." Since baptism stands for the "absolutely decisive event of the Cross and resurrection" this makes it, in Torrance's view, the "primary eschatological act."[191] By it people are "grafted into the wholeness of Christ," and caught up in the "eschatological mystery."[192] If the Lord's Supper signifies "*Christ in us*"; baptism signifies that we are "*in Christ*."[193] As we will see, the deep eschatological and soteriological meaning that Torrance attaches to baptism means that this half of the sacramental relation has a leading role to play in the quest for intercommunion.

c. The Eucharist

The importance of baptism for intercommunion is indicated in Torrance's claim that the Lord's Supper is the "recurring confirmation of Baptism."[194] In other words, it is the baptismal incorporation "materialized in flesh and blood." The sacraments bear an eschatological tension "between the time of the present but hidden reality and the time of the same real-

189. Ibid., 314.

190. Ibid., 315. Cf. Rom 6.3–4.

191. Ibid., 314. In another place he stresses that our baptism is not merely an "action by us," but is an "action on us" (Torrance, "Sacraments," 5.)

192. Torrance, "Eschatology and Eucharist," 314, 316.

193. Ibid., 305.

194. Ibid., 316.

ity revealed in the parousia."[195] But this tension is more palpable in the Eucharist, where you have the "two fundamental moments" that St. Paul refers to: "the night on which He was betrayed"—which reminds us of Jesus' substitutionary blood baptism—and "till He come again." If, as Torrance taught us earlier, the ascension forces us to look to the cross, then the Eucharist makes the cross present. It "reaches into the past, to the death of Christ, and sets it in the present as reality operative here and now in the Church."[196] In doing this it accentuates the eschatological tension between the new reality that is hidden but which will one day be revealed. Yet the Eucharist also "reaches out beyond the present into the future, and becomes the means whereby the Church in the present is brought under the power of the advent of Christ."[197]

Words alone, however, do not give the Eucharist the power to make past and future present. The sacrament signifies an event. This is the supreme ontological event, the *Word made flesh*, the "hypostatic union" of God and Man. Torrance, though, insists on adding a time dimension to the Chalcedonian doctrine. It represents, after all, not only the union of God and Man but the union of the eternal and temporal. Christ is thus the new time as well as the new man. In the resurrection the new man and the new time are consummated, but this consummation is achieved by way of suffering and death.

Baptism signifies that the church is united with Christ, and thus "justified and perfected" in him. It is a new creation. At the same time, baptism signifies that this new creation is hidden in the risen, ascended Christ. The new creation therefore is essentially a *mysterion*. The church's perfection can, therefore, only be "received sacramentally" in the Eucharist. Yet the Eucharist signifies that the church's union with Christ has been inserted into history. This means the church also experiences the "agony of Calvary" as it "proclaims the Lord's death till he comes." The church is at the center of this tension and conflict between the old creation, which is passing away, and the new creation that is emerging. "By means of the Eucharist, so to speak, the agony of Calvary is extended into the ages into which the church goes out as the suffering servant in the mission of the world's redemption."[198] This does not mean the church

195. Ibid., 312.
196. Ibid., 319.
197. Ibid.
198. Ibid., 321.

adds to Christ's once-for-all sacrifice, but that in as much as it shares in the victory of Christ it shares in the sacrifice of Christ. And in doing so, the church "learns to fill up that which is eschatologically in arrears of the sufferings of Christ."[199]

For Torrance, then, the disunity of the church in the world only points to the fact that its perfection or wholeness is received only "sacramentally" within the "brokenness and divisions of history." "The Eucharist speaks both of the fraction of the body on earth . . . and the 'conversion' of the Church into the risen body."[200] These are points, however, that "catholic" churches would have difficulty accepting. For them, the wholeness of the church is an historical fact. Yet this means that there is less need to understand the wholeness of the church eschatologically.

Divisions within the church reflect the tension and conflict that exists between the new creation and the old creation. The church participates in the old creation, yet it must not allow itself to become imprisoned in this creation. The Eucharist is her help, for whenever the church celebrates this sacrament she becomes subject to the ascended Christ, to the "impact of the eschaton," to that "wholeness" that "presses toward its complete unveiling at the parousia."[201] But that means the church is also judged for her divisions, which reflect the degree to which she is still conformed to the world. Because the church has been incorporated into the dying and risen Christ, it "must learn to put off the old as often as through the Eucharist it participates in its new being."[202] If the church refuses to do this, if she ignores the eschatological element, she degenerates into a "human Church."[203] This is a church that is still bound to worldly forms such as historical succession and ethnic and national divisions. It is a church that fails to recognize that the "form of this world is passing away" and that she is part of the new creation.

The words "do this in remembrance of me" and "ye proclaim the Lord's death till he come" evoke the sacrificial character of the Eucharist. Is the Eucharist a sacrifice? Torrance believes it is, but only in the sense that it is an "echo" and a "sacramental counterpart" to Christ's once-for-all sacrifice. This is why the *anamnesis* is more than the exercise of the

199. Ibid., Cf. Col 1:24.
200. Ibid., 322.
201. Ibid.
202. Ibid., 323.
203. Ibid., 330.

church's historical memory. It is the action of the eternal Spirit making Christ's sacrifice a present reality. More precisely, the church's sacramental *anamnesis* is really the Spirit echoing Christ "eternal intercession and oblation in heaven."[204]

The sacramental *anamnesis* is the basis therefore for the proclamation of the Lord's death, which is at the core of the church's *kerygma*. This Eucharistic proclamation "enshrines . . . as its eternal *canto firmo* the Self-consecration of the Lamb of God, the Self-presentation of the Mediator before the face of the Father in His intercession for the Church."[205] Therefore, whenever the church proclaims the Lord's death and communicates in his body and blood, it participates in Christ's unique, vicarious sacrifice. However, this aspect of the Lord's Supper must be understood in light of the "till he come." For then the Lord's Supper will be superseded by the marriage supper of the Lamb.

Torrance's interpretation of the Eucharistic worship owes much to the Chalcedonian formula. The church's Eucharistic offering must neither be confused with Christ's unique offering (a "catholic" tendency) nor separated from it (a "protestant" tendency). The church's Eucharistic action is analogous to Christ's sacrifice. It is like it yet, at the same time, different from it. It is a *"re-actio"* to the *"actio"* of Christ's unique sacrifice.[206] But the *re-actio* can never be on par with the *actio* of Christ. Christ's sacrifice is *sui generis*.

There is one thing that ought to safeguard the Eucharistic sacrifice from becoming either confused with Christ's sacrifice or separated from it. An "eschatological substitution," a *mirifica commutatio*, should take place in the Eucharist.[207] Room in the Eucharistic liturgy, therefore, has to be made for the presence of the Risen Lord. That is why the Maranatha (1 Cor 16:22) is indispensable in the worship of the church. The *actio* of Christ has to displace the *re-actio* of the church. This ensures that the sacrament does not turn into a propitiatory sacrifice, but remains a Eucharistic (thanksgiving) sacrifice. It also ensures that the sacrament remains essentially an "event," the "Christ-event." In Christ's sacrifice

204. Ibid., 324–325.
205. Ibid., 326.
206. Ibid., 327.
207. Ibid.

there is "an identity between the Offerer and the Offering and Him to whom the Offering is made."[208]

We were told that when the eschatological element is displaced from the church it becomes a human church. If it is left out of the Eucharistic sacrifice the consequences are even more tragic. It then becomes a "pagan ceremony."[209] Yet Torrance believes that there is "a point" in every communion service when the "real presence of the *Eschatos* suspends the liturgical action, and makes it point beyond itself for validity and order."[210]

d. Eucharist and Intercommunion

What are the implications of this Eucharistic theology for church unity? This might have been the burning question at Lund, for there it was plain to everyone that the disunity of the church reached its "most painful point at the Lord's Table." Christians could not join together to celebrate and receive Holy Communion.[211] At Lund, though, progress was made towards consensus on the meaning, at least, of the Lord's Supper. In its interim report the commission on Intercommunion concluded that "the great majority of our Churches" were able to accept the following regarding this dominical sacrament: "(a) a memorial of Christ's incarnation and earthly ministry, of His death, and resurrection; (b) a sacrament of His Body and Blood in which He is truly present to give Himself to us, uniting us to Himself, to his eternal Sacrifice, and to one another, through the use of His appointed elements of bread and wine; and (c) eschatologically, an anticipation of our fellowship with Christ in His eternal Kingdom."[212]

Torrance did not have a direct hand in this statement of consensus. He was not a member of the commission on Intercommunion, although his essay for it may have contributed to the progress that was made. He would have concurred with the above points, although he probably would have added a few more. For Torrance, Holy Communion is a sacrament of church unity only as long as the eschatological element in it is

---

208. Ibid., 330.

209. Ibid., 300.

210. Ibid.

211. See Baillie and Marsh, *Intercommunion*, 41.

212. Tomkins, *The Third World*, 280.

recognized. It is this element that prevents the church from degenerating into a merely human church, marked by the conflicts and divisions of the world. Moreover, in the "presence of the eschatological Christ," he adds, "all barriers to intercommunion" are overcome.[213] It is in the Eucharist that the church receives sacramentally "the wholeness of its union with Christ." Indeed, for Torrance, the Eucharist is where the church "really becomes the Church, both as the ontological and eschatological reality and as the visible sacramental fact which is the Church's existence on earth."[214] Now we can understand why Torrance saw intercommunion not just as a goal (as many did) for the church but as the "divinely given means" of unity in the church.

On the other hand, Torrance did not believe that the church could simply institutionalize this unity that is received in the Eucharist. Because the Eucharist is about the One who has triumphed over the world, it cannot be "subordinated" to history or to any "conception of order." This includes, in particular, "catholic" definitions of the church, which are based upon apostolic succession. We have seen how Torrance tried to deal with this issue from an eschatological perspective. Of course, no one could expect the problems associated with apostolic succession to be solved overnight. The Intercommunion report noted that "difference of order" was often a bigger obstacle to intercommunion than doctrine.[215] After all, differences in Eucharistic doctrine do not prevent communion within the Anglican body of churches. That is because unity among these churches is based on a common order of ministry.

"Catholics" and "protestants" have always been divided over the question of the sacrificial element in the Eucharist. Torrance tries to find an ecumenical solution to this problem. His essay is not the only one at Lund that attempted to do this, but it is the only one in which eschatology is a vital part of the solution. He maintains that an "eschatological substitution" needs to occur in the Eucharist to ensure that the church's sacrifice does not become confused with or separated from Christ's unique sacrifice.[216]

---

213. Torrance, "Eschatology and Eucharist," 335.

214. Ibid., 337.

215. Baillie and Marsh, *Intercommunion,* 30.

216. The essay by the A. G. Hebert, an Anglican, on the Eucharist also tries to bridge the differences between Catholics and Protestants. For Hebert, the Eucharist is essentially a sacrifice, but this means that the church participates in "Christ's own sacrifice."

However, it was not Torrance's eschatological interpretation of the Eucharist that caused the biggest stir at Lund, although one could argue it had a seminal influence on Faith and Order. After its Fourth World Conference in 1963, Faith and Order commissioned a full study of the Eucharist, and this included a call for an examination of its eschatological aspects.[217]

It was Torrance's statements about baptism that got the most attention.[218] Specifically, it was his insistence on the unity of baptism and Eucharist and the connection between this unity and the unity of the church. The church has traditionally subordinated baptism to the Lord's Supper, but for Torrance this should never have been done. In his view, baptism is the "supreme eschatological act" by which the church is "grafted into the wholeness of Christ." Thus a refusal to practice intercommunion is a slight against baptism and the unity of the church, which exists in Christ. "Therefore to refuse the Eucharist to those baptized into Christ Jesus and incorporated into His resurrection-body amounts either to a denial of the transcendent reality of holy Baptism or to attempted schism within the Body of Christ."[219] The report from Intercommunion called this statement "challenging" and one that "might provide the starting point for further fruitful ecumenical discussions."[220] It did. In 1960 Faith and Order published *One Lord, One Baptism*, the final report of a three-year long study on the meaning of baptism for the church.

In contrast, though, to the Roman Catholic view he does not see the Eucharist as an "immolation" of Christ. The problem with Hebert's solution is the absence of an "eschatological substitution." The result is that the church's sacrifice becomes confused with Christ's sacrifice. Indeed it also becomes separated from it. For Hebert denies a central element in Christ's sacrifice, that his death was a propitiation for sins. For Torrance, it is the fact that Christ's bore our judgement that sets his sacrifice absolutely apart from the church's sacrifice. See Hebert, "A Root of Difference," 236–54.

217. By this time Torrance was no longer a member of Faith and Order. He resigned in 1963. Geoffrey Wainwright's book *Eucharist and Eschatology* represents an answer to the request from Faith and Order (see Preface).

218. Tomkins, *The Third World Conference on Faith and Order*, 56.

219. Torrance, "Eschatology and Eucharist," 339.

220. Baillie and Marsh, *Intercommunion*, 56.

4. The Third Word Conference of Faith and Order— Lund, Sweden (1952)

That basic division between "catholics" and "protestants" led to a "turning point" at the Third World Conference of Faith and Order. At Lund it became evident that a new methodological approach for overcoming church divisions was desperately needed. Ever since its second world conference (1937), Faith and Order had leaned on the comparative method of study. This method was fruitful. It helped churches to understand one another like never before. But that was about all. It exposed that "deep difference" between "catholics" and "protestants," but it could not help to bridge that difference. Some would even argue, including Torrance, that the comparative method actually fostered a hardening of differences between churches.

The new approach, as outlined by Tomkins, Chairman of the Working Committee, would be more critical and constructive.

> We have seen very clearly that we can make no real advance toward unity if we only compare our several conceptions of the nature of the churches and the traditions in which they are embodied. But once again it has been proved true that as we seek to draw close to Christ we come close to one another. We need, therefore, to penetrate behind our divisions to a deeper and richer understanding of the mystery of the God-given union of Christ with his church. We need increasingly to realize that the separate histories of our churches find their full meaning only if seen in the perspective of God's dealings with his whole people."[221]

This view was echoed by Leonard Hodgson, the theological secretary of Faith and Order, who in his address at Lund pointed out the futility of going endlessly "round and round in the same circle, explaining ourselves to one another."[222] He calls for a "real step forward" to unity by joining "together in seeking light on mysteries which are common to us all."[223]

However, the papers presented at Lund show that Faith and Order had already begun moving forward. Instead of merely outlining their church's position, the contributing authors were asked to write construc-

221. Tomkins, *The Third World*, 15.
222. Ibid., 122.
223. Ibid.

tive theological papers, for the purpose of shedding light, from every direction, on the "fundamental problems involved." "Eschatology and Eucharist" satisfied that demand, by showing how an eschatological understanding of the sacraments could overcome the disunity at the Lord's Table.

Indeed it was at the Lund conference where eschatology began to claim an important place in ecumenical discussions.[224] Torrance's essay may have given impetus to this change. In his introductory statement at Lund on the role of Faith and Order in the upcoming Second Assembly of the WCC, W. A. Visser't Hooft, the General Secretary of the WCC, noted that the "eschatological dimension" of Christian faith had not yet been given "its full place" in the ecumenical discussions.[225] He was not thinking about eschatology in the traditional sense. The church, he adds, "is itself an eschatological reality," for it represents "the new age and the new creation in the midst of the old age and old creation."[226] "We must learn to think of the Church in more dynamic terms, more as belonging to the new world and the coming age . . ."[227]

But the turn to eschatology at Lund probably had more to do with the broad agenda of the World Council of Churches. In 1950, at its meeting in Toronto, the Central Committee of the WCC decided to make Christian *hope* the main theme for its Second Assembly in Evanston, Illinois (1954).[228]

5. *"Ways of Worship"*

"Ways of Worship" was the third theological commission that presented a report at the Lund conference. Although Torrance was not officially

---

224. See the definition for "Eschatology" by E. Clapsis in the *Dictionary of the Ecumenical Movement*, 403f.

225. Tomkins, *The Third World*, 136.

226. Ibid.

227. Ibid.

228. Few things have ever provoked as much interest and debate inside the WCC as the Evanston theme of "hope." European churches generally embraced the theme; whereas churches in North America, where despair was less acute, did not. The report on the theme was crafted by thirty leading theologians (Torrance was not one) over three years. Running over twenty pages, the report contains a remarkably christocentric declaration of hope. True hope, it states, is not a human desire but is the "product in us" of God's acts in history and in Jesus Christ. See Gaines, *The World Council of Churches*, 1140–67.

involved with this commission, he displayed a deep interest in the subject of worship. His essay for the Commission for Intercommunion, "Eschatology and Eucharist," is obviously germane to the subject. For "catholics," the Eucharist represents the heart of Christian worship. This is "liturgical" worship, as opposed to relatively "free" worship of some Protestant churches. Liturgy comes from the Greek word *leitourgia*, which means "public service." According to the root meaning of the word, then, all church worship is liturgical. But liturgical worship has come to mean worship according to "fixed forms," a prescribed set of prayers, hymns, and scriptural readings. It is well known that the Pentecostal movement fostered a revival of "free" worship across church lines. Less well-known is the extent and influence of the liturgical movement in the middle of the twentieth century.[229] It made an impact on many of the member churches of the WCC. This movement was centered on the revival of the "sacramental character" of worship and the restoration of primitive models of worship. Naturally, many members of Faith and Order saw this movement as something that could bring churches closer together. Some even expected the church's renewal to "come from the altar."[230]

Torrance backed the liturgical movement, but he also expressed concerns about the theology undergirding some liturgical forms. The Report on Worship stated that "all worship is by and within the family of God's people, alike in heaven and on earth."[231] Torrance acknowledged that the "earthly liturgy" in some sense participates in the "heavenly liturgy," but he felt that this participation needed to be defined more precisely. Should it be understood in a platonic or an eschatological way? Torrance insists on the latter way of understanding, going against the tide in British liturgical renewal.[232]

---

229. Three of the most important scholarly works to stem from this movement are: Gregory Dix, *The Shape of the Liturgy*; Gabriel Hebert, *Liturgy and Society*; and Jean Daniel Benoit, *The Liturgical Renewal*.

230. Tomkins, *The Third World*, 272.

231. Ibid., 40.

232. According to Torrance, Dix interprets the history of the church's worship as the "transmutation of eschatology into liturgy" (Torrance, "Liturgy and Apocalypse," 3). Dix appears to conflate the ascension and parousia. "In the primitive conception there is but *one eschaton, one* 'coming,' the 'coming *to* the Father' of redeemed mankind, which is the realization of the Kingdom of God" (Dix, *The Shape*, 265).

He bases his case on the Apocalypse of Saint John, the "most liturgical and most eschatological" book in the Bible in his view.[233] The Apocalypse does not posit an identity between the earthly liturgy and the heavenly liturgy, as the Orthodox Church believes, but instead reveals the uniqueness of the heavenly liturgy. Nor does Christ simply unite the earthly liturgy with the heavenly one. What we get in the Apocalypse, he argues, is an "echo" of the heavenly liturgy, since the heavenly liturgy cannot be translated into earthly language.[234] One needs the Spirit to understand it. In fact, Torrance's words here *echo* points he made in his essay "Eschatology and Eucharist."

He did not write anything on worship for Faith and Order, but he did for the Church Service Society of Scotland in 1953. "Liturgy and Apocalypse" was written in response to disappointment over the fact that the theological revival in Scotland had not had a measurable effect on the liturgical life of the church there. Torrance was sympathetic, but he maintained that sound theology is the key to liturgical renewal. Further, a renewed liturgy would be an eschatologically oriented one. "The crucial point in this relation between theology and liturgy is the inter-relation between liturgy and eschatology."[235] It is the point where our hearts should be raised "above and beyond our theological and liturgical expressions in wonder and expectation."[236]

In order to get to this stage, however, one must pay close heed to the Book of Revelation. Revelation, for Torrance, is essentially the "unveiling" of Jesus Christ. At Alyth this meant that Christ is the "clue to history." Here Christ is the clue to true Christian worship. The "essence of Christian liturgy," he writes, is the "celebration of the resurrection."[237]

Liturgy should lead to doxology. It should be a gateway into heaven, to the Lamb upon the throne and the hosts of angels, to the kingdom of God and the new age. These things are eschatological realities; however, that means they cannot be fully revealed before the advent of Christ

---

233. Torrance, "Liturgy and Apocalypse," 4. In regard to the relationship between the Revelation and the liturgies of the early church, see Piper, "The Apocalypse of John," 10–21. Rather than being simply the source of the liturgies of the early church, Piper argues that Revelation reflects the liturgies of the early church. This view is echoed by Cabaniss in "A Note on the Liturgy," 78–86.

234. Torrance, "Liturgy and Apocalypse," 13, 14.

235. Ibid., 3.

236. Ibid.

237. Ibid., 10.

and the close of this age. The Apocalypse tells us that the new age has broken into the present age, but it also tells us that this age is essentially veiled until the final advent of Christ. That explains why we must still use the language and symbols of the old age to describe the new age. Liturgists have a daunting task. They have to try and put "new wine into old wineskins," while this age is slipping away and the "old wineskins" are breaking down. They have suffered the judgment of the cross. If a liturgy is platonically conceived, the final result is an earthly liturgy that purports to be an image of a perfect heavenly liturgy. But when a liturgy is eschatologically conceived, it will epitomize the sharp conflict between the kingdom of God and the kingdoms of the world.

This kind of liturgy will also yield to the advent presence of Christ. Liturgical language will be "transfigured in the Spirit on the Lord's Day."[238] The heavenly liturgy will supervene upon the earthly liturgy. According to Saint John, the heavenly liturgy is given to the church as the Song of Moses and the Lamb. It is a song that "looks back" and "looks forward." For Torrance, the liturgy of heaven "centres on the self-presentation of the Lamb of God before the Father," as our "Advocate and Intercessor."[239]

This explains why the Eucharist is the heart of the church's liturgy. However, contrary to Anglo-Catholic assumptions, the Spirit does not unite the eucharistic liturgy with the heavenly liturgy. The Eucharist is not about the sacrifice of Christ or the church's spiritual offering in Christ. As we learned earlier, the eucharistic liturgy "echoes" the heavenly liturgy. It is sacrifice, though, in that it is a "counter-sacrifice of praise and thanksgiving," in response to Christ's once-for-all sacrifice for sins and his ongoing work of intercession before the Father.[240]

Yet even this echo of the "New Song" is "essentially imperfect and fragmentary." The reason is that the church's liturgy is mingled with apocalyptic. While the liturgy discloses something of the new age, it cannot help giving us a distorted picture of it. For the liturgy itself suffers from the judgment upon this corrupt age. This leads to a "conflict" between the "perfect liturgical form of Heaven and the liturgical forms of earth."[241] This conflict will be resolved in the final advent, when all the "forms and fashions" of the world will have passed away, when the Eucharist will be

238. Ibid., 8.
239. Ibid., 13.
240. Ibid.
241. Ibid., 15.

supplanted by the marriage supper of the Lamb. However, that conflict can be suspended now. In order for that to happen an "eschatological substitution" must takes place in the church's liturgy. After all, Christian worship is really about the "celebration of the resurrection." Liturgy must be geared towards the advent presence (*parousia*) of Christ. Then the Holy Spirit will lift Christian hearts and minds (*sursum corda*) above the liturgy, in contemplation of the heavenly chorus. The Spirit can literally turn earthly language into a heavenly language (*glossolalia*).

Torrance does not doubt that liturgical worship can bring churches together. He even thinks it can bring the whole world closer together. The liturgy's eschatological orientation includes a universal orientation. It should pertain to the "whole creation," since all creation cries out for redemption (cf. Rom 8:22). The Eucharistic liturgy should also "anticipate *and echo* that final Messianic Supper," where everyone who thirsts is invited to come and drink.[242] In other words, it should reflect the "world-mission" of the church, which includes evangelism and ecumenism.

In sum, Torrance insists that "true" Christian liturgy must be "open toward heaven," to the advent presence of the risen Christ, and "open to the whole world of men, in prayer for their salvation, and the whole creation in prayer for its renewal."[243]

6. A New Beginning: Faith and Order after Lund

Lund was also the birthplace of a new Faith and Order commission on Christ and the church. Its maxim would be "the way to the Centre is the way to unity." Torrance played a key role in its formation. At the conference his committee got a request for two memoranda on the subject of the church in relation to the doctrine of Christ and the Holy Spirit.[244] Torrance agreed to submit the one that would deal with the church and Christ. The outcome of this was "Where do we go from Lund?" (1953). The title betrays the pessimism that Lund produced; yet the contents manifest optimism as well. "Lund marks the end of an old era in ecumenical theology, and the beginning of a new era in which we have promise of a development in modern times that may well correspond

---

242. Ibid., 17.

243. Ibid., 16.

244. Minutes of the Meeting of Commission of Faith and Order, and of the Working Committee, 28 August 1952, Lund, Sweden.

eventually to the development of ecumenical theology in the fourth and fifth centuries."[245]

Torrance was optimistic because he was convinced that the unity of the church was much more profound that the divisions within it. He points to the general acceptance of "all the great doctrines of faith." He attributes this progress to the influence of biblical theology and to the renewed interest in classical and Reformation theology. Still he urges the churches to go further, building on the unity they already have. However, he does not think this is feasible without a new ecumenical method. Such a method, he adds, would have to be "analogous to the nature of theological truth."[246] This tells us that even at this relatively early point in his career, Torrance is something of a "scientific" theologian. The central theological truth for him is, of course, the doctrine of Christ, and it is through it that other theological doctrines such as the church are to be studied.

"Where do we go from Lund?" represents a new phase in Torrance's approach to the problem of church unity, but it is one he believes was sanctioned at Lund. "Because we believe in Jesus Christ we believe also in the Church as the Body of Christ." This statement is found in its report.[247] Torrance feels that the time is ripe to think out the implications of it. He would like to make it the "starting point" of a doctrine of the church. He notes that this has been attempted before, in the fifth century and sixteenth century, through Calvin especially, but he says it is time to attempt this afresh in order to "set forth in truly dogmatic form" the doctrine of the church "as the Body of Christ."[248]

This will require overcoming the tendency to think of the Body of Christ as a "mere image or metaphor" for the church. For Torrance, it refers to an "essential reality."[249] Yet, at the same time, it is an *analogous* reality. The Body of Christ refers to an "analogical relation" between Christ and his church; so that the relation is neither one of an "identity" nor of a "difference" between the church and Christ.[250] The relation has

245. Torrance, "Where Do We Go," 53.

246. Ibid., 54.

247. Tomkins, *The Third World Conference.*

248. Torrance, "Where Do We Go," 57.

249. Ibid.

250. Ibid., 58.

to be modeled naturally after the hypostatic union of the two natures in the one person of Christ.[251]

First, he argues that the "hypostatic union" needs to be made more dynamic, in accord with the whole mission and work of Christ.[252] This includes thinking in terms of the death, resurrection, and second advent of Christ. This dynamic, christological approach to theological loci has become a refrain in Torrance. We heard it in his treatment of the sacraments and worship and in his response to the modern eschatological debate.

There is another reason why he thinks a study of the church as the Body of Christ is imperative. It has to do with safeguarding the humanity of Christ in the church. At Lund Torrance sensed a tendency in some quarters to think about the church as the Body of the Trinity or as the Body of the Holy Spirit. The Holy Spirit is the effective cause of the church's participation in Christ, and the relation between Christ and the church is grounded on the Trinitarian relations, but the "'divine nature' of the church is not God, nor the Spirit, but the *Word made flesh*, who is True God and True Man."[253] A doctrine of the church as the Body of Christ, then, must be informed by a "triangular relation between the church and the historical Christ, the risen and ascended Mediator, and the Christ who will come again in His full Humanity as well as Deity."[254]

"Where do we go from Lund?" also deals with church tradition, another divisive issue that emerged at the conference. In fact a new commission was set up to deal with the subject. Torrance was not on this commission but offers a way forward on the subject by means of a tentative application of his doctrine of the church.

---

251. Karl Barth is Torrance's inspiration here. The "whole question of the analogical relation between Christ and his church has undergone the most ruthless scientific searching and criticism particularly at the hands of Karl Barth" (ibid., 57). However, he indicates that his interpretation of Barth in this regard has come by way of von Balthasar's perceptive study, *Karl Barth, Deutung und Dartsellung seiner Theologie* (1951).

252. Torrance, "Where Do We Go," 59.

253. Ibid., 58. An example of the error Torrance refers to is found in a book he reviewed. See William Robinson's *The Biblical Doctrine of the Church*. Robinson contends that "like" Christ the Church is "both human and divine" (ibid., 119). And just as in Christ there are "two natures in one Person," so in the Church, there are "two natures in one body."(ibid.).

254. Torrance, "Where Do We Go," 58.

Every church is prone to make dead traditions, instead of the living Christ, its "clothing." Yet a church cannot simply discard tradition (*paradosis*) without falling into a docetic ecclesiology. The notion that the church is the Body of Christ (the Word made flesh) dictates an outer "ecclesiastical" form for the church. But in Torrance's view, this outer form must be regulated by the "inner" or "dogmatic" form of the church, just as the sacrament is given its meaning through the Word (*kerygma*). In other words, there is a need for a church *Tradition*, a "*traditio corporis*" that "takes place through the whole *kerygmatic* continuity of the Church."[255] In this case the church will be regulated by its inner form, so that the growth of the church as the Body of Christ will be in accord with the growth of the church "into the Mind of Christ." Church dogma is not identical to the mind of Christ, but is an expression both of the church's spiritual capacity to know this mind and to bring the Body of the Christ into conformity with it. Dogma functions to ensure the Body is not separated from the Head, that the Head in not made subject to the Body, but that the Body is made subject to the Head (Eph 1:21). Through baptism and the Holy Spirit the church *is* the Body of Christ. But in another sense, it has to *become* the Body of Christ, since it still participates in the fallen creation. Thus it has to "put off" those human traditions and the forms of the world that it has accumulated.

This notion of the growth of the church as the Body of Christ is one of the things Torrance takes from Calvin's ecclesiology. It is really the teleological aspect of the church's existence. When we think about the growth of the church as a Body, we are reminded of the parable of the mustard seed in the Gospels (Matt 13:31–32, par.). Yet, for Torrance, there is no real analogy in nature to the growth of the church. The secret of the church is that its "teleological growth" must be understood in terms of its "eschatological fulfillment."[256] In other words, the real analogy for growth is the life of Jesus Christ, a life that is fulfilled in death, resurrection, and advent.

As for church tradition, Torrance thinks the Orthodox Church approximates the ideal. There he sees the unity of "the dogmatic and ecclesiastical forms."[257] Yet he also detects serious flaws. The unity in this church is not understood in dynamic terms. In other words, eschatologi-

255. Ibid., 61.
256. Ibid., 62.
257. Ibid.

cal fulfillment is not balanced by teleological growth. This explains why Orthodox theology and liturgy have changed little over the course of a thousand years. There is certainly growth in the Roman Catholic Church, but the growth in this case is separated from eschatological fulfillment. As a consequence, you have an ecclesiastical form in divergence from the dogmatic form. Torrance points to the recent papal dogma on the Assumption of the Virgin Mary as a glaring illustration of this problem.[258]

With the Lutheran church the situation is nearly the reverse. Dogmatic form overshadows ecclesiastical form. Hence this Church is, in Torrance's view, the "most confessional Church in the world."[259] While tradition counts for little in the Lutheran Church, it is the exact opposite in the Anglican Church. This church prides itself on the preservation of the true ecclesiastical form. Yet that is not balanced by dogmatic efforts to have this form subject to the mind of Christ. Here it appears that neither teleological growth nor eschatological fulfillment is taken seriously.

Torrance gives a mixed review of his own church tradition, the Reformed. On one hand he lauds Calvin for allowing the inner and outer forms of the church to penetrate one another under the impact of the Word of God. His efforts at trying to restore the ancient Catholic Church testify to his balanced approach. On the other, he argues that the Reformed church suffered because of the influence of Schleiermacher. This theologian believed in dogmatic and ecclesiastical integration, but unfortunately he did not conceive this integration in light of its eschatological fulfillment. Instead it was understood as "immanent" in the consciousness and experience of the church.

258. Read Torrance's review of "Evangelisches Gutachen," 90–96. He claims that it is "contrary to the unique eschatological character of Christ's Resurrection and ascension, and the unique relation this bears to the resurrection of all who will rise again at the Parousia" (ibid., 92).

259. Torrance, "Where Do We Go," 63.

5

Eschatology and the Church, Part II

The Theological Commission on Christ and the Church, 1955–1963

A. Atonement and the Church

THIS COMMISSION WAS SET UP BY THE WORKING COMMITTEE OF FAITH and Order in 1953. It was divided into a North American and a European section, which Torrance led as secretary until 1955. The Theological Commission on Christ and the Church (TCCC) marked the beginning of that new era in ecumenical theology. Its mandate was to explore the "nature and work of Christ and the Holy Spirit" within a "united Church of thought."[1] It held its first meeting at Evanston in 1954, in conjunction with the Second Assembly of the WCC. The starting point for discussion was Torrance's paper "The Atonement and the Oneness of the Church" (1954). The paper builds upon that christological approach to church unity he had sketched out in "Where do we go from Lund?" But that is not the only explanation for it. According to a letter he wrote to Barth in 1953, it was also meant to head off Anglican misappropriations of a christological doctrine of the church.

> In thinking over the work we tried to do at Lund, and since I wrote my article in SJT on it, I am very convinced that what the Ecumenical movement needs more than anything else in its Christological approach to the doctrine of the church is a proper doctrine of atonement, with the radical substitution which that involves—for that will cut away from them all false notions of ecclesiasticism, liturgy, sacrifice, etc., and assert the sole lord-

1. Commission on Faith and Order: Minutes, Commission and Working committee, n. 21 (1954) 18.

ship of Christ in the most fundamental way-otherwise many will misread a Christological doctrine of the Church as the Body of Christ and interpret it in the direction of *Christus prolongatus* or *coredemptio*—both are which constant temptations of the Anglicans and devastatingly harmful.[2]

It is safe to say that Barth would have welcomed this theological decision, though we should not believe that the idea of Christ's "radical substitution" is a brand new idea in Torrance. In that same year Barth published *Die Kirchliche Dogmatik* IV/1, the first part of his doctrine of atonement, which is grounded on the radical substitution of Christ as *vere Deus* and *vere homo*.[3] We cannot be sure if Torrance had this latest volume of the *Dogmatik* in his hands, but we know for certain that he was inspired by Barth's early ideas on the atonement.[4] An essay by F. W. Camfield offers us a clue.[5] Torrance's own piece, "The Atonement and the Oneness of the Church" takes a paragraph from it. But the most important point is that Camfield's essay is inspired by Barth. This is indicated by the author's first words in it. "'I believe that we have to learn anew what the Holy Scriptures say and mean by substitution of Jesus Christ and satisfaction.' These words, spoken by Barth in the course of a discussion on the 'Christian Witness,' provide much food for reflection."[6]

However, unlike Camfield and Barth, Torrance is concerned in his article with the application of the atonement to the disunity of the church. It is about *at-one-ment*, how Christ makes the church one in him. It all begins with the act of Christ. The "oneness of the Church is grounded in the incorporating and atoning action of Christ."[7] Earlier he postulated the church's incorporation into Christ through the sacra-

2. Torrance to Karl Barth, 13 March 1953. Torrance was undoubtedly aware too of Barth's stress on the church's utter dependence on the Word of God. This utter dependency could be forgotten if all focus is on the church as the Body of Christ through sacramental incorporation. "The Real Church is the assembly which is called, united, held together and governed by the Word of her Lord, or she is not a Real Church" (Barth, "The Real Church," 342).

3. See especially section 58.3,4 "Jesus Christ the Mediator," 122–28.

4. Torrance, as is well known, spearheaded the translation of *Die Kirchliche Dogmatik* into English. Along with G. W. Bromiley, he was the editor of most of the series. *KD* IV/1, *Die Lehre von der Versohnung* was published in English in 1956 by T. & T. Clark, Edinburgh.

5. Camfield, "The Idea of Substitution in the Doctrine of the Atonement."

6. Ibid., 282. The quote is from Barth's *God in Action*, 123.

7. Torrance, "The Atonement," 246.

ments. Now he postulates Christ's incorporation with us through his life, death, and resurrection.

At first blush, it looks like Torrance is opening the door to the thing he desperately wants to fend off, a *Christus prolongatus*! Yet in fact he gets what he is after, and the hypostatic union is his key. But not so simply. He follows through on his desire to give this classical concept more dynamic expression. He speaks of Christ's "incorporating and atoning action." Earlier he drew our attention to a "mutual involution" between the "gathering up" and the "incorporation" that happens through Word and Sacrament, now he propounds a "mutual involution" between the hypostatic union and the atonement, based on the history of Jesus Christ. "It is one of the most pressing needs of theology," he writes, "to have the hypostatic union restated much more in terms of the mission of Christ, much more from the perspective of the cross and resurrection."[8] In effect, Torrance wants us to understand the hypostatic union in terms of *teleological development* and *eschatological fulfillment*.

The "hypostatic union" is not a concept found in the Bible, but Torrance believes it is one that accurately sums up the biblical account of Jesus' life and ministry; although when it comes to the biblical account, Torrance is indebted to modern biblical theologians, especially William Manson.[9]

Christ's incorporation with us began with his baptism, and it was consummated in his death on the cross. In between, he gathered the twelve disciples around him, forging his union with us, the "Body of sinners." He sealed this union when he celebrated the Passover meal with his disciples. Jesus' life and ministry, then, is really about the "One" incorporating himself into the "Many," thus forming a new Israel out of the twelve from old Israel. Torrance also finds support for his thesis in the Epistle to the Hebrews. Here he sees Christ "learning obedience" and at the same time "bringing His relation to sinners to their *telos* through suffering."[10]

The critical point is that the church, as the Body of Christ, is "grounded" on this "mutual involution" between the hypostatic union and atonement.[11] Whereas the "One and the Many is the doctrine of the

---

8. Torrance, "The Atonement," 246.

9. See Manson, "The Norm," 33–42.

10. Torrance, "The Atonement," 247.

11. Ibid., 248.

Christ," the "Many and the One is the doctrine of the Church, the Body of Christ."[12] At Pentecost the church is sent into the world as the Many representing the One. The church, though, does not merely try to represent Christ. The cross and resurrection are pivotal. On Torrance's view, the breathing of the Spirit after the resurrection (John 20:22) signifies the transfer of the hypostatic union from Christ to church, an act that enables it to participate in the mystery of Christ.

In order to guard the church against all impulses that would naturalize it, Torrance adds two more classical concepts to the hypostatic union, the *anhypostasia* and *enhypostasia*. They assert that the atonement is the one complete act of the God-man. Jesus Christ is "at once the One and the Many." The *anhypostasia* asserts that the atonement is an act of God. [13] The *enhypostasia* asserts that it is an act of God *as man*—and something else. It indicates that a "concrete substitution" of our humanity takes place; hence Christ does not enter into the relationship between God and man as a "third party."[14] The one Son of God becomes also the one Son of Man. Christ atones as God and Man, not as God alone. He is at once the *judge* who condemned sin in the flesh, and the *judged* who was obedient onto death.

Christ's substitutionary atonement has profound implications for our doctrine of the church, as the Body of Christ. For what is true for the One is true for the Many. The church therefore has to yield to Christ. It can only do this by imitating him. "The only way the Church can follow Him is by way of *anhypostasia*, by way of self-denial and crucifixion, by letting Christ take its place and displace self-assertion; and by way of *enhypostasia*, by way of incorporation and resurrection."[15] Sacramentally, this means it must live out the meaning of baptism and Eucharist. The way of the cross is the way to resurrection. Likewise it is the way to reunion for the church.

This brings us back to the church's analogical relation to Christ. The incarnation is *sui generis*. Therefore the *anhypostasia* and *enhypostasia*,

12. Ibid., 249.

13. Torrance points to Gustaf Aulen's *Christus Victor* model as an example of an *anhypostatic* doctrine of atonement. If this model of Christ's work is right, he says, then he says the "deed of atonement would be a pure act of God over the head of man" apart from any act of incorporation (Torrance, "The Atonement," 250).

14. Torrance, "The Atonement," 251. Regarding these notions, see Camfield, "The Idea of Substitution," 285; also Barth, *Church Dogmatics* IV/1 58.3, 123.

15. Torrance, "The Atonement," 252.

like the hypostatic union itself, has to be applied gingerly to the church. Torrance is aware that he is pushing the envelope (another reason to exercise caution), and he gives only a tentative outline of the approach that is needed. "*Logically*" this involves recognizing that the relationship between the church and Christ is neither one of "identity" nor "difference," but rather one of "*proportionaliter.*"[16] "*Christologically*," it means that the terms *inconfuse* and *inseparabiliter* need be applied to the relation between Christ and the Body of Christ in a "secondary and cognate sense."[17] *Soteriologically*, this demands recognition of Christ's *mirifica commutatio* (wonderful exchange), even in the church's work of reconciliation. *Pneumatologically*, this involves seeing the church's relation to Christ as effectuated through the work of the Spirit.

When the *anhypostasia* is applied to the church as the Body of Christ then it has "no *per se* existence, no independent hypostasis, apart from atonement and communion through the Holy Spirit."[18] When the *enhypostasia* is applied, the church "is given in Christ a real *hypostasis* through incorporation, and therefore concrete function in union with Him."[19]

As we noted, Torrance's decision to bring to bear the doctrine of substitutionary atonement on the church safeguards the eschatological nature of the church. Although in this context, he thinks about eschatology in an unusual way. The church has no independent existence but only an "eschatological relation" to Christ. This means it is utterly dependent upon God's free actions "for and in the Church": the substitutionary death of Christ, Pentecost, and the *kerygma*. Meanwhile the *enhypostasia*

16. Ibid., 253.

17. Ibid.

18. Ibid., 254. The christological use of this classical formula can be traced back to the sixth-century monk Leontius of Byzantium, but there is no evidence that he used it in the way Torrance uses it. For Torrance, the *anhypostasis-enhypostasis* means that the Christ's human nature has no independent existence and that it exists only in the *hypostasis* of Christ. According to Le Ron Shults, though, Torrance's application of the formula owes more to nineteenth-century Protestant scholastics (although there is some precedent for Torrance's use of it in John of Damascus [c.652–c.750]). For Leontius, the *enhypostasis* meant simply "to have a concrete existence," not to have existence *in another* (Shults, "A Dubious," 438). Therefore even the *Logos* could be described as *enhypostatic* (ibid., 440).

19. Torrance, "The Atonement," 255.

asserts a "teleological relation between the Church and Christ in terms of a real continuity of being."[20]

Like the *anhypostasia* and *enhypostasia* relation, the eschatological and teleological relation should not be separated. Otherwise one is left with a strange dichotomy, an "eschatological view" and an "ontological view" view of the church.[21] In the first case, the church is conceived as an "event" that depends strongly on the free movement of the Word and Spirit, but not so strongly on incorporation into Christ. This view also tends to foster a separation between the visible church and Christ. In the second case, the church is conceived as a reality dependent on the incarnation and the sacraments. However, this view can produce a confusion of Christ and the church, so that the church becomes an "extension of the incarnation." The continuity of the church is thus defined in terms of historical succession, because the extension is not viewed in light of the resurrection of Christ but only in terms of time and history as commonly perceived.

Torrance does not furnish us with examples of these views of the church. They seem, though, to correspond roughly to that basic division between "evangelical" and "catholic" understandings of the church; more specifically, a hyper-Barthian view and an Anglo-Catholic view respectively.[22]

His ecumenically unifying solution is to have us think of the church's relation to Christ *anhypostatically* and *enhypostatically* at the same time. Then we have an ontology of the church that is also understood eschatologically, in terms of the death and resurrection of Christ; and an eschatology that is understood ontologically, in terms of its "substantial union" with the "Risen, Ascended and Advent Lord."[23] Here we have a solution that is parallel to Torrance's solution to the modern eschatological debate. This involves interpreting the "eschatological end" teleologically and the "teleological end" eschatologically.

---

20. Ibid.

21. Ibid., 256.

22. See Karl Barth, "The Church." We say "hyper Barthian" because in Torrance's view this would be a distortion of Barth's doctrine of the church. Even in this essay Torrance sees an inchoate ontology of the church; and he would probably see *KD* IV/1 as the development of this idea. A better representative of the "eschatological view" of the church might be Gustaf Aulen (see n. 14).

23. Torrance, "The Atonement," 256.

The church's oneness is grounded in the oneness of Christ and his atoning and incorporating action for the church. Torrance calls the oneness of the church in Christ the "final and commanding truth . . . the enduring reality, the eternal indicative."[24] Clearly the New Testament and primitive Christianity give us every reason to confess that the church is "one, holy and catholic." Yet we still need an explanation for the apparent disunity of the church.

The "impossible seems to have happened," Torrance exclaims; the Body of Christ, the church, is divided.[25] To be sure, the church is not divided because members of the Body want it divided. Division is the often the unintended consequence of the saints trying to preserve the church's oneness, its holiness and its unity in Christ. For Torrance, the "enigma of sin" and the "mystery of iniquity" are ultimately to blame for the disunity of the church on earth.[26] Nonetheless, he believes that all Christians are "culpably implicated" in this sin and this iniquity. How so? Strangely, the reason lies in the fact that the church is the Body of Christ—which is "no mere figure but reality." Christ's incarnation means he took on the "body of the flesh" in order that through this body he might reconcile us to him. "For He made Him who knew no sin to be sin for us, that we might become the righteousness of God in Him" (2 Cor 5:21). He reconciled us through the cross, and the cross is where the church's oneness is "consummated." There Christ put to death the body of sin, and all divisions between him and us and between one another (Eph 2:11f.) within the Body. The cross is the point of our reconciliation, but it is also the point of the revelation of our sinful divisions within the church. "Confession of Oneness with Christ carries with it confession of oneness with our fellows in sin. As we acknowledge that we are guilty of the breaking of His body on the Cross, so we cannot but acknowledge that we are implicated in the guilt of rending the Church."[27]

It is not enough, however, to confess our division before the cross. The church must allow the judgment of the cross to put an end to those divisions. In one very real sense, it has put them away. In baptism the church is also incorporated into the risen and ascended Christ. One cannot forget, then, that the church's oneness is both a mystery hidden in

---

24. Ibid., 268.
25. Torrance, "Our Oneness," 275.
26. Ibid.
27. Ibid., 277.

Christ and an eschatological reality that will be fully revealed at the final *parousia*. The *parousia* will also be the final judgment that puts away all sin and all remaining divisions. This is why Torrance feels that intercommunion is instrumental for the healing of church divisions. When we proclaim, at the Communion table, the Lord's death till he comes, "we eat and drink judgement to our sin and division."[28] It is there that hope of unity triumphs over the despair caused by our disunity; because here too we are given a foretaste of the marriage supper of the Lamb and of that a participation in the perfect oneness of the church in Christ.

Torrance thinks of the unity of the church as being "eschatologically in arrears."[29] However, this does not mean the unity of the church is something that lies entirely in the future. The future unity of the Church with Christ refers less to a product of progressive development and more to a "revelation of what is a present but hidden reality."[30] In this age we receive a partial revelation of that hidden reality through the Lord's Supper and the Holy Spirit.

B. Ministry and the Church

At its meeting in 1955, the Working Committee of Faith and Order concentrated its attention on the subject of priesthood. It discussed three essays on the subject. Why the sudden interest? About this time ecumenical meetings were taking place between Anglicans and other churches in Britain, and Torrance believed that a union between the Church of Scotland and the Church of England was in the offing. He also staked hope on the discussions taking place between Anglicans and the Lutheran and Reformed churches on the continent, but was worried that the Anglican priesthood would pose a serious problem for "continental Christians."[31] Thus it was high time to clarify this subject. In the end, the Committee agreed that priesthood was one of those "fundamental issues" over which Anglicans are divided from other Protestants. For Torrance, what was needed was a proper understanding of the priesthood. He was thus impelled towards an intensive study of the theological significance

---

28. Ibid., 278.

29. Ibid.

30. Ibid., 279.

31. Commission on Faith and Order: Minutes, Commission and Working committee, n. 22 (1955) 16.

of the priesthood. The fruit of his labor was *Royal Priesthood*, which he presented to the Faith and Order committee the following year.[32]

There is no doubt that the existence of a special priesthood in the Anglican Church would have hampered union talks with other Protestant churches. Even the word "priest" is problematic. Outside the Gospels, it is rarely used in the New Testament. It is associated more with Judaism than the emerging Christian community. Neither Jesus nor the apostles referred to themselves as priests. "Priest" is the Latin equivalent of "presbyter," the Greek word for *elder*. Elder, of course, was frequently used in the New Testament church. Even the apostle Peter refers to himself as an elder. But "priest" is a poor translation of "presbyter," since its actual meaning makes it closer to the New Testament word for priest, *hiereus*. A presbyter in the New Testament is either a ruler and/or a teacher, but a "catholic" presbyter, in many cases, is much more than that. He (or she) has a sacerdotal ministry. Thus the presbyter absolves Christians of their sins and presides over the "sacrifice" of the Eucharist.

However, the priesthood need not divide Anglicans from other Protestants. Luther, after all, was not against the priesthood *per se*. He was only opposed to a mediatorial priesthood, set apart from the rest of the church. He championed the "priesthood of all believers" (Exod 19:6; 1 Pet 2:9; Rev 1:6; 5:10), those who sacrifice their love for the world and instead offer glory to God through a life of faith. Calvin, and Reformed theologians after him, drew attention to the *munus sacerdotale*, the priestly office of Christ (Ps 110:4; Heb 6:20—10:25). For Calvin, it was important to distinguish the true priesthood of Christ from the false "Popish" priesthood with its sacrificial Masses for sins.

Although *Royal Priesthood* addresses a modern ecumenical problem, we may also see it as an attempt to integrate the particular interests of Luther and Calvin. For while Luther extolled the priesthood of believers, he did not study its connection with the priesthood of Christ; and Calvin's appreciation for the priesthood of Christ was not matched by an appreciation of the priesthood of the church as the Body of Christ. *Royal Priesthood*, however, is equally about the priesthood of Christ and the priesthood of the church. Torrance sees an intimate (though not identi-

---

32. The expressed aim of *Royal Priesthood* was to foster unity between the Church of Scotland and the Church of England. In his dedication he writes: "To the CHURCH OF ENGLAND, the church of my mother and my wife, and the CHURCH OF SCOTLAND, the church of my father, in earnest prayer that they may soon be one."

cal) relation between the two. It is an instance of that relation between the One and the Many, which is the doctrine of Christ, and the Many and the One which is the doctrine of the church, the Body of Christ. Indeed Torrance avoids the phrase "priesthood of believers." It is responsible, he feels, for a "ruinous individualism" that characterizes much of Protestantism.

In order to appreciate fully *Royal Priesthood*, it is important to recognize two related points. First, it builds upon principles enunciated in the essay "Atonement and the Oneness of the Church."[33] Thus the priesthood of the church and the priesthood of Christ do not complement one another. In fact the former is wholly dependent on the latter. That is because Christ's priesthood is substitutionary. This brings us to the second point. While the essay relies upon Barth's doctrine of substitutionary atonement, *Royal Priesthood* relies on Barth's treatise on Christ's priesthood as expounded in *Die Kirchliche Dogmatik* IV/1,2 (1953–55). There are important differences, though. The ascension and eschatology are more prominent in *Royal Priesthood* than in *KD IV*; while the work of the Holy Spirit is more prominent in *KD IV* than in Torrance's monograph. Torrance also does something that Barth fails to do. He relates the royal priesthood of Christ to the church's worship and ministry.

1. The Royal Priest

While the church's priesthood is wholly grounded in Christ's priesthood, Christ's priesthood has roots in the priesthood of ancient Israel. His priesthood is first of all a fulfillment of the priesthood found there. According to Torrance, this was a "dual priesthood" represented by Moses and Aaron. But he makes the case that the priesthood of Moses was primary. He was "priest par excellence." For Torrance, we must remember, every part of salvation begins with the Word of God. This is even true of the priesthood. In the case of Moses, then, his main priestly function was not the offering of sacrifices but the "mediation of God's Word." He was the "high-priestly Logos."[34] Aaron's priesthood, on the

---

33. For more on the relation between the priesthood of Christ and the atonement see James B. Torrance's "The Priesthood of Jesus: A Study of the Doctrine of the Atonement." Although James does not focus on the church's corporate priesthood, his definition of Christ's priesthood clearly echoes (and shows the influence of) that of his elder brother.

34. On this point, Torrance is indebted to Schrenk's definition of ἱερεύς in Kittel's *Theological Dictionary of the New Testament* (257–83). However, Schrenk implies that

other hand, was basically one of "witness to God's Will." This was the liturgical, sacrificial priesthood. However, this priesthood could not stand alone. It was dependent on the prophetic priesthood of Moses.

Over time, though, that changed, according to Torrance. Israel rebelled against the Word of God and began to idolize the liturgical, sacrificial priesthood. But with the coming of Jesus Christ, the true nature of the priesthood was restored. It was "primarily as Word of God" that Jesus went to the cross. Jesus confesses our sins before God and pronounces God's judgment upon them (Heb 3:1; 4:14; 10:23). Moreover, the dual nature of the priesthood was restored. "The significant fact is that, while in Word Jesus exercises his prophetic ministry, in his action he exercises His priestly ministry."[35] The Word becomes incarnate, becomes the Suffering Servant of God.

The crucial point is that Jesus fulfilled once-and-for-all the priesthood of Israel, because he is the Son of God in the flesh.[36] For Torrance, this is the main lesson of Hebrews (cf. Heb 1:2–3). Jesus fulfilled it perfectly because he is the union of God and man, person and work, word and action. "He is Priest in final reality, fulfilling the Mosaic priesthood because His Word is identical with Kingly act; fulfilling the Aaronic priesthood because his offering is identical with His Person."[37] These features, then, make Jesus' priesthood a "Royal Priesthood." What is more, he not only fulfills the old priesthood, he fulfills it "for us." It is a substitutionary priesthood. As one of us in every way except sin, Christ "has done for us what we could not do." "For every high priest taken from among men is appointed for men in things pertaining to God" (Heb 5:1). He fulfilled all God required from his covenant partner in terms of "life, worship, and prayer." God still demands sacrifice and worship and from his covenant people, but (as we have learned) these things can only be an

---

the "high-priestly Logos" concept has more to do with the influence of the Jewish philosopher Philo (272–73). In his important study, Cyril Eastwood also argues that the priesthood in the Old Testament was essentially didactic, centred on the Word or the Law. "The priest is the mouthpiece of God," he writes. And this is what Moses was and remained. *The Royal Priesthood of the Faithful*, 19–21.

35. Torrance, *Royal Priesthood*, 9.

36. It is strange that in *Royal Priesthood* Torrance fails to even mention Melchizedek, "King of Salem, priest of the most High God." He defines Jesus' priesthood as "another order," but according to *The Epistle to the Hebrews* this is the order of Melchizedek (Heb. 6:20—7:17).

37. Torrance, *Royal Priesthood*, 14.

echo or counterpoint to Christ's one and eternal offering on our behalf. It is only fitting that this is done through words of thanksgiving and praise (cf. 1 Pet 2:5), since Christ's priestly action was foremost a proclamation of the Word.

Now this brings us to the priesthood of the church. This priesthood can be no more than a "participation" in Christ's priesthood. If we want to be schooled in the priesthood of the church, though, Torrance believes we must turn to St. Paul's epistles—despite the fact the apostle never mentions priests. The main point is that the liturgy (*leitourgos*) of this priesthood extends beyond the eucharistic celebration. As such it includes works of love in the church and suffering witness to the gospel outside the church. In Manson's words, "we must therefore 'go out' to Jesus, to where He was crucified 'outside the camp,' and must take our share of the shame he bore."[38] In short, it is a "liturgy done in the flesh, enacted in the body, as sacrificial oblation to God."[39] The model for this liturgy is the Suffering Servant. "The way in which the Church draws near to God is the way of the Son of Man."[40]

The priesthood of the church cannot neglect its eschatological side. Indeed, what Torrance says about the Eucharist can be said about the priesthood of the church. If we deny the eschatological element in it, we run the risk turning the church into a human church. The priesthood has several eschatological dimensions. After all, eschatology is not just about things that lie in the future. Eschatology is about gathering up the past too. This happens through the church's ministry, which involves a filling up in the Body of Christ of "that which is eschatologically in arrears of the sufferings of Christ."[41]

We have seen how the church's liturgical worship is bound up with apocalyptic. We must bear in mind, though, that eschatology cannot be divorced from teleology, which is "rooted" in the "prophetic view of the Kingdom" in the Bible. Christian worship thus represents a teleological fulfillment. Christ's one sacrifice abrogates all human sacrifices. It signals the beginning of the new age. This age is the endless Sabbath, or eternal worship in "spirit and truth." This kind of worship is delineated in the last two chapters of Hebrews. "Here we have a new understanding of

38. Manson, *The Epistle to the Hebrews*, 151.

39. Torrance, *Royal Priesthood*, 17. Cf. Rom 12:1; 15:16; Eph 5:2.

40. Ibid.

41. Torrance, "The Atonement," 257.

worship in terms of the finished work of Christ and in terms of the Spirit, in which we are free to worship God in true fear and love, in new obedience to the commandment of love."[42]

2. *The Body of Christ*

Like Barth (even more so, perhaps), Torrance is vulnerable to the charge of christomonism. The Holy Spirit does not stand out in his early writings, although he certainly does not ignore it. This is obvious in *Royal Priesthood*. "We cannot pay too much attention to the fact that the Holy Spirit was sent upon the church after crucifixion, resurrection, and the ascension. In that series Pentecost belongs as one of the mighty salvation events, and to that series the *parousia* will belong as the last."[43] Torrance also demonstrates a deep appreciation for the way the Reformers treated the Holy Spirit. Calvin's eschatology is described as "the doctrine of the Spirit and all that union with Christ through the Spirit involves."[44] He takes note of the "strong charismatic element" in Butzer's eschatology, which makes it an "eschatology of love." In *Royal Priesthood* we can see the influence of these two Reformers.

Notwithstanding these facts, there is no mistaking the fact that in Torrance the doctrine of the Holy Spirit plays a subordinate role to Christology—even in comparison to Karl Barth, who is routinely criticized for not paying enough attention to the third person of the Trinity. "The Church is not . . . the Body of the Holy Spirit"; it is "the Body of Christ."[45] "The 'divine nature' of the Church is not . . . the Holy Spirit, but the Word made flesh."[46] In *Royal Priesthood* we are told that the doctrine of the Spirit must have "Christology for its content (John 14:17, 26; 15:26; 16:13f)."[47] It is hard to take issue with this principle, but this means that pneumatology is "really Christology applied to the Church as

---

42. Torrance, *Royal Priesthood*, 19. In his commentary on Heb 13:15, Calvin describes the sacrifice of praise as the "finest worship of God, and the one which is to be preferred to all other exercises." "This, I say, is the rite of sacrifice which God commends to us today." Torrance, David and T. F. Torrance, *Calvin's Commentaries: The Epistle of Paul the Apostle to the Hebrews*, 211.

43. Torrance, *Royal Priesthood*, 23.

44. Torrance, *Kingdom and Church*, 101.

45. Torrance, "Where Do We Go," 58.

46. Ibid.

47. Torrance, *Royal Priesthood*, 25.

the Body of Christ."[48] The Creator Spirit "operates by creating out of the world a body (*soma*) which St. Paul calls the Body of Christ."[49] The body that the Spirit creates is the "sphere" where the new creation is formed out of the old creation.

When Torrance links the work of the Spirit to Christ and his church, he also links it closely to the work of redemption, and thus to eschatology and teleology. We might think that the Spirit is what gives the church its forward motion (cf. John 3:8), but in Torrance's view it is really Christ who gives the Spirit a forward motion in the church. He believes that a powerful Christology (i.e., biblical and Chalcedonian) is the only way to correct static doctrines of the Spirit.[50] Christology allows us to see the Spirit as "formed Spirit" and as "quickening Spirit." This Spirit is behind the "intensive" movement to fulfillment (*pleroma*) within the body (*soma*) and the "extensive" movement of the body to the "ends of the earth and to the ends of the ages."[51] Here in fact is a teleological description of the ministry and mission of the church.

This notion of the body's movement toward *pleroma* is found in Ephesians.[52] Given Torrance's firm belief that the church is the real Body of Christ, it is only natural that he is drawn to this concept. But there is another explanation for his interest. The concept was important to Anglican ecumenists, too. For the "catholic" ones, the solution to disunity in the church was the "recovery of the *wholeness* of tradition."[53] On

---

48. Ibid.

49. Ibid., 23.

50. See Torrance, Review of *The Letters of Saint Athanasius*, 205–8. Torrance draws a straight line from Athanasius' biblical Christology to his "formal treatise on the doctrine of the Spirit." Still, in his view, Athanasius' Christology was not biblical enough—"somewhat static and metaphysical." His doctrine of the Spirit is deprived of those "dynamic qualities" and that "future tense" which are so much a part of the New Testament (ibid., 207). He faults Athanasius for leaving in the "background" the "inseparable relation between the doctrine of the Spirit and eschatology so marked in the Pauline and Johannine literature" (ibid., 206).

51. Torrance, *Royal Priesthood*, 24.

52. It is likely that his interpretation of Ephesians owes something to Butzer. He tells us that his commentary on Ephesians 4 "became dominant in the Reformed doctrine of the Church" (Torrance, *Kingdom*, 73). Torrance also sees a teleological movement toward *pleroma* in Butzer. On one hand the kingdom of heaven has broken into the world, but on the other the church is the "sphere where that kingdom is progressively realised by a "*mirificum incrementum*" and is more and more apparent in this world" (ibid., 77).

53. The Church of England, *Catholicity*.

the other hand, the evangelicals spoke of the need for the "growth of the Church into the fullness of Christ."[54] Torrance, however, criticized the catholics for seeing this "wholeness" in terms of the "historical continuity of the Body of Christ." For him the only "wholeness" is the "once-and-for-all," eschatologically conditioned wholeness of Jesus Christ; and instead of the evangelicals' notion of what he calls "biological growth" into Christ, he contends for the church's "eschatological fulfillment" in Christ.[55]

When Torrance takes up this notion of the church's movement toward fulfillment/fullness (*pleroma*) he not only counterbalances his emphasis on eschatological fulfillment, he addresses the concerns of his Anglican counterparts. However, he does not want them to construe this movement toward *pleroma* as a validation of their understanding of the historical continuity of the Body of Christ (i.e., *Christus prolongatus*). The church's movement toward *pleroma*, therefore, is grounded in Christ's substitutionary atonement, beginning with his incarnation, and in the work of the Spirit of Christ.

This means the movement of the Body of Christ is correlative to the action or movement of Christ. It is not a matter of linear growth but of a "desperate struggle," since the church bears the cross in the world. It lives as the church Militant. Yet the end (*telos*) of this movement, this struggle, is the resurrection of the body and redemption of creation. However, Christ himself embodies that end as eschatological fulfillment (*eschatos*). He is the "New Man," the "Head of a new race," who gathers up "all Humanity in Himself (Eph 1:10; Rom 5:15f; 1Cor 15:21f, 45)."[56]

Indeed Torrance feels that the humanity of Christ and our ability to participate in it is, at this period, the "crucial issue in eschatology."[57] He is referring here to the risen Jesus Christ. While in the past the church struggled for the humanity of the historical Jesus, today, he says, it must struggle for the "humanity of the risen Jesus ascended to the right hand of God the Father Almighty."[58] This is not a new motif in Torrance's eschatology. It goes back to Ayth, where eschatology had much to do

---

54. The Church of England, *The Fulness of Christ*. As the title indicates, this work is inspired by Eph 4:10–15.

55. Torrance, "Catholicity," 87; Torrance, "The Fulness of Christ,"94.

56. Torrance, *Royal Priesthood*, 25.

57. Ibid., 43.

58. Ibid.

with the "personal touch of the risen Lord; and also to Auburn, where he stressed the need to uphold the person of Christ, not just the work of Christ.

There is no question that the de-mythologizing of Bultmann left the humanity of Christ in the dust, but Torrance also blames C. H. Dodd, Reinhold Niebuhr, and Paul Tillich for leaving us with a docetic risen Christ.[59] And even the Evanston statement on the theme of Hope, for all its focus on Christ, fails to highlight the humanity of the risen Christ. Torrance tries to redress this problem in a post-Evanston sermon on Heb 6:17–20: "Our Sure and Certain Hope."[60]

For Torrance, it is not only the humanity of Christ that is at stake, but our humanity too. After all, it is Christ, "the New Man," who gathers up humanity in himself through his movement from descent to ascent. This final stage is vitally important. It means that Christ goes on to "fill all things" (Eph 1:23; 4:10), thence the "new humanity is pressed toward its univeralisation or catholicization."[61]

Torrance suggests that the word *pleroma* in Eph 1: 23 and 4:10 refers to both Christ and the church, although most interpreters would identify the church only in the first case. He believes the church is implied in Eph 4:10 because the church is the Body of Christ. And, since it is filled with the Spirit of Christ, the church "is caught up" in the ascended Christ's movement to fill all things.

Ephesians 1:23 is a passage fraught with difficulties.[62] One of them is the question whether *pleroma* is in apposition to *soma* (the nearest noun) or to *auton* in the preceding verse. If it is the first, then the church, his Body, is the fullness or completion of Christ. If it is the second, then Christ is the fullness that fills all. On Torrance's view, this ambiguity is theologically justified. The church is the Spirit-filled Body of Christ. Yet its relation to Christ, following the Chalcedonian formula, is one of

59. Torrance, "The Place of the Humanity of Christ," 2.

60. He writes: "[W]e do not worship some inhuman Ghost, we worship and adore Jesus—and that belongs to the very essence of our hope: that Jesus wearing our humanity, Jesus bone of our bone and flesh of our flesh, is at the right hand of God, Lord and King of All. Because it is our humanity that Jesus wears, you and I are anchored to Him within the veil" (Torrance, "Our Sure and Certain Hope,"154). The sermon was delivered originally in October 1954.

61. Torrance, *Royal Priesthood*, 25.

62. There are at least five major interpretations of the verse. For a survey of them, as well as a proposed new one, see Roy Yates, "A Re-examination," 146–51.

likeness and difference. Unlike Christ, the church is an object of the filling. Like Christ, the church is engaged in the "filling of all things" (cf. Col 1:24). However, Christ's atonement and substitution for the church would mean that the church's work of filling is really the actualization of Christ's filling. Its movement in the world is correlative to Christ's movement in ascension. It fills only as it is filled by Christ. Through Christ the church becomes a Spirit-filled Body, as it "reaches out through the Spirit to fulfillment (*pleroma*)."[63]

The church's movements to *pleroma* takes place "intensively" within the Body of Christ, as members who are "rooted and grounded in love" grow up into the "perfect man, to the measure and stature and fulness of Christ." Withal, it happens "extensively" as the church carries out its world mission to all corners of the earth, until the end of time. Rightly, Torrance sums up the church's fulfillment as both "a teleological and an eschatological movement."[64] Its teleology is really a function of the church's ontological union with the Christ, who as the new creation has a relation to space and time. On the other hand, the church's eschatology reminds us that this movement is not natural but is due to the actions of God in Christ—to the resurrection, ascension, and the operation of the Holy Spirit. In sum, the church's teleological and eschatological movement represents the "interpenetration" of the church's being and mission, and Christ's person and work.

The movement to *pleroma*, then, is the growth and spread of the new humanity of Christ, for the church is really the "new humanity in concentrated form."[65] Love is essential to this new humanity. Jesus Christ is the "concrete embodiment of the Love of God."[66] Christ "loved the Church and gave himself for it" (Eph 5:25). But these facts bring us back to Christ's substitutionary atonement for the church. The relation between Christ and the church is a love union, but this love is his love, which the church participates in through the Communion of the Spirit. The church thus becomes a "communion filled and overflowing with the divine love."[67]

---

63. Torrance, *Royal Priesthood*, 24.
64. Ibid.
65. Ibid., 26.
66. Ibid., 30.
67. Ibid., 29.

3. Church, Space, and Time

Royal Priesthood hardly strikes us as being an eschatological work; yet it is deeply embedded with eschatological ideas, and the book is one of the few places where he plainly defines eschatology. *"Eschatology properly speaking is the application of Christology to the Kingdom of Christ and to the work of the Church in history."*[68] The definition is peculiar, but felicitous at the same time. It reminds us of one of his most important works on eschatology, *Kingdom and Church*, and it reveals the extent to which his eschatology has been shaped by his reading of the Reformers. Indeed these are the words he uses to define Calvin's eschatology.[69] Also, the definition encapsulates Torrance's entire eschatology. In the 1940s, under the pressure of historical events, this eschatology largely deals with the work of the church in history. It was mainly an eschatology of judgment. In the 1950s, under the pressure of the ecumenical movement, his eschatology is largely concerned with the kingdom of Christ. Here, though, there is less emphasis on judgment but more emphasis—following Calvin and Butzer—on resurrection and new creation. This explains Torrance's interest at this time in the humanity of the risen Christ and our participation in this humanity through Word and Sacrament.[70] This is another reason why he holds fast to the image of the church as a Body.[71] Human nature, after all, requires a body (*soma*).

However, just as the priesthood of the church is corporate, so is this human nature. The scars on Christ's risen body testify to his everlasting human nature. Yet if the church is really his Body, and no metaphor, then we have to think of Christ's humanity as corporate as well. But the

---

68. Ibid., 43. Italics are mine. We have a foreshadowing of this definition in the essay "Atonement and the Oneness of the Church." There we learn that the best way to reconcile the "eschatological view" and the "ontological view" of the church is to see them representing the "analogical transposition of Christology and soteriology to the Church" (Torrance, "Atonement," 256).

69. "Calvin's main teaching about eschatology can be formulated by saying that eschatology is the application of Christology to the work of the church in history." Forward to Quistorp, *Calvin's Doctrine*, 8.

70. Earlier, he defines the church as the "atonement becoming actual among men in the resurrection of a new humanity" (Torrance, "Atonement," 268). On this subject see also Torrance, "The Place of the Humanity." Torrance credits Calvin with restoring faith in the vicarious humanity of Jesus Christ in the sacraments. On the other hand, the vicarious humanity of Christ is probably more vital to Torrance's sacramental theology than it was to Calvin's (Stamps, "The Sacrament," 389f.).

71. See "What is the Church?" 6–21.

church, as collective entity, does not actually constitute this corporate nature, even though it is baptized into Christ. Remember, the church has no real existence apart from Christ's action toward it. His atonement is substitutionary. The corporate nature of the church, therefore, is derived from his baptism. He is "at once the One and the Many." Thus Torrance boldly asserts that "Christ is the Church."[72] He is also the "concrete embodiment" of love. Love is of the essence of humanity, but this love (*agape, philia*) is necessarily relational.

The church, then, is "the New Man" (Eph 2:15) by virtue of the fact it has "put on Christ" and put on this new man through baptism. Jesus Christ is also the "humanizing Man" by means of the Body's movement toward *pleroma*, "till we all come . . . to a perfect man" (Eph 4:13).[73] However, following the analogy of Christ, one would suppose there is a difference as well as a likeness between the humanity of the church and the humanity of Christ.

Now if the church is the New Man, then the problem of church disunity is more serious than we think. Our sinful divisions not only show contempt for the one faith, the one Lord and the one baptism. They are also dehumanizing. For schism, as Calvin points out, can be traced to a lack of brotherly charity (*Inst.* IV.2.5). However, the ascension of Christ means this New Man must be understood eschatologically as well. "And it has not yet been revealed what we shall be, but we know that when He is revealed, we shall be like Him, for we shall see Him as He is" (1 John 3:2). The Holy Spirit and the sacrament mean that the church participates in this New Man here and now, but the ascension and *parousia* of Christ tell us that the church has still to become this New Man, just as the church has still to become One Body.

It is evident that the church has a relation to time and space. But we must not regard the church in terms of time and space as normally perceived. This would be tantamount to regarding Jesus "according to the flesh." One needs to regard the church as the Body of the risen and ascended Christ, who has restored and renewed time and space. The church thus "participates in a reality of creation and time beyond all threat of decay and transience."[74] This new relation helps to explain the two-fold eschatological tension in the New Testament, between the "new

72. Torrance, "What is the Church?" 9.

73. Torrance, *Royal Priesthood*, 45.

74. Ibid., 49.

creation and the old creation here and now" and between the "present and the future" manifestation of this new creation. The tension is not merely subjective. It refers to the growth of the Body of Christ through the Holy Spirit. Torrance speaks of the "supernatural life of Christ" flowing into the church to renew and quicken it. This sounds like he has torn a page from the *Mystici Corporis Christi*.[75] Actually, he gets this picture from Ephesians, where Saint Paul describes the church as an "*oikodomē*" (building) which undergoes "*auxēsis*" (increase, growth) from above.[76] Here again we have the image of the church's movement toward *pleroma*, but in this case it is conceived in terms of space and time.

Since the church participates in a new time, it must not define its ministry on the basis of the old, fallen time. In Torrance's view, this is precisely the problem with the Anglican doctrine of apostolic succession. Ministry, and thus the continuity of the church, is understood as an extension of Jesus' ministry on the plane of "secular history" (the "schema of this *aeon*").

The church is still surrounded by fallen time, but it must not surrender to it, for this is a "guilt-ridden" time that falls "under judgement" and "passes irreversibly away into vanity and death."[77] But the new time of the church is a "continuous reality flowing against the stream of crumbling time." Thus the church gets "younger and younger." Consequently the church must guard against growing old along with the rest of the world. It must "redeem the time" (Eph 5:16), and "keep awake and keep vigil" (Matt 25:1ff.) for the advent of Christ.

Torrance thinks about space here as the "structural forms or schemata of the cosmos."[78] But these, along with time, are part of the sin-infested creation. They have undergone a "hardening into rigidity." He is not thinking about physical realities here but about the "power of the law (*nomos*)." Law, for Torrance, is the "form" that this "passing age assumes under divine judgment and the means by which it seeks to entrench itself in finality."[79] Law is therefore the anti-thesis to eschatological fulfillment.

---

75. Cf. *Mystici Corporis Christi*, nos. 49, 51, 77. "Thus the Church becomes, as it were, the filling out and the complement of the Redeemer, while Christ in a sense attains through the Church a fulness in all things" (no. 77).

76. See Eph 2:20f.; also Eph 4:15f.; Col 2:19.

77. Torrance, *Royal Priesthood*, 50.

78. Ibid., 52.

79. Ibid.

Torrance does not have in mind only the moral law. Law refers to the basic principles of the world (*ta stoicheia tou cosmou*) which enslave people (Gal 4:3), such as the "whole *nomos* of the Jewish tradition and succession."[80] When the church defines itself in terms of temporal succession and tradition it is not only enslaved to "crumbling time." It is enslaved to *nomos,* too.

The church of course cannot simply extricate itself from the power of *nomos.* It is still involved in the structural forms of this fallen world, and it has its mission within this world. But these forms must be "relativized," since the church is given a "new orientation within" them. This is an eschatological orientation. After all, the church "lives a life from beyond itself, and therefore looks beyond the historical forms of its orders to find its true being and form in the risen Humanity of Christ."[81] The church should have no more confidence in the time and form of the world than the individual should have in the "flesh." If the church has been crucified with Christ, then it is "crucified to the world and crucified to the law."[82]

The church is no longer in bondage to law. Rather, it has the freedom of the Spirit. Indeed, Torrance goes so far as to insist that the contrast between law and Spirit belongs to the "essence of eschatology."[83] The church must be led by this Spirit, so that it can partake of that life that is "from beyond itself." This involves a new time-form. It is one that is "bound up with a new structure, the Spiritual Body of Christ."[84] This explains why Paul defines "orders in terms of the *charismata* of the Spirit."[85] These are signs also that the new world is breaking into the old.

However, the new world will not completely break in before the final *parousia.* Even the *charismata* are provisional. In the new creation tongues and prophecies will have ceased. We must bear in mind that the church lives between the times, between ascension and final *parousia.* It is a "passing time," yet it is the time of church's "meeting with Christ as

80. Ibid., 54.

81. Ibid., 56.

82. Ibid., 55.

83. Torrance, "Christ the First," 314. "From this point of view," he adds, Torrance argues, the Epistle to the Galatians is the "most eschatological of all Paul's epistles" (Torrance, "Christ the First," 314).

84. Torrance, *Royal Priesthood*, 53.

85. Ibid., 56.

His Body," the time of "the mission of the Christ through His Body."[86] It is the time for decision, for repentance, for faith. Above all, it is a time of grace. If the new world were to break in completely now, Christ's glory would overwhelm humankind. There would be no time anymore for repentance, for growth in faith. Final judgment would come upon all.

4. The Priesthood of the Church

The Priesthood of the church is a royal priesthood. It is essentially a corporate priesthood, because the church "is formed by One Spirit into One Body with Christ."[87] But the church's priesthood is not an extension of Christ's priesthood. It only "participates" in this priesthood, which is the royal priesthood par excellence. It participates by "serving Him as Prophet, Priest and King."

The church's ministry needs to be governed by Chalcedonian Christology, so that its ministry is neither identified with nor separated from Christ's ministry. While the difference between identification and separation may often be a fine one, Torrance feels that "catholic" doctrines of ministry tend to confuse the church's ministry with Christ's ministry. Priests, thus, are thought of as continuing Jesus' earthly ministry and as fulfilling a mediatorial role between the church and God. What is more, the Eucharist is seen as a repetition or continuation of Christ's sacrifice.[88] On the other hand, the church's ministry is not essentially different from the ministry of Christ. As the body is answerable to the head, so the church's ministry is one of "subordination and obedience." Participation is really a matter of the church serving Christ.

More broadly, Torrance believes the church's whole ministry is a "reflex" of the "whole incarnational movement of Christ," his "descent

---

86. Ibid., 59.

87. Ibid., 35.

88. For a "catholic" view of ministry, see Kirk, *The Apostolic Ministry.* Cf. especially the essays by L. S. Thorton and Gregory Dix. Thornton sees the mission of the apostles as one with Christ's mission, and similarly the historic episcopate as one with the mission of the apostles (ibid., 99, 104, 109). For Dix, an apostle by definition represents not just the name of the one who sent him, but his very person (ibid., 228). One might also want to consult the classic work by R. C. Moberly, *Ministerial Priesthood.* For this author, the priesthood of the Church is sacrificial and "is really an identification with the priesthood and sacrifice of Christ" (ibid., 254). Out of her "proceeds the aroma of perpetual offering towards God" (ibid., 255).

and ascent, his *katabasis* and his *anabasis.*"[89] These movements stand for Christ's death and resurrection, but also for Christ's "incorporating and atoning actions." *Anabasis* refers to the ascension of Christ and the fact that he now bears our new resurrected humanity. Yet, after he ascended, Christ endowed the church with spiritual gifts (Eph 4:8). These ensure that the church's ministry is "correlative" with Christ's movement toward *pleroma* (Eph 4:10).

But is there any place for a distinct priesthood within the church? This is the really important question, for it is this kind of priesthood that divides Anglicans from other Protestants. The New Testament does not explicitly call for one. Eph 4 and 1 Cor 12 describe a division of ministry within the one corporate priesthood for the edification of the Body, but priests are not included within this division. Nonetheless, Torrance argues for a special priesthood, although his argument is also a defense of the ordained ministry within the Reformed churches. Nor does the New Testament specify a ministry for the celebration of the Lord's Supper; yet Torrance sees a need for one. This is not because the sacrament is really a bloodless sacrifice. It is because there is a need for order at the Lord's Table (cf. 1 Cor 10–14), which, in his view, is the focal point of the order of the whole church.

This need for order in the church explains the distribution of spiritual gifts (*charismata*) at the Table. The ministerial priesthood does not create order in the church, but it has the responsibility of maintaining it. The presence (*parousia*) of Christ in the Eucharist is what creates order. "The order of the priesthood is itself ordered by the Sacrament of the Eucharist."[90] But the divine order of the sacrament does not happen *ex opere operato*. It is revealed only through the church's obedience to the Word, which, with and through the Spirit, begets and maintains the church.

The main theme of the First Assembly of the WCC (1948) was "Man's Disorder and God's Design," but for Torrance the solution to disorder is not so much a recovery of God's design as a hope in the order of God's new creation. The Eucharist is the locus for this hope, for it is

---

89. Torrance, *Royal Priesthood*, 39. See Phil 2:5ff. The influence of Barth's doctrine of reconciliation (CD IV) on Torrance is obvious here. This doctrine is based squarely on the Christ's *katabasis* and *anabasis*: IV/1 ("Jesus Christ, the Lord as Servant") and IV/2 ("Jesus Christ, the Servant as Lord").

90. Torrance, *Royal Priesthood*, 77.

a sign of the in-breaking of the new creation, of the new divine order.[91] The nature of this "new order" is love, but we know that Christ himself is the "concrete embodiment" of this love. It is noteworthy that in the early church, the Eucharist was part of an agape meal or "love feast" (Jude 12). In the new creation many things will have passed away, including the sacraments and ministry of the church; even faith and hope will no longer be. But love will remain forever (1Cor 13).

The Eucharist is about *love* because it is for the edification of the Body of Christ. The spiritual gifts (*charismata*) at the table are for "the profit of all." According to Torrance, love, as expressed in humble service, is of the "very *esse*" of the church, and that is why it "reaches out to the divine *telos* of the eternal Kingdom (1 Cor 15:28, etc.)."[92] The Eucharist is about love also because it is a foretaste of the Heavenly Banquet—that eternal communion of the church and Christ (1 Cor 10:16).

Yet the church cannot possess the divine order. The ordering of the Eucharist must not be confounded with the divine order itself. This order is really the coming of the new creation. The purpose, then, of order in the church, and of obedience to the Word and the Spirit, is to make way for the new creation. It exists to "to make room in the midst for the presence of the risen Christ so that the church's fellowship becomes the sphere where the resurrection of Christ is effectively operative here and now."[93] Indeed Torrance sees the risen Jesus, in his new humanity, as the personification of order. In him, "everything has its proper order, proper time, proper place, proper sequence and proper end."[94]

Credo . . . carnis resurrectionem. Torrance never tires of discussing the resurrection of Christ's body, but, strangely, he rarely mentions the general resurrection of Christians. He mentions it in *Royal Priesthood*, but he does not think about it as an event at the end of this age. Nor does

---

91. This principle of order is perhaps another example of the influence of Calvin on Torrance. Benjamin Milner avers that "order" is one of the governing themes in Calvin's doctrine of the church. This means that redemption for him "is essentially the restoration of the order established in the creation" (Milner, *Calvin's Doctrine*, 9). While he correctly observes that for Calvin order is procured through the Word and the work of the Spirit, he completely ignores the eschatological aspect of order. But this should be expected, since Milner does not share Torrance's Christological definition of the church and redemption.

92. Torrance, *Royal Priesthood*, 66.

93. Ibid., 67.

94. Torrance, "The Doctrine of Order," 23.

he think of it in an individual sense. In keeping with his definition of humanity, it involves the whole church as the Body of Christ.[95] "Thus the whole ordering of the Church on earth must be poised upon its expectation of the resurrection in the body (1 Cor 15:23), and must therefore be an ordering of the Church as *soma pneumatikon*."[96] It must be ordered according to the risen Christ, the "first fruits" of the resurrection. There is an anticipation of the resurrection in the church only because the risen Christ, the *Eschatos,* is actively present in the Eucharist. For these reasons, Torrance insists that order in the church has to be "eschatological." "Apart from the eschatological perspective, order is dead for it does not serve the resurrection, and does not manifest the love of Christ or His coming again to reign."[97]

It should be no surprise that Torrance connects the Eucharist and the resurrection of the body. Recall that he connected the "first resurrection" of Rev 20 with Christian baptism (see chapter 3). Baptism *is* the "first resurrection." He also insisted on seeing the sacrament as an *event,* rather than as a sign of grace. And for Torrance there is no greater event than the resurrection.

However, it is important to recognize an eschatological reserve even in the divine order of the church. Christ's presence is not fully revealed in the Eucharist, so neither is the divine order of the new creation. There can be no "direct reading," Torrance maintains, of order from the Eucharist "on this side of the *parousia*."[98] Not even the *charismata* provide us with a full revelation of order, since they will cease on the other side of the final *parousia.*

Still less can the order of the church be derived from the "particular" priesthood. For the order of this priesthood "is itself ordered by the Sacrament of the Eucharist."[99] And just as the Eucharist will pass away at the *parousia,* so will this particular priesthood. It is not an everlasting reality, but a functional one, which is eschatologically and teleologically

95. On this matter Torrance appears to be influenced by J. A. T. Robinson's *The Body*. It is another work in biblical theology that Torrance mined (despite the author's modernist Christology). The Anglican bishop concludes that it is "quite impossible to think of the resurrection hope in terms of the individual unit" (Robinson, *The Body,* 81). That is because the "carrier of glory . . . is not the individual but *the Church* (Eph 5:27)" (ibid., 82).

96. Torrance, *Royal Priesthood,* 66.

97. Ibid., 68.

98. Ibid., 73

99. Ibid., 77.

determined. It exists only to build up the "real priesthood," the whole Body of Christ until it "reaches the fullness of Christ." The form it takes is no different from that of the corporate priesthood. This is the form of the Suffering Servant. But while the particular priesthood will disappear at the *parousia*, the "real priesthood of the one Body will be fully revealed."[100]

5. *Episcopacy*

Torrance is even willing to compromise with Anglicans on the subject of bishops. While he rejects apostolic succession, and the idea that the episcopate is an "effectual sign" of the church ("no bishop, no church"), he does recognize a need for oversight (*episkopoi*) in the church. Relying on Calvin (and his use of Cyprian), Torrance interprets the episcopate in terms of the priesthood of Christ. Christ himself is really the only bishop over the church. The episcopate in the church, however, is not identical to Christ's episcopate. Like the priesthood of the church as a whole, the episcopate can only participate in Christ's oversight. Or, as Calvin expressed it, the episcopate in the church is really a "subministration" of that One Bishop. And like the priesthood of the church, the episcopate of the church involves the whole Body of Christ. It is a "corporate episcopate."

This does not mean that oversight is diffused throughout the whole church, so that every member of the church is a bishop. Just as within the corporate priesthood, there is a particular priesthood or presbyterate (ordained ministers of the Word and Sacrament), there is a "membering" within the corporate episcopate. But this takes place within the particular priesthood. Thus the episcopate is held "in *solidum* by the ministers."[101] The bishop can only act "in *presbyterio*," as a "president" of the Body in which the "corporate episcopate is gathered up to a head."[102]

Like the "particular priesthood," Torrance believes the "corporate episcopate" is functional and provisional. It is exists to build up the Body of Christ in this time of grace. Unlike the Body, however, it does not perdure. It will cease to be in the new creation. The episcopate bears witness to the "eschatological ordering of the whole Church in Christ."[103]

100. Ibid., 81.

101. Ibid., 91.

102. Ibid., 104.

103. Ibid., 102.

This divine order, however, is given to us only in part. Its full revelation is reserved for the final advent, when "the Chief Shepherd will be manifested in His *episkopai* or visitation."[104]

In any event, Torrance's doctrine of episcopacy would not have satisfied many leading Anglicans. For the authors of *The Apostolic Ministry* (1946), in particular, the real issue is not oversight in the church but a renewal of the apostolic ministry through a mono-episcopacy. And this renewal would entail restoration of the bishop's priestly function in the church.[105]

C. The Communion of the Spirit

In the last section we commented on the role of pneumatology in Torrance's eschatology. We need to say more about this doctrine. While it is subordinate to Torrance's Christology, it becomes an increasingly important part of his thought in the late fifties. As he says at one point, the Spirit is the "abiding Parousia of Christ," the "link between the two advents" which gives rise to a "trinitarian understanding of the Parousia."[106]

There is an historical explanation for Torrance's sudden interest in the Holy Spirit. Between 1957 and 1963—the year it concluded its work—the Theological Commission on Christ and the Church (TCCC), concentrated its attention on two topics in succession: Baptism and the Work of the Holy Spirit in the church. Although the Commission did not begin its official study of the Holy Spirit until 1959, the subject was on its agenda at its founding in 1953. The original mandate of the Commission was to study "the doctrine of the Church in close relation to both the doctrine of Christ and to the doctrine of the Holy Spirit."[107] This mandate helps to explain Torrance's resolve to give the doctrine of the Holy Spirit christological content as well as a clear relation to the Body of Christ. At the first meeting on the new commission, Torrance agreed that the "full-

104. Ibid.

105. Torrance was one of the authors of the Bishop Report, which recommended episcopacy for the Church of Scotland as a first step toward union with the Church of England. He knew the difficulties; he compared raising the word "bishop" in Scotland to raising a "red rag to a bull" (Torrance, "The Problem," 7). Not surprisingly, the report was overwhelmingly rejected by the General Assembly of Scotland. See Henderson, *Power Without Glory,* 114–21.

106. Torrance, "Christ the First," 309.

107. Commission on Faith and Order: Minutes, Commission and Working committee, n. 17 (1955) 19.

est place" had to be found for "the relation of the Church to the Spirit." At the same time, he concurred with George Florovsky (a fellow committee member) when he stressed the need to uphold the *filioque* in the face of a modern "tendency" in some quarters to "de-christologize ecclesiology."[108]

The "Word made flesh" is the starting point for Torrance's theology, determining its "matter and method." This accounts for his theological objectivism and realism, but it also accounts for his reticence on the subject of pneumatology. He knew too well that all talk about the spirit was not talk about the Holy Spirit sent by God the Father and God the Son. Protestants, he observes, are prone to confuse the human spirit with the Spirit of God ("a *homineque*"); while the Roman Church is prone to confuse the spirit of the church with the Spirit of God ("an *ecclesiaque*").[109] Hence the pressing need, in his view, to ground pneumatology in Christology before exploring its operation in humankind and the church.

Torrance's only paper on the Holy Spirit is in fulfillment of the agenda of the TCCC. Written in 1963, part of it is included in his book *Theology in Reconstruction* under the heading "The Foundation of the Church: Union with Christ through the Spirit."[110] It is really about salvation history in terms of the foundation and the development of the church. There is only one church of God, with one people, but it has three stages: a "preparatory form" that predates the incarnation and extends back to Adam and the old covenant of Israel; the church's renewal and fulfillment in Jesus Christ; and the church's "final and eternal form," which will be the new creation that Christ will create at his advent. Pentecost plays a critical role in salvation-history. It is the power behind the "new birth" of the church. But Torrance interprets the effect of Pentecost in light of the Transfiguration. It stands for the "transformation" of the church "into the Body of the risen Lord," which is then "quickened and filled with his Spirit."[111] He reminds us that the church is not the "Kingdom of the Spirit" or the "Body of the Spirit." It is the "spiritual Body of Christ on earth and in history."[112] The work of the Spirit in the church is correlative

108. Commission on Faith and Order: Minutes, Commission and Working committee, n. 17 (1955) 18.

109. Torrance, *Theology in Reconstruction*, 228.

110. Ibid., 192–208.

111. Ibid., 204.

112. Ibid., 205.

to the work of Christ for the church, so that the church may be "rooted" and "grounded" in him.

Yet the Spirit's relation to Christ and his church extends further back than Pentecost, back to a point which reveals the indissoluble connection between them. The Spirit is fundamentally and finally the Communion of the Spirit. The church's real foundation is not Adam but the immanent Triune God. "The Church is grounded in the Being and Life of God, and rooted in the eternal purpose of the Father to send his Son, Jesus Christ, to be the Head and Savior of all things."[113] And that means that "both the source and goal" of the church are in the eternal love of God which has "overflowed" in the creation and redemption of the world. The church expresses God's desire for fellowship with people. Through the church he pours out his Spirit on them, in order to transmit his divine nature to them, so that he as Father, Son, and Holy Spirit can truly be at home among his people eternally.

This picture of the church as a communion of love was brought out in more detail in an earlier essay for the TCCC, "What is the Church?" (1958). There was debate within the Working Committee over the most suitable biblical image for the church.[114] Some felt that no image should be given priority. For Torrance, though, one image had to take precedence. He strongly insisted that the church "is the Body of Christ." That is not to say other images are to be ignored. *Royal Priesthood* plainly attests to that fact. But in his view, these other images only serve the image of the Body of Christ. What made Torrance favor this image? Robinson's *The Body* certainly helped him to understand the richness of its biblical meaning.[115] On top of that, the image reinforced his belief in the ontological nature of the church, a nature that is in a kind of hypostatic union with Christ. The image also brought attention to the humanity of Jesus Christ. Most importantly, out of all biblical images he finds this one to be

---

113. Ibid., 192.

114. The book *Images of the Church in the New Testament* (1960) by Paul Minear (another member of the TCCC) reveals just how difficult it is to find an appropriate image for the church. The author identifies up to *one hundred* images of the church in the New Testament.

115. For Robinson, the "body" is the "keystone of Paul's theology." The implication is that Paul's doctrine of the church is really an extension of his Christology, i.e., of the risen body of Jesus Christ (Robinson, *The Body*, 9, 49). The church for Paul is not "like" Christ's body but "is" his Body (ibid., 51). A key text for Robinson is Acts 9:4, which indicates the close identity between the risen Jesus and the church.

the most profoundly christological. Like no other, it directs us to an ultimate truth, namely that "Christ is the Church."[116] Although the reverse is not true, this statement reveals a lot about the church. The "Church participates in Christ."[117]

We have learned the significance of this proposition for the ministry of the church. Now we see its significance for the general life of the church. Participation in this case is understood as a "communion-in-participation in Christ."[118] There is a historical-contextual explanation for this new notion in Torrance. It is a response to a new tendency in Faith and Order to understand the church as a social, institutional reality in line with such images as the People of God, the Household of God, and the Family of God. Correspondingly, sociology was looked upon by some theologians, especially in North America, as an essential tool for understanding the church. One member spoke of the "blessed marriage" of sociology and theology as "part of the eschatological hope."[119] By contrast, Torrance values the Body image because, among others things, it "does not" make us think of the church as a "sociological or anthropological magnitude," but instead as the "immediate property" of Christ.[120]

Nonetheless, Torrance uses other images to convey the fact that the Body of Christ is a social reality, not a biological reality. The church is the New Man, but at the same time it is the "city of the Living God" and the "heavenly Jerusalem." The reason is that the Body of Christ is about *koinonia* (communion and participation). Right away we think about the communion between members in the Body, but Torrance contends that *koinonia* refers "primarily" to the church's "participation in Christ," in his "New Humanity," and "only secondarily" to the communion between people in the church.[121] The church's participation is really a participation in union with Christ, a union however that is analogous to that unique union in Christ. The church's "communion-in-participation" with Christ

116. Torrance, "What is the Church?" 9.

117. Ibid.

118. Ibid., 10.

119. From Dean W. G. Muelder, member of the Theological Commission on Institutionalism. Commission on Faith and Order: Minutes, Commission and Working committee, n. 23 (1956) 13.

120. Torrance, "What is the Church?" 7

121. Ibid., 10. On *koinonia* as an objective participation in Christ through the Spirit, see George, *Communion with God* and Lohmeyer, *Der Brief an die Phillipper.*

is not a right, but a privilege granted through Christ. The church is not to be separated from Christ, but neither is it to be confused with Christ. It is not an *"alter Christus."*

Baptism and Holy Communion "enshrine" this *koinonia* the church has with Christ. Baptism in particular highlights the closeness of this union; while Holy Communion in particular highlights the separation that still exists. The church is wholly justified, yet it constantly needs to be "cleansed" in Christ. The sacraments remind us that this *koinonia* has to be understood dynamically and eschatologically. The church, as the Body of Christ, has "communion-in-participation" in the "crucified, risen, ascended and advent Christ."[122] The church is not called to look forward to a full hypostatic union with Christ, but it is called to look forward to a much closer union with him in the new creation. "We shall be like him" (1 John 3:2). "It is the Advent which reminds the Church that although it is already one Body with Christ through the Spirit, it has yet to be made one Body with Him in the consummation of His Kingdom."[123]

Now there is also the communion within the church, between believers in Christ. Torrance calls this the church in its "horizontal dimension." This is not simply the human dimension of the church. Natural social relations do not complete the church. Christ's atonement means that he is the substitute even for human social relations. So when the church participates in Christ, it participates in "His very Life as the Son of the Father in the communion of the Holy Spirit."[124]

This actually fills out the horizontal dimension, for it connects the saints on earth with the saints in heaven. As the church's High Priest and Mediator, Christ not only intercedes for the church on earth but has opened the doorway to the community of heaven. This last activity is especially important in the Orthodox Church. When we are brought into the church then, "we come to 'Mount Zion, and unto the city of the living God, the heavenly Jerusalem, and to the innumerable hosts of angels, to the general assembly and church of the first-born.'"[125] It is in light of this that the church is to be seen as a "communion of love" through Christ and the Holy Spirit. The fellowship between one another in the church

122. Torrance, "What is the Church?" 13.
123. Ibid., 15.
124. Ibid., 9.
125. Ibid., 16. Cf. Heb 12:22–23.

is really a participation in the "overflow of divine Life and Love."[126] The church's fellowship is therefore overflowing. It is marked by a teleological movement toward fulfillment. It is an "ever-widening communion in which the Body (*soma*) presses out in expansion toward a fullness (*pleroma*) in the love of God in all its height and depth and length and breadth which more and more gathers into itself men and women from the ends of the earth."[127] This expansion also makes the church a peace-making community, a "community of reconciliation."

For more on the place of the "Communion of the Spirit" in eschatology, we have to turn to the introduction of Torrance's *The School of Faith* (1959). Here he discusses the doctrine of God, but a preponderant amount of space is given to the Holy Spirit. His starting point is the "union with Christ through the Communion of the Spirit." The Communion of the Spirit is "correlative to the union of God and Man wrought out in the Work and Life of Jesus Christ."[128] The "heart" of the church's eschatology is found in this special union and communion. The church is where people now partake of the "New Humanity of Christ" and share in the "life and love of the Father and Son and the Holy Spirit, that is in the Communion of the Spirit."[129] It is precisely here that we get a foretaste of the new creation within the old.

This union and communion is also the foundation of the world's hope. Since our union with Christ is predicated on Christ's "carnal union"[130] with us, all men and women are in one sense united to Christ. They also share in the Communion of the Spirit. Incarnation and resurrection mean that the Spirit of Christ is "poured out upon 'all flesh' and operates on 'all flesh.'"[131] The crucial point is that our spiritual union with Christ is not something that is annexed to our physical union with him (*contra* Westminster Catechism). Nor does our carnal union with Christ depend on our spiritual union with him. There is only "one union with Christ . . . which He gives us to share through the gift of the His Spirit."[132]

126. Ibid.

127. Ibid., 17.

128. Torrance, *The School of Faith*, cvi.

129. Ibid., cxvii, cxxi.

130. This phrase in *The School of Faith* is the cornerstone of Rankin's thesis: "Carnal Union with Christ."

131. Torrance, *The School of Faith*, cxvii.

132. Ibid., cvii.

This is why the Spirit, for Torrance, represents the "abiding Parousia" of Christ.

The Spirit is operative now upon all people. Torrance does not intend to mean that everyone is a Christian, but only that the whole world is the sphere of the Spirit's reconciling work. In the church there is an "intensive fulfilment" of the new life in the Spirit, but by way of the church's mission to the world this new life moves towards an "extensive fulfilment" in all creation. "Today that universal Communion of the Spirit has its provisional and proleptic form in the historical Church, but then the Church attaining to the fulness of Christ will be coincident with the whole Kingdom spanning the new heaven and new earth."[133] This statement reminds us of that "eschatological conception of love" that Torrance discovered in Butzer.[134]

Teleology stands out in *The School of Faith*. The Spirit, we learn, is "already reaching out toward victorious triumph and consummation."[135] The Spirit, though, cannot be separated from Christ. The Communion of the Spirit, after all, is "correlative to the incarnational union in Christ," and together they form the basis of the church's hope. Neither can the movement toward "extensive fulfilment" be detached from the final coming of Christ. *Pleroma* (fullness), then, cannot be separated from the *parousia* (coming-presence). As we learned, the "teleological end must be interpreted eschatologically, and the eschatological end must be interpreted teleologically." So at the "decisive hour," he writes, Christ will "come again to take up His reign, to judge and renew His creation."[136] Now, however, we get a prolepsis of this "decisive hour," since the extensive growth of the church entails God's judgment upon the world, upon its resistance to the love of God. This creates a tension between the church and the world, and this tension is a "sign of the end"—a sign the Spirit is moving towards victory and that the coming of Christ is imminent.

133. Ibid., cxxvi.

134. Butzer, he writes, "insists that Christians must translate their faith in "a true faithful and active love to all men," for they are to live out among men the communion of love to which they belong to Christ" (Torrance, *Kingdom and Church*, 81).

135. Torrance, *The School of Faith*, cxxv.

136. Ibid.

Conclusion

THE FOREGOING CHAPTERS PROVE THAT TORRANCE WAS AT THE FORE-
front of the modern renaissance of eschatology. It is now time for scholars to reckon with his contribution to this subject. We can understand
why this has not been done already. His early theology in general has
been overshadowed by his later scientific theology. Then there is the elu-
siveness of his eschatology. Torrance did not leave us with a systematic
treatment of the subject. Instead, eschatology is diffused throughout his
early corpus: scattered among his many lectures, essays, sermons, articles, and reviews. It is woven together with other theological loci such
as the church, the sacraments, ministry, and especially Christology. That
is why instead of Torrance's eschatology it is better to speak about the
"eschatological orientation" in his theology. Now, finally, we have captured that orientation.

Yet not only do we have Torrance's eschatology before us, we have it
in its historical context. It is important that we view it in this way, for his
eschatology—more than any other aspect of his thought—is historically
conditioned. World War II, the spread of Communism, and the general
crisis of civilization engendered the practical and apocalyptic sides of his
eschatology. Eschatology is, first of all, a part of the ministry of word and
sacrament. It is meant to give direction, comfort and hope to the people
of God in times of distress. But in the midst of these times Torrance
realized that the individual, realized eschatology which characterized his
early ministry was missing something. In order to keep people grounded
in hope, eschatology had to take into account disturbing historical events.
Likewise, the ecumenical movement engendered the ecclesial emphasis
that marks his eschatology in the 1950s. It is impossible to make sense
of Torrance's eschatology in these years without an appreciation for the
universal drive for church unity; in particular, the drive for it on British
soil. When we realize the degree to which historical circumstances
shaped Torrance's eschatology, then we realize also that his theology in

this period is not a straightforward application of Barthian theological principles.

1. Significant Features of Torrance's Eschatology

Although Torrance's eschatology is historically conditioned, we should not relativize it to history. There are features of it that are of lasting significance. Paramount is its christocentrism. Eschatology for Torrance has to do with the *parousia* (presence and coming) of Christ, and this entails his redeeming work in history and in the church. Karl Barth may have inspired a generation of theologians to take seriously the relationship between Christ and eschatology, but Torrance appears to be the first theologian to try to do this consistently. One might contend that Jürgen Moltmann, with his *Theology of Hope*, deserves this credit. However, Moltmann's approach is more *eschato-centric* than christocentric; more Old Testament than New Testament. Eschatology, he states, is "Christology in an eschatological perspective."[1] Hope depends on what God will do, not on what he has done. "Jesus is recognized in the Easter appearances as what he really will be."[2] What is fundamental to Torrance's eschatology, eschatological fulfillment and teleological development in Christ, is quite alien to Moltmann's *Theology of Hope*.

Another Reformed theologian, Adrio König, was more successful (though far less influential) at constructing a Christ-centered eschatology. His book *The Eclipse of Christ in Eschatology: Toward a Christ-Centred Approach* (1989) offers a "new approach to 'last things.'" "Only when Christ himself, his birth, ministry, crucifixion, resurrection, ascension and working through the Holy Spirit, is understood as wholly and in every sense the last," he writes, "have we heard correctly the Bible's message about eschatology."[3] But after having examined Torrance's eschatology, we can hardly call this Dutch Reformed theologian's approach "new." Besides, König's eschatology lacks the balance and sophistication of Torrance's. The result is a blunt christomonism. In contrast to Torrance, König undervalues the Old Testament perspective, as well as the church and the sacraments. Finally, in stark contrast to König's,

1. Moltmann, *Theology of Hope*, 192.
2. Ibid.
3. König, *The Eclipse of Christ*, 35.

Torrance's eschatology points ultimately in a trinitarian direction. Our union with Christ leads to a "communion of the Spirit."

A second important feature is the way in which Torrance attempts to translate New Testament eschatology into a modern idiom. Finding a way to do this has been a formidable challenge for modern theologians. Rudoph Bultmann's "de-mythologizing" project represents one solution. The trade off, however, is that the historical and apocalyptic aspects of biblical eschatology are cut loose and eschatology is reduced to a divine existential encounter.

Long before Moltmann and Pannenberg sought to reconnect eschatology with history, Torrance tried to do this through his sermons on the Apocalypse. This meant resisting the tendency to view apocalyptic as a vestige of an ancient Jewish cosmology rather than as a feature of Christ's revelation and redemption. Apocalyptic, for Torrance, has to do with the tense boundary between the old creation and new creation, the old time and new time, the kingdoms of the world and the kingdom of God. Apocalyptic reveals the connection between eschatology and history. Yet at the same time it safeguards eschatology from becoming identified with an ideology of progress.

Central to New Testament eschatology is the dual sense that the kingdom is both a present reality and something yet to come. For Torrance, this suggests that eschatology needs to be understood in terms of fulfillment in Christ and development in time through him. Hence, the eschatological end and the teleological end must be held together in balance. God's work of redemption through Christ must not be detached from the world that God created through his Son. Yet Torrance observed this happening in modern eschatology. "Realized eschatology," for example, concentrated on the eschatological end at the expense of the teleological end, so that one was left with an eschatology that seemed detached not only from its biblical moorings but also from the modern world, which had acquired an understanding of biological evolution and was imbued with an acute sense of history. However, Torrance's understanding of teleology does not come from modern ideas of evolutionary progress. It comes from his insight into Jesus' history. While Jesus Christ's resurrection and ascension stand for eschatological fulfillment, that fulfillment takes place only by way of his incarnation and death. The incarnation reveals Christ's entry into history, while his death on the cross tells us that his life in time was one of suffering service and witness.

Thus the church as the Body of Christ finds fulfillment only by participating in this ministry of suffering service and witness to the world.

Now that brings us to a third important feature, and one that sets this eschatology apart from that of other Protestant theologians.[4] This is the organic connection between Torrance's eschatology and his ecclesiology. A good illustration of this relationship is the way he sees apocalyptic eschatology enshrined in the liturgy of church.

In order to appreciate this particular contribution of Torrance, we must bear in mind that the findings of Weiss and Schweitzer had cast serious doubt on the relationship between the eschatology of the church and eschatology of Jesus. And following in their footsteps, Martin Werner portrayed the entire doctrinal system of the historic church as a contrivance in place of the kingdom that never arrived.[5] In his view the eschatology of Jesus had been supplanted by the ecclesiology of a Hellenized Christianity. As a consequence, the church's ministry bears little relation to Christ's ministry on earth. For Torrance, eschatology is essentially about Christ, the Last One (*Eschatos*), but it also centers around the church, since it is truly Christ's Body. If the church ignores the eschatological element in its ministry, sacraments, worship, and its *kerygma*, it loses more than its visionary outlook. It loses sight of its union with Christ. Instead of existing as an eschatological reality the church exists only as a social or institutional reality.

Far from replacing eschatology with an ecclesiology, Torrance holds to an ecclesiology that is shaped by eschatology. The eschatological element in the church ensures that it does not become conformed to the old age, to its "crumbling time," as is the case when the church seeks to extend the incarnation of Christ by means of historical succession. For through its union with the risen and ascended Christ, the church participates in the new time of the new creation. The church's sacraments are also filled with eschatological significance. Baptism is a sign of the church's union with the risen Christ, of its eschatological fulfillment in Christ, of its participation in the new creation. However, all this is hidden from the church on earth. This is why the church is given the Lord's

---

4. This propensity to think about eschatology in virtual isolation from the church continues up to the present day. Cf. Schwarz, *Eschatology*; and Fergusson and Sarot, *The Future as God's Gift*. The additional essay in this book by Farrow ("Eucharist, Eschatology," 199–215) is the one important exception.

5. Werner, *The Formation of Christian Dogma*.

Supper, for here the Christian community encounters the advent presence (*parousia*) of Christ and enjoys a foretaste of the Marriage Supper
of the Lamb.

Eschatology is interwoven also with Torrance's ecumenism. His two
most important works, *Kingdom and Church* and *Royal Priesthood,* are
proof of this. Torrance firmly believes that the eschatological element
in Christianity can be fully captured only in an undivided church. For
Christ is one; and his Body is one. Although he could be sharply critical,
for example, of Anglican doctrines of the church, he nonetheless believed that their stress on both the "wholeness" of the church's tradition
and the church's "growth into fulness" witnessed to a core element of
the church's eschatological reality. This is the teleological movement of
the Body towards fullness (*pleroma*) in Christ. Moreover, when Torrance
refers to the church as a great communion of the saints that spans heaven
and earth this indicates his desire to accommodate an important dimension of Orthodox eschatology.[6]

The ecumenical perspective in Torrance's eschatology means that
the church is called to look beyond its sinful divisions to its true nature
in Christ. It has been made one in Christ through baptism, but this oneness is hidden with the risen and ascended Christ. Hence this oneness
can only be received sacramentally on this side of the Eschaton. Yet intercommunion is essential to the actualization of the church's unity on
earth.

A fourth notable feature of Torrance's eschatology is its accent on
the humanity of Christ: the bodily resurrection, ascension, and advent of
the man Christ Jesus. Indeed Torrance came to see the humanity of the
risen Christ, and the church's participation in it, as the crucial issue in
modern eschatology. He was disturbed by the prevalence of docetism in
modern eschatology, and in his view the only defense against this heresy
was a new emphasis on the humanity of the risen Christ. Early on, when
his eschatology was more personal and existential, Torrance tended to
think about Christ's humanity in individual terms. At Alyth he stressed
the "personal touch" of the risen Lord, who is "bone of our bone" and
"flesh of our flesh." He even defines Christianity as "a Person." Further,
his sermons on the Apocalypse show a vehement antagonism toward the
de-humanizing forms of modern collectivism, where every man is but

---

6. On the importance of this dimension in Orthodox eschatology, see Louth,
"Eastern Orthodox Eschatology," 234–36.

"a number." In the 1950s, though, his focus shifts to the corporate side of Christ's humanity and ours. In light of his ecumenical work, this is a logical development. But not only did this new focus help to promote the unity of the church, it helped to fend off the threat of collectivism, by pointing to a much better alternative.[7] The church is regarded as the *New Man*, the new humanity "in concentrated form," whose essence is *agape* love. The Eucharist, moreover, is where we have a real anticipation of the resurrection of this Man; for here we encounter the eucharistic *parousia*, the "humanizing man."

2. Critical Observations

The strength of Torrance's eschatology comes from its christocentric and scientific approach to the subject. The content of this eschatology does not derive from speculation but from a rigorous obedience to its chief subject matter: the nature of Christ and his saving action in and for the world. His approach aims at objective theological knowledge and a central role for eschatology in the life of the church.

Yet we must reckon with the weak points of Torrance's eschatology. One obvious problem is his narrow description of it. His way of defining eschatology ensures that this topic is no longer peripheral to Christianity (Barth's famous dictum is upheld!). On the other hand, it also means the traditional "four last things"—the *resurrection, last judgment, heaven and hell*—are peripheral to his eschatology. In many respects, Torrance's is a quintessentially modern eschatology. It is more concerned with the relevance of eschatology for the present than about speculating on things in the future. His approach, then, raises the question whether there is a need any longer for a doctrine of "last things," if everything we need to know can be ascertained through Christology.[8] In any event, Torrance's

---

7. An important influence on Torrance's doctrine of the Body of Christ was Robinson's *The Body*. The book was intended as an answer to the challenge of communism. Robinson was convinced that the world had just entered the age of the "socialised man." Christians, he adds, "should be the last people to be found clinging to the wrecks of an atomistic individualism, which has no foundation in the Bible. For their hope does not lie in escape from collectivism: it lies in the resurrection of the body—that is to say, in the redemption, transfiguration, and ultimate supersession of one solidarity by another" (ibid., 9).

8. Recently, there have been attempts to renew the traditional understanding of eschatology as a discussion about "last things." See Braaten and Jenson, *The Last Things*.

method only proves that eschatology, unlike Christology, is a "word with many meanings."[9]

The revival of eschatology in modern times is attributable to a great extent to the rediscovery of the biblical foundations of this subject. This is certainly true in the case of Torrance's eschatology. It relies heavily on the results of the biblical theology movement. On the other hand, one could argue that his eschatology becomes less biblical as it becomes more christocentric, especially when he turns towards classical Christology in order to fortify his doctrine of the church as the Body of Christ. We need only to consider the theme of judgment.

Torrance develops the doctrine of the Body of Christ in order to uphold both the unity of the church and Christological nature of it (as well as the growth of it toward *pleroma*). This involves taking the expression the "body of Christ" more literally and less metaphorically.[10] We must not, therefore, think of the real church as an abstraction or "mystical body." The Body of Christ is, rather, a concrete ontological reality. It is in fact the new Man. The Body of Christ indicates an ontological union between Christ and the church that is analogous to the hypostatic union of the human and divine natures in Christ. "The Church *is* the Body of Christ." However, this statement should not be made the basis for an ecclesial triumphalism. The Body of Christ is not a mystical reality; yet it is very much an eschatological reality. The church is the Body of the "crucified, risen, ascended and advent Christ." In another sense, then, the church still has to become the Body of Christ.

Yet we have to ask whether Torrance presses this Body image too far, so that the relationship between the Christ and the church becomes too close. The net effect of his procedure is that the doctrine of final judgment is left debilitated. It is difficult, after all, to imagine Christ judging his own body. That is why Peter speaks about judgment beginning at the "house of God" (*oikou tou Theo*) (1 Pet 4:17). Moreover, the New Testament suggests that a final judgment is essential to eschatological fulfillment. Indeed judgment and the final *parousia* appear concomitant (see 1 Cor 4:5; 2 Thess 1:5–10; Rev 19:11—20:15). It is judgment, moreover, that does not pass by the church (1 Cor 3:12–15; 2 Cor 5:10;

---

9. Sauter, *What Dare We Hope*, 1.

10. For an argument in defence of the metaphorical interpretation of the "body of Christ," see Gundry, *Soma*. For Gundry, the body of Christ can only be a metaphor, since this body (the church) is "non physical."

1 Pet 4:17).[11] In *Apocalypse Today* Torrance insists that all judgment happens through the cross of Christ, and that all judgment is ultimately redemptive. But this view, coupled with his doctrine of the Body of Christ, leaves us with the impression that the final judgment is already past. There is no reserved judgment.

Torrance also employs the *anhypostasis/ enhypostasis* dialectic in order to defend the oneness and unity of the church. However, the use of this ancient dialectic also stultifies any notion of a final judgment. The *anhypostasis* and *enhypostasis* assert Christ's substitutionary atonement for the church. Yet this means that the church has no *per se* existence except in the person of Christ. The end result is that we cannot think of the church *only* as the Body of Christ. "Christ *is* the Church." He is both "the One and the Many." As the God-Man he is the one mediator between God and humankind. But as a mediator he does not merely stand *between us* and God. His incarnation, life, ministry, and sacrificial death show that he has stood *in our place* in order to reconcile us to God.

Torrance stressed the need to hold in balance the "teleological end" and the "eschatological end." However, the balance appears to tip in favor of the eschatological end when he employs the *anhypostasis* and *enhypostasis*, despite the fact he uses the terms in a "more dynamic way" in accord with the atoning action of Jesus Christ. If on the basis of these terms Christ *is* the church, then that impoverishes the idea that the church is on its way to becoming one Body at the *eschaton*. In other words, the eschatological nature of the church tends to be reduced to an unveiling of what already is, namely Christ in his glory.

Torrance's doctrine of the Body of Christ could use a salutary dose of his own apocalyptic eschatology. The Apocalypse points to the inadequacy of all our earthly language including the *anhypostasia* and *enhypostasia*, since it is taken from the world that has come under judgment and which is therefore passing away. Apocalyptic also involves, in his words, the "eschatological suspension of logical form in order to keep our thought ever open to what is radically new."[12]

---

11. Emil Brunner was one to stress the fact that the New Testament expectation of the parousia included the expectation of a final judgement. See his chapter on judgement in *Eternal Hope*, 170–84. Edmund Schlink, who served alongside Torrance in the Working Committee for Faith and Order, also underlines the final judgement in his eschatology. See Schlink, *The Coming Christ*, 114–16; 257–58. "The end of the world," he writes, "is the day of divine judgement" (ibid., 257).

12. Torrance, *Theological Science*, 280.

For the past half century the theme of hope has occupied a preeminent place in eschatology (and in theology in general). The main theme of the Second Assembly of the World Council of Churches (Evanston, 1954), and the immediate popularity of Moltmann's *Theology of Hope* (ET, 1967) marked the ascendance of the theme.[13] In Sauter's words, eschatology "starts with amazement about the fact that human beings are allowed to hope."[14] Yet the theme of hope takes a far back seat in Torrance's eschatology. This is ironic when one considers that a large part of his eschatology was constructed in the shadow of the Evanston assembly. To be sure, hope is not absent in his eschatology. It comes into view in his sermons on the apocalypse. Yet it recedes from view in the late growth stages of his eschatology. While Torrance's contemporaries churned out volumes in response to the main theme at Evanston, he has only a sermon. In it he stresses only the objective, christological side of hope. Christ is our "sure and steadfast hope," the "anchor of the soul" (Heb 6:19). But in order to maintain that eschatological tension between the present and the future, the already/not yet, one should not ignore the subjective aspect—the "hope that is in you" (1 Pet 3:15). In the New Testament hope involves both "confidence in God" and "patient waiting" for him (cf. Rom 5:4f.; 14:4; 1 Thess 1:3).[15] It is something, moreover, that depends as much on the promises of God as on that "anchor of the soul."

How do we explain the neglect of hope in Torrance's eschatology? We could point to historical factors. His preoccupation with ecumenical issues in the 1950s would certainly have trammeled serious reflection on individual hopes. Yet even when Torrance's eschatology was highly practical and personal (c. 1940–43), hope was not a dominant theme. Much more attention was paid to the "Eternal Now." We have to search for a theological explanation.

His relative neglect of the work of the Holy Spirit is one.[16] New Testament hope is linked with the presence of the Spirit in believers

13. The long list of books on hope include Brunner, *Eternal Hope*; Minear, *Christian Hope*; Fison, *The Christian Hope*; Berkhof, *Well-Founded Hope*; Gogarten, *Despair and Hope*; Caird and Pannenberg, *The Christian Hope*; Macquarrie, *Christian Hope*. For recent contributions to the theme, see Sauter's *What Dare We Hope?*; Volf and Katerberg, *The Future of Hope*.

14. Sauter, *What Dare We Hope*, 217.

15. See Bultmann and Rengstorf, *Hope*, 33–40.

16. Cf. Barth's sustained treatment of hope in CD IV/3, 2. It is noteworthy that the title of this section is "The Holy Spirit and Christian Hope."

(Rom 5:5; 8:23–25; 15:13; Gal 5:5). Indeed it should be understood as a gift of the Spirit. A better explanation might be the basic nature of Torrance's eschatology. It is, in his words, an "application of Christology." Yet one could argue that his eschatology is *christologically over-determined*. Even its pneumatological aspect is determined strongly by the person and work of Christ. Christ, for Torrance, represents eschatological fulfillment. Christ is therefore the realization of all our hopes. Granted, this eschatological fulfillment is balanced by a teleological development toward fullness. There is a growth, upward and outward, of the Body of Christ towards fullness. But growth is not the same as hope. It has more to do with sanctification.

Finally, Torrance's doctrine of the atonement obviates the need to say much about hope as a Christian response. His idea of the radical substitutionary atonement of Christ means that he is not only the fulfillment of our hopes. He is in his vicarious humanity the concrete substitute for them. He is not only the *object* of our hope but the only true *subject* of hope, too. This doctrine of atonement means that the church's response in terms of worship and priestly service is fulfilled by Christ in his vicarious humanity. This is another reason why the humanity of the risen Christ is crucial to Torrance's eschatology. The church's priesthood is really a participation in Christ's royal priesthood. The church's priestly action is, as a result, only an "echo" or a "counterpoint" to his priesthood. In fact the individual Christian does not have a prayer of his own to stand on. As Robert Stamps, in his study of Torrance's Eucharistic theology, discovered "there is no prayer," not even an *amen*, "save that which is 'through him.'"[17] Likewise, any discussion of Christian hope would logically lead to a discussion about our participation in Jesus' fulfilled hope for us.

3. The Genesis of a "Scientific" Eschatology

We followed the development of Torrance's eschatology through the 1940s and 50s. There is the personal-existential phase, the historical-apocalyptic, and finally the ecumenical-ecclesial phase. But what direction does his eschatology take after this?

---

17. Stamps, "The Sacrament," 411. Torrance examines the role of Christ in the mediation of the human response to God in *The Mediation of Christ*, 83–108. He identifies five responses. Faith is one. It is telltale that hope is not one of the five.

Our study has uncovered another important fact. This is the genesis of a scientific eschatology. It is often assumed that Torrance's scientific theology represents a major turning point in his career, and that this theology bears little connection to whatever precedes it. The publication of *Theological Science* in 1969 introduced his scientific theology to the world. This book, however, is the product of at least two decades of study, going back to the period when he was heavily engaged with eschatology and ecumenism. While McGrath correctly traces the origins of Torrance's scientific theology back to earliest years of his career (Basel, Auburn), he does not identify the relation between his work in the 1950s and his scientific theology. He even suggests that his ecumenical work only distracted him from his work in that area.[18] But a closer investigation reveals a continuous line between his theology in the fifties and his later scientific theology, although here we can only show the lineaments of this continuity.

For Torrance, the first requirement of a scientific theology is to think in accord with that unique object of theology, *"God in His Revelation."* This means his theology is fixed on Jesus Christ, the accommodation of God to us in human form. "Scientific theology is therefore the systematic presentation of its knowledge through consistent faithfulness to the divine, creaturely objectivity of God in Christ."[19] Negatively, it is a theology that consistently avoids speculation and a priori convictions about God. It is clear that Torrance's early eschatology meets the basic requirements of a scientific theology.

This scientific approach helps to explain why Torrance does not tell us much about heaven and hell, the final judgment, and life in the new creation—the traditional fare of eschatology. Our scientific knowledge of these things is severely restricted.

His early theology foreshadows another important element of his scientific theology. This is the principle of unity, which Torrance insists upon in order to overcome the epistemological and cosmological dualisms that have dominated Western thought for centuries. This principle should not be confused with monism. Rather, it is about the relation and interaction between seemingly diverse realities: the empirical and theoretical, the physical and spiritual, the temporal and eternal, the divine and the human, and God and the natural world. For Torrance, this prin-

---

18. McGrath, *T. F. Torrance*, 195.

19. Torrance, *Theological Science*, 138.

ciple derives ultimately from the doctrine of the incarnation (*hypostatic union*) and the doctrine of the Trinity (*homoousion*). Later in his career, he explored the unity of God in terms of the integration of God's Being-in-his-Acts and Acts-in-his-Being.

In Torrance's early theology we can find illustrations of the principle of unity, although the principle itself is not clearly articulated. At Auburn, recall, he insisted on understanding the "Person and Work of Christ" together—as well as understanding revelation and redemption, incarnation and atonement, together. His emphasis on unity is also apparent in his ecumenical work. Here he attempts to hold together Christ and his Body (the church), "catholic" and "evangelical" doctrines, baptism and Eucharist, creation and redemption, the presence of Christ and coming of Christ, and the teleological end and the eschatological end.

The principle of unity helps to explain Torrance's attraction to modern science. He believed twentieth-century natural scientists were leading the way in the eradication of dualisms as they disclosed the "rational unity of the universe."[20] More significantly, he also observed a convergence between theology and natural science on the basis of this kind of unity. For the natural world that scientists study is the same world in which God has revealed himself concretely and objectively in Jesus Christ. This explains why Torrance was passionate about establishing a proper relation between theology and space and time, and why, in the process, he had no qualms about utilizing Einstein's revolutionary concept of "space-time."

Two of Torrance's best knows works, *Space, Time and Incarnation* (1969) and *Space, Time and Resurrection* (1976), indicate the importance of space and time to his theology. But his analysis of these subjects actually begins in the early 1950s. In the "Modern Eschatological Debate" (1953) he maintains that a proper eschatology requires an apprehension of Christ's relation to time, on the basis of his incarnation, death, and resurrection. If that can be done, then the church would be in a better position to quell arguments in support of the "delay of the Parousia" and apostolic succession. In *Royal Priesthood* his examination of the church's

---

20. Torrance, *The Ground and Grammar*, 52. At this point we should mention another link between Torrance's early eschatology and his scientific theology. He highlights the fact that many of the scientists (most importantly, Albert Einstein) who led this revolt against dualism were Jewish. This reminds us of the influence that the biblical theology movement had on him in the 1950s. One of its features was a belief in a distinctive Hebraic mindset. See David Torrance, *The Witness of the Jews God*, 98–103.

ministry forces him to think more deeply about the church's relation to both time and space. Time and space together comprise the "*schemata* of the cosmos*.*" The problem with apostolic succession, he argues, is that it involves enslavement to the fallen, corrupted "schemata of the cosmos." This is signaled by an attachment to law (*nomos*) instead of the Spirit, who is the true "Law" behind the "new divine order."

Space, Time and Incarnation and *Space, Time and Resurrection* also reveal Torrance's debt to the "new physics," although he argued that it was really the Christian doctrine of creation that prepared the way, centuries before, for the modern advances in physics. Modern science, though, does help Torrance to see that the root cause of the problem of apostolic succession is a bifurcation of space and time.[21] Apostolic, historical succession can be redeemed, therefore, if we begin to think in terms of a four-dimensional space-time. And if this is done we would also make progress toward understanding the integration of redemption and creation.

Eschatology is not prominent in Torrance's scientific theology. Still, it occupies an important place. To be sure, his eschatology at this later stage reflects different interests. Whereas his early eschatology is mainly the product of his attempt to understand how redemption takes place *in* creation, his later eschatology is the product of his attempt to understand the redemption *of* creation.

The premise behind *Space, Time and Incarnation* is the interrelation of incarnation and creation. They form, in his words, "the great axis in God's revelation with the world of space and time," without which we could not make sense of God's revelation.[22] What is the significance of this "great axis" for eschatology? The incarnation points to the creation of a "coordinate system between two horizontal dimensions, space and time, and one vertical dimension, relation to God through His Spirit."[23] This means that God operates through his own "space-time track." He is not subject to this track, but in his freedom travels through it, "fulfilling the divine purpose within it and pressing that fulfilment to its consummation in the new creation."[24] He sees this movement, as a result, as both "teleological" and "eschatological" movement. It is one as well in which

21. Torrance, *Theology in Reconciliation*, 274.

22. Torrance, *Space, Time and Incarnation*, 68.

23. Ibid., 72.

24. Ibid.

"the incarnate Word calls space and time, as it were, into contrapuntal relation to the eternal rationality of God . . ."[25]

In *Space, Time and Resurrection* we learn that the resurrection of Christ entails the "redemption" of space and time. This redemption, however, cannot be understood apart from the ascension and final *parousia* of Christ. The resurrection, like the nature of the church, must be understood "*enhypostatically*" and "*anhypostatically*." If we understand it only in light of the latter, then the resurrection becomes a "sort of super-history, touching our history only in a tangential manner," which would only disqualify it as historical.[26]

For Torrance, the new theory of space and time (space-time) helps to explain why we perceive a "delay" in the *parousia* of Christ. The one indivisible *parousia* is a "sort of space-time *parousia*," unlike the *parousia* that we "split apart . . . as we do space and time in our ordinary every day experience, due to the speed of light."[27] In other words, it is a *parousia* in which space and time are brought back together, so that it is "neither spaceless nor timeless."[28] Thus it is not a *parousia* in Spirit only. Nor is it a *parousia* that is ephemeral. It is one that is tied to the nature and mission of the church, and the "new heaven and earth."

Even this brief introduction to Torrance's later eschatology raises questions that need to be answered. What should we make of his proposed partnership between science and theology, a partnership based on a supposed common ground? In order to be successful, both science and theology have to submit to the intrinsic rationality of the universe, to its "space-time" structures. They diverge, of course, since science is concerned only with the contingent rationality and structure of the universe, while theology is concerned with the "transcendent source" of this universe. Yet, at the same time, Torrance argues that the resurrection of Christ reveals a "profound interrelation between redemption and creation."[29] In other words, there is a profound interrelation between the "eschatological end" and the "teleological end." Is the "new physics," then, pointing to the actual redemption of creation that has taken place (is taking place) through Jesus Christ?

25. Ibid., 73.
26. Ibid., 95.
27. Ibid., 144.
28. Ibid.
29. Ibid., 175.

At any rate, Torrance also insists that the redemption of creation cannot be completed apart from the final *parousia* of Christ. It is necessary, then, to explore Torrance's understanding of this relation between the "eschatological end" and the "teleological end" in light of the "new physics." Does the "Einsteinian cosmology" help him to integrate these "ends"? Or does it compromise the eschatological end, just as his heavy reliance on classical Christology in his early eschatology appears to compromise the teleological end?

Now that we have a clearer picture of Torrance's early theology, we are hopefully in a better position to answer these and other questions pertaining to his later theology.

Works Cited

Works by Thomas F. Torrance

Published Works

"Answer to God." *Biblical Theology* 2.1 (1951) 3–16.

The Apocalypse Today. London: Clark, 1960.

"The Atonement and the Oneness of the Church." *Scottish Journal of Theology* 7 (1954) 245–69.

Atonement: The Person and Work of Christ. Edited by Robert T. Walker. Milton Keynes, UK: Paternoster, 2009.

Calvin's Doctrine of Man. London: Lutterworth, 1949.

"Christ the First and the Last." In *Conflict and Agreement in Church, vol. 1. Order and Disorder*, 304–15. London: Lutterworth, 1959.

"Concerning Amsterdam. I. The Nature and Mission of the Church." *Scottish Journal of Theology* 2 (1949) 241–70.

"Concerning the Ministry." *Scottish Journal of Theology* 1 (1948) 190–201.

"The Divine Vocation and Destiny of Israel in World History." In *The Witness of the Jews to God*, edited by David W. Torrance, 85–104. Edinburgh: Hansel, 1982.

The Doctrine of Grace in the Apostolic Fathers. Edinburgh: Oliver and Boyd, 1948.

The Doctrine of Jesus Christ. Eugene, OR: Wipf & Stock, 2002.

"The Doctrine of Order." *Church Quarterly Review* 160 (1959) 21–36.

"Eschatology and the Eucharist." In *Intercommunion,* edited by D. M. Baillie and J. Marsh, 303–50. London: SCM, 1952.

"The Eschatology of the Reformation." In *Eschatology: Four Occasional Papers read to the Society for the Study of Theology*. Scottish Journal of Theology Occasional Papers, No. 2, edited by T. F. Torrance et al., 36–90. Edinburgh: Oliver & Boyd, 1953.

Gospel, Church, and Ministry. Thomas F. Torrance Collected Studies 1. Edited by Jock Stein. Eugene, OR: Cascade, 2012.

The Ground and Grammar of Theology. Charlottesville, VI: University Press of Virginia, 1980.

"History and Reformation." *Scottish Journal of Theology* 4 (1951) 279–91.

"Hugh Ross Mackintosh: Theologian of the Cross." *The Scottish Bulletin of Evangelical Theology* 5 (1987) 160–73.

Incarnation: The Person and Life of Christ. Edited by Robert T. Walker. Milton Keynes, UK: Paternoster, 2008.

"*In Hoc Signo Vinces*." *The Presbyter* 3.2 (1945) 13–20.

"The Israel of God." *Interpretation* 10 (1956) 305–20.

Karl Barth, Biblical and Evangelical Theologian. Edinburgh: T. & T. Clark, 1990.

"Kierkegaard on the Knowledge of God." *The Presbyter* 1.3 (1943) 4–7.

Kingdom and Church: A Study in the Theology of the Reformation. 1956. Reprint. Eugene, OR: Wipf & Stock, 1996.

"Liturgy and Apocalypse." *Church Service Society Annual* 24 (1954) 1–18.

"The Meaning of Baptism." *Canadian Journal of Theology* 2 (1956) 125–32.

The Mediation of Christ. Grand Rapids: Eerdmans, 1983.

"The Modern Eschatological Debate." *Evangelical Quarterly* 25 (1953) 45–54, 94–106, 167–78, 224–32.

The Modern Theological Debate, pamphlet issued for private circulation by the Theological Students' Union of the Inter-Varsity Fellowship of Evangelical Unions, London, 1941.

"Our Oneness in Christ and Our Disunity as Churches." In *Conflict and Agreement in the Church, vol. 1. Order and Disorder,* 263–83. London: Lutterworth, 1959.

"The Place and Function of the Church in the World." Alyth, UK: Alyth Printing Works, 1942.

"The Place of the Humanity of Christ in the Sacramental Life of the Church." *Church Service Society Annual.* The Church of Scotland. no. 26 (1956) 1–10. *Royal Priesthood.* London: Oliver & Boyd, 1955.

Review of *Calvin's Sermons,* translated by Leroy Nixon et al. *Scottish Journal of Theology* 5 (1952) 424–27.

Review of *Catholicity,* edited by Geoffrey F. Fisher. *Scottish Journal of Theology* 2 (1949) 85–93.

Review of *The Earliest Christian Confessions,* by Oscar Cullmann. *Scottish Journal of Theology* 5 (1952) 85–87.

Review of *The Epistle to the Hebrews,* by William Manson. *Scottish Journal of Theology* 5 (1952) 309–13.

Review of *Evangelisches Gutachen zur Dogmatisierung der leiblichen Himmelfahrt Mariens,* by Edmund Schlink et al. *Scottish Journal of Theology* 4 (1951) 90–96.

Review of *The Fulness of Christ: The Church's Growth into Catholicity,* a report by a group of Anglican ministers presented to the Archbishop of Canterbury. *Scottish Journal of Theology* 5 (1952) 90–100.

Review of *The Letters of Saint Athanasius concerning the Holy Spirit.* Translated with introduction and notes by C. R. B. Shapland. *Scottish Journal of Theology* 2 (1951) 205–8.

Review of *The Oracles of God: An Introduction to the Preaching of John Calvin,* by T. H. L. Parker. *Scottish Journal of Theology* 1 (1948) 212–14.

Review of *Reformed Dogmatics,* by Heinrich Heppe. *Scottish Journal of Theology* 5(1952) 81–85.

"Salvation is of the Jews." *The Evangelical Quarterly* 22 (1950) 164–73.

The School of Faith: The Catechisms of the Reformed Church. London: Clarke, 1959.

Space, Time and Incarnation. London: Oxford University Press, 1969.

Space, Time and Resurrection. Grand Rapids: Eerdmans, 1976.

"A Study in New Testament Communication." *Scottish Journal of Theology* 3 (1950) 298–313.

Theological Science. London: Oxford University Press, 1969.

Theology in Reconciliation. Grand Rapids: Eerdmans, 1975.

Theology in Reconstruction. London: SCM, 1965.

"Toward a Doctrine of the Lord's Supper." In *Conflict and the Agreement in the Church, vol. 2. The Ministry and the Sacraments of the Gospel.* London: Lutterworth 1960.

"Universalism or Election." *Scottish Journal of Theology* 2 (1949) 310–18.

"What is the Church?" *The Ecumenical Review* 11 (1958) 6–21.

When Christ Comes and Comes Again. London: Hodder & Stoughton, 1957.

"Where Do We Go from Lund?" *Scottish Journal of Theology* 6 (1953) 53–64.

Unpublished Works

Unless indicated, all materials are held in Special Collections, Princeton Theological Seminary Library, Princeton, N.J.

"And there was no more sea." Sermon on Rev 21:1. Alyth Barony Parish, Scotland, 3 May 1942.

"Aberdeen, 1947–50." Memoir.

"Ascension and Advent." Sermon on Eph 4:8–10. Alyth Barony Parish, Scotland, 18 May 1947.

"Behold I stand at the door on knock." Sermon on Rev 3:20. Alyth Barony Parish, Scotland, 8 February 1942.

"But now Christ is risen from the dead." Sermon on 1 Cor 15:20. Alyth Barony Parish, Scotland, Easter evening, 1941.

Communion Sermon on 1 Cor 2:2. (Heb 12:2). Alyth Barony Parish, Scotland, 18 October, 1942.

"Communion." Sermon on 1 John 1:1–3. Alyth Barony Parish, Scotland, 16 February 1941.

"Cursed is the man who trusted in man." Sermon on Jeremiah 17:5. Alyth Barony Parish, Scotland, 31 May 1942.

Easter Sermon on Luke 24:30f. Alyth Barony Parish, Scotland, March, 1940.

Easter Sermon on Rev 1:9,10. Alyth Barony Parish, Scotland, 1942.

"God's arrows." Sermon on Phil 3:8, 12–14. Alyth Barony Parish, Scotland, 1942.

"'If Christ be not risen.' What then?" Easter Sermon on 1 Cor 15:17–18. Alyth Barony Parish, Scotland, 1941.

"In a straight betwixt the two." Sermon on Phil 1:23. Alyth Barony Parish, Scotland, 18 January 1942.

"It is expedient that I go away." Sermon on John 16:20. Alyth Barony Parish, Scotland, 17 May 1942.

"The Leaven and the Loaf." Sermon on Matthew 13:33. Alyth Barony Parish, Scotland, 1941.

"The Lion and the Lamb." Sermon on Rev. 5:5ff. Alyth Barony Parish, Scotland, 1940.

"Marks of the true Church." Sermon on Acts 2:42. Alyth Barony Parish, Scotland, 30 November, 1941.

"My Parish Ministry—Alyth, 1940–43."

New College Lectures on Eschatology. Edinburgh. January–March, 1952.

New Year's Sermon on Acts 1:7. Alyth Barony Parish, Scotland, January, 1941.

"Our Sure and Certain Hope." Sermon on Hebrews 6:17–20. October, 1954.

"Peace of Christ." Sermon on John 14:27. Alyth Barony Parish, Scotland, April, 1940.

"The Problem of Presbyterian-Anglican Relations in Britain." n.d.

"The Sacraments and Eschatology." n.d.

"The Second Advent." Sermon on Luke 17:20–37. Alyth Barony Parish, Scotland, 10 January, 1943.

Sermon on 2 Peter 3:8. Alyth Barony Parish, Scotland, 1940.

"Student Years—Edinburgh to Basel, 1934–38." Memoir.

"Then opened He their understanding." Sermon on Luke 24:39–45. Alyth Barony Parish, Scotland, April, 1942.

"Theology in Action." Lecture, Assisi, Italy, 1945.

Thomas F. Torrance to Karl Barth, 30 March 1949. *Karl Barth-Archiv*, Basle, Switzerland.

Thomas F. Torrance to Karl Barth, 13 March 1953. *Karl Barth-Archiv*, Basle, Switzerland.

"The three tenses of Communion—past, future, present." Sermon on Luke 22:19–John 6–1 Cor 11. Alyth Barony Parish, Scotland, 21 February 1943.

"War Service: Middle East and Italy, 1943–45."

Secondary Literature

Achtner, Wolfang. *Physik, Mystik and Christentum: Eine Darstellung und Diskussion der naturlichen Theologie bei T. F. Torrance.* European University Studies, Series 23 Theology, vol. 438. Frankfurt: Lang, 1991.

Addison, Paul. *The Road to 1945.* London: Quartet, 1977.

Augustine, Aurelius. *The City of God.* Translated by Henry Bettenson. New York: Penguin, 1972.

Aulen, Gustaf. *Christus Victor.* Translated by A. G. Hebert. London: SPCK, 1961.

Baillie, D. M., and J. Marsh, eds. *Intercommunion: The Report of the Theological Commission Appointed by the Continuation Committee of the World Conference of Faith and Order.* London: SCM, 1952.

Baillie, John. *And the Life Everlasting.* London: Oxford University Press, 1934.

———. *The Belief in Progress.* New York: Scribner, 1951.

———. *The Place of Jesus Christ in Modern Christianity.* New York: Scribner's Sons, 1929.

———. *What is Christian Civilization?* London: Oxford University Press, 1945.

Balthasar, Hans Urs von. "Eschatologie." In *Fragen der Theologie heute*, edited by J. Feiner, et al., 403–21. Einsiedeln, Switzerland: Benziger, 1957.

———. *Karl Barth: Darstellung und Deutung seiner Theologie.* Cologne: Hegner, 1951. E.T. *The Theology of Karl Barth.* Garden City, NY: Doubleday Anchor, 1972.

Bandstra, A. J. "History and Eschatology." *Calvin Theological Journal* 5.2 (1970) 180–83.

Barr, James. *The Semantics of Biblical Language.* London: SCM, 1961.

Barth, Karl. *Against the Stream.* London: SCM, 1954.

———. *Die Auferstehung der Toten.* München: Kaiser, 1924. E.T. *The Resurrection of the Dead.* New York: Hodder & Revell, 1933.

———. *Church Dogmatics*, vols. 1–4. Translated by G. W. Bromiley, edited by G. W. Bromiley and T. F. Torrance. Edinburgh: T. & T. Clark, 1956–75.

———. "The Church—The Living Congregation of the Lord Jesus Christ." In *The Universal Church in God's Design*, 67–76. Vol. 1 of *Man's Disorder and God's Design.* 5 vols. London: SCM, 1948–49.

———. *Credo.* Translated by J. Strathearn McNab. London: Hodder & Stoughton, 1936

———. *The Epistle to the Romans.* Translated from 6th ed. by E. Hoskyns. London: Oxford University Press, 1933.

———. *God in Action.* Edinburgh: T. & T. Clark, 1936.

———. *The Heidelberg Catechism for Today*. Translated by Shirley Guthrie, Jr. Richmond, VI: John Knox, 1964.

———. *The Humanity of God*. E.T. Richmond, VA, 1960.

———. *Die Kirkliche Dogmatik*. Zollikon: Evangelischer, 1942–51.

———. "The Real Church." *Scottish Journal of Theology* 3 (1950) 337–51.

Bartsch, Hans Werner, ed. *Kerygma and Myth: A Theological Debate*. Translated by R. H. Fuller. 2nd ed. New York: SPCK, 1962.

Baumann, Michael. *Roundtable: Conversations with European Theologians*. Grand Rapids: Baker House, 1990.

Beardslee, William. "New Testament Apocalyptic in Recent Interpretation." *Interpretation* 25.4 (1971) 419–35.

Beckwith, I. T. *The Apocalypse of John*. New York: Macmillan, 1922.

Benoit, Jean Daniel. *The Liturgical Renewal*. London: SCM, 1958.

Berkhof, Henrikus. *Christ, the Meaning of History*. Translated by L. Buurmann. Richmond, VA: John Knox, 1966.

Berkhof, Henrikus. *Well-Founded Hope*. Richmond, VA: John Knox, 1969.

Berkhof, Louis. *Systematic Theology*. Grand Rapids: Eerdmans, 1939.

Bollier, John. "Judgement in the Apocalypse." *Interpretation* 7.1 (1953) 14–25.

Boring, M. Eugene. "Narrative Christology in the Apocalypse." *The Catholic Biblical Quarterly* 54.4 (1992) 702–23.

———. "The Theology of Revelation." *Interpretation* 40.3 (1986) 257–69.

Bousset, Wilhelm. *Die Offenbarung Johannis*. Gottingen: Vandenhoeck & Rupect, 1906.

Braaten, Carl. "The Kingdom of God and Life Everlasting." In *Christian Theology: Introduction to its Traditions and Tasks*, edited by P. Hodgson & R. King, 328–52. Philadelphia: Fortress, 1982.

Braaten, Carl, and Robert Jenson, eds. *The Last Things: Biblical and Theological Perspectives on Eschatology*. Grand Rapids: Eerdmans, 2002.

British Council of Churches. Minutes from meetings: 3 March 1949, 4–5; 3 November 1949, 8–11; 30 March 1950, 12–13; 5 October 1950, 20–21; The Church of England Record Centre. London, UK.

Brunner, Emil. *Christianity and Civilization*. New York: Scribner's Sons, 1948–49.

———. *Dogmatics,* vols. 1–3. London: Lutterworth, 1963.

———. *Eternal Hope*. London: Lutterworth, 1954.

———. *The Mediator*. Philadelphia: Westminster, 1947.

Bultmann, Rudolph. *History and Eschatology*. Edinburgh: Edinburgh University Press, 1957.

———. "New Testament and Mythology." 1941. In *Kerygma and Myth*, edited by H. W. Bartsch and translated by R. H. Fuller, 1–44. 1953. Reprint. London: Harper, 1961.

Bultmann, Rudolph, and Karl H. Rengstorf. *Hope*. Translated D. M. Barton and P. R. Akcroyd, 33–40. London: Black, 1963.

Cabaniss, Allen. "A Note on the Liturgy of the Church." *Interpretation* 7.1 (1953) 78–86.

Cahill, Brendan J. *The Quotable Churchill*. Philadelphia, London: Running, 1998.

Caird, G. B. *A Commentary on the Revelation of St. John the Divine*. London: Black, 1966.

Caird, G. B., Wolfhart Pannenberg, et al. *The Christian Hope*. London: SPCK, 1970.

Calvin, John. *Institutes of the Christian Religion.* Translated by Henry Beveridge. Grand Rapids: Eerdmans, 1989.

———. "Psychopannychia." In *Tracts and Treatises of the Reformation,* vol. 3. Translated by Henry Beveridge with historical notes and introduction added to present addition by Thomas F. Torrance, 419–90. 1844–51. Reprint. Grand Rapids: Eerdmans, 1958.

Camfield, F. W. "The Idea of Substitution in the Doctrine of Atonement." *Scottish Journal of Theology* 1 (1949) 282–93.

Carey, Kenneth Moir, ed. *The Historic Episcopate.* London: Dacre, 1954.

Carmer, Carl, ed. *The War Against God.* New York: Holt, 1943.

Carrington, Philip. *The Meaning of Revelation.* London: SPCK, 1931.

Charles, R. H. *A Critical and Exegetical Commentary on the Revelation of St. John.* 2 vols. Edinburgh: T. & T. Clark, 1920.

Childs, Brevard. *Biblical Theology in Crisis.* Philadelphia: Westminster, 1970.

Church of England. Archbishop of York's Conference, Malvern. *Malvern 1941: The Life of the Church and the Order of Society: Being the Proceedings of the Conference.* London: Longmans, 1941.

———. *Catholicity.* Westminster: Dacre, 1949.

———. *The Fullness of Christ.* London: SPCK, 1952.

Church of Scotland. *The Challenge of Communism.* London: SCM, 1951

———. *The Church under Communism.* London: SCM, 1952.

———. *God's Will for the Church and Nation.* Reprinted from the reports of the Commission for the interpretation of God's Will in the present crisis. London: SCM, 1946.

———. *God's Will in Our Time.* Being the report presented to the General Assembly of the Church of Scotland in 1942, by the Commission for the Interpretation of God's Will in the Present Crisis. London: SCM, 1942.

Clapsis, Emmanuel. "Eschatology." In *Dictionary of the Ecumenical Movement,* edited by Nicholas Lossky et al., 403–4. Geneva: World Council of Churches, 2002.

Collins, Adela Yarbro. "Reading the Book of Revelation in the Twentieth Century." *Interpretation* 40.3 (1986) 229–42.

Colyer, Elmer. *How to Read T. F. Torrance: Understanding his Trinitarian and Scientific Theology.* Downer's Grove, IL: InterVarsity, 2001.

Commission on Faith and Order of the World Council of Churches. *Faith and Order Findings: The Final Report of the Theological Commission to the Fourth World Conference on Faith and Order, Montreal 1963.* London: SCM, 1963.

———. Minutes of the Working Committee. Papers no. 22. Davos, Switzerland, 1955.

———. Minutes of the Working Committee. Papers no. 21. Evanston and Chicago, 1954.

———. Minutes of the Working Committee. Papers no. 23. Herrenalb, Germany, 1956.

———. Minutes of the Working Committee. Papers no. 15. Lund, Sweden, 1952.

———. *One Lord, One Baptism.* London: SCM, 1960.

Considine, J. S. "The Rider on the White Horse, Apoc. 6:1–8." *Catholic Biblical Quarterly,* 8 (1946) 406–22.

Conzelman, Hans. *An Outline of the Theology of the New Testament.* London: SCM, 1969.

Cullmann, Oscar. *Christ and Time: The Primitive Conception of Time and History*. Translated by Floyd Filson. London: SCM, 1964.

———. *The Christology of the New Testament*. Translated by S. Guthrie and C. Hall. London: SCM, 1963.

———. *Early Christian Worship*. Translated by A. S. Todd and J. B. Torrance. London: SCM, 1953.

———. *The Immortality of the Soul or the Resurrection of the Dead? The Witness of the New Testament*. London: Epworth, 1958.

Demant, V. A. *What is Happening to Us?* London: Dacre, 1952.

Dix, Dom Gregory. *The Shape of the Liturgy*. London: Dacre, 1945.

Dodd, C. H. *The Apostolic Preaching and its Development: Three Lectures with an Appendix on Eschatology and History*. London: Hodder & Stoughton, 1936.

———. *The Coming of Christ*. Four broadcast addresses for the season of Advent. Cambridge: United, 1951.

———. *The Parables of the Kingdom*. New York: Scribner's Sons, 1936.

Drucker, Peter. *The End of Economic Man: The Origins of Totalitarianism*. New York: Day, 1939.

Eastwood, Cyril. *The Royal Priesthood of the Faithful*. Minneapolis: Augsburg, 1963.

Ellul, Jacques. *The Meaning of the City*. Translated by Dennis Pardee. Grand Rapids: Eerdmans, 1970.

Fallaw, Wesner. "Atomic Apocalypse." *The Christian Century* 63.39 S25 (1946) 1146–48.

Farrer, Austin. *Rebirth of Images: The Making of the St. John's Apocalypse*. London: Dacre, 1949.

———. *The Revelation of St. John the Divine*. Oxford: Clarendon, 1964.

Farrow, Douglas. "Eucharist, Eschatology and Ethics." In *The Future as God's Gift: Explorations in Christian Eschatology*, edited by David Fergusson and Marcel Sarot, 199–215. Edinburgh: T. & T. Clark, 2000.

Fergusson, David, and Marcel Sarot, eds. *The Future as God's Gift: Explorations in Christian Eschatology*. Edinburgh: T. & T. Clark, 2000.

Feuillet, Andre. *L'Apocalypse: État de la question*. Brussels: Desclee de Brouwer, 1962.

Fison, J. E. *The Christian Hope*. London: Longmans, Green, & Co, 1954.

Flew, R. Newton. *The Nature of the Church: Report of the Theological Commission of the World Council of Churches*. London: SCM, 1952.

Forell, George W. "Justification and Eschatology in Luther's Thought." *Church History* 38.2 (1969) 164–74.

Forsyth, P. T. *This Life and the Next*. London: Independent, 1918.

———. *The Person and Place of Christ*. London: Hodder & Stoughton, 1909.

———. *The Work of Christ*. London: Independent, 1910.

Fosdick, H. E. *Christianity and Progress*: New York: Associated, 1922.

Gaines, David. *The World Council of Churches: A Study of its Background and History*. Peterborough, Smith, 1966.

George, Alfred. *Communion with God in the New Testament*. London, 1953.

Gogarten, Friedrich. *Despair and Hope for Our Time*. Translated by Thomas Weiser. Philadelphia: Pilgrim, 1970.

Gray, Bryan J. A. "Theology as Science: An Examination of the Theological Methodology of Thomas F. Torrance." Sacred theology doctorate diss. Katholieke Universiteit te Leuven, 1975.

Gundry, Robert. *Soma in Biblical Theology with Emphasis on Pauline Anthropology.* Society for New Testament Studies Monograph Series 29. Cambridge: Cambridge University Press, 1976.

Guthridge, Johannes. *The Christology of T. F. Torrance: Revelation and Reconciliation in Christ.* Excerpta ex diss. ad Lauream. Melbourne: Pontificia Universitas Gregoriana, 1967.

Habets, Myk. *Theosis in the Theology of Thomas Torrance.* Farmhan, UK: Ashgate, 2009.

Hebblethwaite, Brian. *The Christian Hope.* Grand Rapids: Eerdmans, 1984.

Hebert, Arthur G. *Liturgy and Society.* London: Faber & Faber, 1935.

———. "A Root of Difference and of Unity." In *Intercommunion,* edited by Donald Baillie and J. Marsh, 236–54. London: SCM, 1952.

Henderson, Ian. *Power without Glory: A Study in Ecumenical Politics.* Richmond, VA: John Knox, 1969.

Hendriksen, William. *More than Conquerors.* Grand Rapids: Eerdmans, 1939.

Heppe, Heinrich. *Reformed Dogmatics.* Translated by G. T. Thomson. London: George Allen & Unwin, 1950.

Hesselink, John. "A Pilgrimage in the School of Christ." *Reformed Review* 39 (1984) 49–64.

Hodgson, Peter C., and Robert King, eds. *Christian Theology: An Introduction to its Traditions and Tasks.* Philadelphia: Fortress, 1985.

Hunsinger, George. "The Dimension of Depth: T. F. Torrance on the Sacraments of Baptism and the Lord's Supper." *Scottish Journal of Theology* 54.2 (2001) 155–76.

Jenson, Robert. *Alpha and the Omega.* 1963. Reprint. Eugene, OR: Wipf & Stock, 2002

Jeske, Richard, and David Barr, "The Study of the Apocalypse Today." *Religious Studies Review* 14.4 (1988) 337–44.

Kang, Phee Seng. "The Concept of the Vicarious Humanity of Christ in the Theology of Thomas Forsyth Torrance." PhD diss., University of Aberdeen, 1983.

Käsemann, Ernst. "The Beginnings of Christian Theology." In *Apocalypticism,* edited by Robert W. Funk, 17–46. New York: Herder & Herder, 1969.

Keller, Adolph. *Christian Europe Today.* 2nd ed. New York: Harper, 1942.

Kierkegaard, Søren. *Philosophical Fragments.* 2nd ed. Translated by David F. Swenson and Geoffrey F. Fisher. Princeton, NJ: Princeton University Press, 1962.

Kirk, Kenneth, ed. *The Apostolic Ministry.* London: Hodder & Stoughton, 1946.

Kittel, Gerhard, ed. *Theological Dictionary of the New Testament.* 10 vols. Translated and edited by Geoffrey Bromily. Grand Rapids: Eerdmans, 1964–1976.

Klassen, William. "Vengeance in the Apocalypse of John." *Catholic Biblical Quarterly* 28.3 (1966) 300–311.

Koch, Klaus. *The Rediscovery of Apocalyptic.* Translated by Margaret Kohl. London: SCM, 1972.

König, Adrio. *The Eclipse of Christ in Eschatology: Toward a Christ-Centered Approach.* Grand Rapids: Eerdmans, 1989.

La Due, William. *The Trinity Guide to Eschatology.* New York: Continuum, 2004.

Lang, August. *Der Evangelienkommentar Martin Butzers und die Grundzuge seiner Theologie.* Leipzig: Dieterich, 1900.

Lee, Kye Won. *Living in Union with Christ: The Practical Theology of T. F. Torrance.* New York: Lang, 2003.

Leitch, J. W. *A Theology in Transition: H. R. Mackintosh as an Approach to Karl Barth.* London: Nisbet, 1952.

Lindsay, Hal. *The Late Great Planet Earth*. Grand Rapids: Zondervan, 1970.

Lohmeyer, Ernst. *Der Brief an die Phillipper, an die Kolosser und die Philemon*. Gottingen: Vandenhoeck und Ruprecht, 1961.

Louth, Andrew. "Eastern Orthodox Eschatology." In *The Oxford Handbook of Eschatology*, edited by Jerry L. Walls, 234–36. Oxford: Oxford University Press, 2008.

Luoma, Tapio. *Incarnation and Physics: Natural Science in the Theology of Thomas F. Torrance*. Oxford: Oxford University Press, 2002.

Lüthi, Walter. *The Church to Come*. London: SPCK, 1939.

Mackintosh, H. R. *The Doctrine of the Person of Jesus Christ*. 2nd ed. Edinburgh: T. & T. Clark, 1913.

———. *Immortality and the Future*. London: Hodder & Stoughton, 1915.

———. *Types of Modern Theology*. 1937. Reprint. London: Collins, 1964.

MacLean, Stanley S. "*Regnum Christi:* Thomas Torrance's Appropriation of John Calvin's Ecclesiology." In *John Calvin's Ecclesiology: Ecumenical Perspectives*, edited by Gerard Mannion and Eduardus Van der Borght, 185–202. London: T. & T. Clark, 2011.

MacLeod, George F. *Only One Way Left: Church Prospect*. Glasgow: The Iona Community, 1956.

Macmurray, John. *The Clue to History*. London: SCM, 1938.

MacPherson, John. *The Doctrine of the Church in Scottish Theology*. Edinburgh: T. & T. Clark, 1903.

Macquarrie, John. *Christian Hope*. New York: Seabury, 1978.

Manson, William. *The Epistle to the Hebrews: An Historical and Theological Reconstruction*. London: Hodder & Stoughton, 1951.

———. *Jesus the Messiah*. London: Hodder & Stoughton, 1943.

———. "The Norm of the Christian Life in the Synoptic Gospels." *Scottish Journal of Theology* 3 (1950) 33–42.

McConnnachie, John. *Significance of Karl Barth*. London: Hodder & Stoughton, 1931

McCormack, Bruce L. *Karl Barth's Critically Realistic Dialectic Theology: Its Genesis and Development, 1909–1936*. Oxford: Clarendon, 1995.

McGrath, Alister, *T. F. Torrance: An Intellectual Biography*. Edinburgh: T. & T. Clark, 1999.

McLeod-Campbell, John. *The Nature of the Atonement*. 6th ed. New York: Macmillan, 1886.

Milligan, William. *The Book of Revelation*. 2nd ed. London: Hodder & Stoughton, 1891.

Milner, Benjamin. *Calvin's Doctrine of the Church*. Leiden: Brill, 1970.

Minear, Paul. *Christian Hope and the Second Coming*. Philadelphia: Westminster, 1954.

———. *Images of the Church in the New Testament*. Philadelphia: Westminster, 1960.

Moberly, R. C. *The Ministerial Priesthood*. London: Murray, 1899.

Moffatt, James. "The Revelation of St. John the Divine." In *The Expositor's Greek Testament*, vol. 5, edited by W. Robertson Nicholl, 279–494. London: Hodder & Stoughton, 1905–1910.

Moltmann, Jürgen. *The Coming of God*. Translated by Margaret Kohl. Minneapolis, MN: Fortress, 1996.

———. *Theology of Hope: On the Ground and the Implications of a Christian Eschatology*. New York: Harper and Row, 1967.

Morrison, John Douglas. *Knowledge of the Self-Revealing God in the Thought of Thomas Forsyth Torrance.* New York: Lang, 1997.

Mounce, Robert. *The Book of Revelation.* Grand Rapids: Eerdmans, 1977.

Orr, James. *The Progress of Dogma.* London: Hodder & Stoughton, 1901.

Pannenburg, Wolfhart. *Revelation as History.* New York: MacMillan, 1968.

Paton, William. *The Church and the New Order.* London: SCM, 1941.

Payne, Ernest. *Thirty Years of the British Council of Churches: 1942–62.* London: British Council of Churches, 1972

Pelling, Henry. *Britain and the Second World War.* London: Collins, 1970.

Piper, Otto. "The Apocalypse of John and the Liturgy of the Ancient Church." *Church History* 20 (1951) 10–22.

Pope Pius XII. *Mystici Corporis Christi.* No pages. Online: http:// www.papalencyclicals .net/pius12/P12MYSTI.HTM.

Prigent, Pierre. *Apocalypse et Liturgie.* Neuchâtel, Switzerland: Delachaux & Niestlé, 1964.

Quistorp, Heinrich. *Calvin's Doctrine of Last Things.* Richmond, VA: John Knox, 1955.

Rankin, William. "Carnal Union with Christ in the Theology of T. F. Torrance." PhD diss., University of Edinburgh, 1997.

Reddish, Mitchell. "Martyr Christology in the Apocalypse." *Journal for the Study of the New Testament* 33 (1988) 85–95.

Richardson, Kurt. "Trinitarian Reality: The Interrelation of Uncreated and Created Being in the Thought of Thomas F. Torrance." PhD diss., University of Basel, 1993.

Ritschl, Albrecht. *The Christian Doctrine of Justification and Reconciliation.* 1874. E.T. edited by H. R. MacKintosh and A.B. MacAuley. Edinburgh: T. & T. Clark, 1900.

Robinson, John A. T. *The Body: A Study in Pauline Theology.* London: SCM, 1952

Robinson, William. *The Biblical Doctrine of the Church.* St. Louis, MN: Bethany, 1948.

Rodger, P. C., and L. Vischer, eds. *The Fourth World Conference on Faith and Order, Montreal, 1963.* London: SCM, 1964.

Rouse, Ruth, and Stephen Neill. *History of the Ecumenical Movement 1517–1948.* London: SPCK, 1954.

Rowley, H. H. *The Relevance of Apocalyptic.* London: Lutterworth, 1944.

———. "The Voice of God in Apocalypse." *Interpretation* 2.4 (1948) 403–18.

Samuelson, Paul. *Economics.* 8th ed. New York: McGraw-Hill, 1970.

Sansom, Dennis. "Scientific Theology: An Examination of the Methodology of Thomas Forsyth Torrance." PhD diss., Southwestern Baptist Theological Seminary, 1981.

Sauter, Gerhard. *What Dare We Hope? Reconsidering Eschatology.* Harrisburg, PA: Trinity, 1999.

Schlink, Edmund. "Church and the Churches." *Ecumenical Review* 1.2 (1949) 150–68.

———. *The Coming Christ and the Coming Church.* Translated by I. H. Neilson et al. Edinburgh: Oliver & Boyd, 1967.

Schrenk, Gottlob. "ἱερός." In *Theological Dictionary of the New Testament.* 10 vols., 3:221–83. Translated and edited by Geoffrey Bromily. Grand Rapids: Eerdmans, 1964–1976.

Schwarz, Hans. *Eschatology.* Grand Rapids: Eerdmans, 2000.

Schweitzer, Albert. *The Decay and Restoration of Civilization.* Dale Memorial Lectures, 1922. 2nd ed. London: Lutterworth, 1960.

————. *The Quest of the Historical Jesus: A Critical Study of Its Progress from Reimarus to Wrede.* 1906. Translated by W. Montgomery. Reprint. New York: MacMillan, 1961.

Scott, E. F. *The Book of Revelation.* London: SCM, 1939.

Shepherd, Massey. *The Paschal Liturgy in the Apocalypse.* Ecumenical Studies in Worship 6. London: Lutterworth, 1960.

Shults, F. Leron. "A Dubious Christological Formula: From Leontius of Byzantium to Karl Barth." *Theological Studies* 57.3 (1996) 431–46.

————. "An Open Systems Model for Adult Learning in Theological Inquiry." PhD diss., Walden University, 1991.

Skoglund, John, and J. Robert Nelson. *Fifty Years of Faith and Order.* New York: Committee for the Interseminary Movement of the National Student Christian Federation, 1963.

Spengler, Oswald. *The Decline of the West.* 1922. Translated with notes by C. F. Atkinson. New York: Knopf, 1973–76.

Stamps, Robert Julian. "'The Sacrament of the Word made Flesh': The Eucharistic Theology of the Thomas F. Torrance.' PhD diss., University of Nottingham, 1986.

Stendahl, Krister. *Immortality and Resurrection: Four Essays by Oscar Cullmann, Harry Wolfson, Werner Jaeger, and Henry J. Cadbury.* New York: MacMillan, 1965.

Stephens, W. B. *The Holy Spirit in the Theology of Martin Bucer.* London: Cambridge University Press, 1970.

Strobel, August. *Kerygma und Apokalyptik, Ein religionsgeschichtlicher und theologishcher Beitrag zu Christusfrage.* Gottingen: Vandenhoeck und Ruprecht, 1967.

Swete, Henry. *The Apocalypse of St. John.* Grand Rapids: Eerdmans, 1951.

Temple, William. *Christianity and Social Order.* Toronto: Pelican, 1942.

————. *The Hope of the New World.* London: SCM, 1940.

Tomkins, Oliver, ed. *The Third World Conference on Faith and Order held at Lund, Aug. 15–28, 1952.* London: SCM, 1953.

Torrance, David, and T. F. Torrance, eds. *Calvin's Commentaries: The Epistle of Paul the Apostle to the Galatians, Ephesians, Philippians and Colossians.* Translated by T. H. L. Parker. Grand Rapids: Eerdmans, 1965.

————, eds. *Calvin's Commentaries: The Epistle of Paul the Apostle to the Hebrews; and the First and Second Epistles of St. Peter.* Translated by W. B. Johnson. Edinburgh, Grand Rapids: Eerdmans, 1963.

Torrance, David, ed. *The Witness of the Jews to God.* Edinburgh: Handsel, 1982.

Torrance, James B. "The Priesthood of Jesus: A Study of the Doctrine of the Atonement." In *Essays in Christology for Karl Barth*, edited by T. H. L. Parker, 155–73. London: Lutterworth, 1956.

Toynbee, Arnold. *Civilization on Trial.* New York: Oxford University Press, 1948.

Troeltsch, Ernst. *The Social Teaching of the Christian Churches.* 1912. Translated by Olive Wyon. Reprint. New York: Harper, 1960.

Trook, Douglas. "The Unified Christocentric Field: Toward a Time-Eternity Relativity Model for Theological Hermeneutics in the Onto-Relational Theology of Thomas F. Torrance." PhD diss., Drew University, 1986.

Visser't Hooft, W. A., ed. *The First Assembly of the World Council of Churches held at Amsterdam, 22 Aug.–4 Sept. 1948.* Amsterdam Assembly Series, Vol. 5. London: SCM, 1948.

Volf, Miroslav, and William Katerberg, eds. *The Future of Hope*. Grand Rapids: Eerdmans, 2004.

Wainwright, Geoffrey. *Eucharist and Eschatology*. London: Epworth, 1971.

Weightman, Colin. *Theology in a Polanyian Universe: The Theology of T. F. Torrance*. New York: Lang, 1994.

Weiss, Johannes. *Jesus' Proclamation of the Kingdom of God*. 1892. Translated and edited by Richard Hiers and David Holland. Reprinted. Philadelphia: Fortress, 1971.

Werner, Hans. *The Formation of Christian Dogma: An Historical Study of its Problem*. Translated by S. G. F. Brandon. New York: Harper, 1957.

West, Charles. *Communism and the Theologians*. London: SCM, 1958.

Westminster Confession of Faith. Online. http://www.creeds.net/reformed/Westminster/contents.htm.

Wilson, Bryan. "Millennialism and Sect Formation in the Nineteenth and Twentieth Centuries." In *Apocalyptic in History and Tradition*, edited Christopher Rowland and John Barton, 212–32. London: Sheffield Academic, 2002.

World Conference on Faith and Order. Minutes of the Continuation Committee. Papers no. 102 (Series 1). Clarens, Switzerland, 1947.

World Council of Churches. *Man's Disorder and God's Design*. 5 vols. London: SCM, 1948–49.

———. *Official Pamphlets and Publications*. Geneva, 1910–79. Microfilm.

Yates, Roy. "A Re-examination of Ephesians 1:23." *The Expository Times* 83 (1971–72) 146–51.

Yeung, Jason Hing-Kau. *"Being and Knowing: Thomas Torrance's Christological Science."* PhD diss., London University, 1993.